How to Use This Book and Its Media

A Pocket Style Manual, APA Version, is a quick reference for writers and researchers who use the style guidelines of the American Psychological Association (APA). As a researcher, you can turn to it for details about finding, evaluating, and documenting sources and about writing papers in APA style. As a writer, you will find advice on revising sentences for clarity, grammar, punctuation, and mechanics.

Here are the book's key features.

- **The brief and detailed contents** inside the front and back covers allow you to quickly spot the help you need.

- **The index** at the back of the book includes user-friendly terms like "*I* vs. *me*" to point to common problems like pronoun case.

- **Charts and checklists** throughout the book and at the end of the book provide quick advice on revising a draft or preparing for a writing center visit.

- **Writing and formatting APA-style papers** is covered in sections 1–12, which provide advice about using APA conventions, supporting a thesis, avoiding plagiarism, and integrating sources when you write papers in APA style. The handbook includes sample pages from 11 types of student papers. Annotations on the sample pages point out appropriate writing as well as correct formatting of the parts of an APA-style paper.

- **Documenting sources in APA style** is covered in sections 13–15, which provide models for APA-style in-text citations and reference list entries. Directories to documentation models are on pages 104 and 111–12 and in the back of the book.

- **The glossaries** in the Appendices offer useful definitions and help with commonly confused or misused words such as *affect/effect.*

If your instructor has assigned this book with LaunchPad Solo, use the activation code to access exercises, model papers, and LearningCurve game-like quizzing. Visit **hackerhandbooks.com/pocket** to log in.

- **Grammar and research exercises** help you improve your writing and integrate sources.

- **11 model papers** in 7 disciplines provide guidance in writing and formatting your work.

- **LearningCurve quizzes** offer game-like sentence-level practice and let you track your progress.

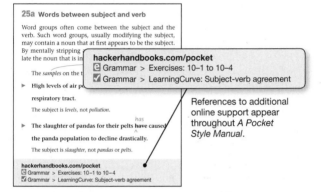

25a Words between subject and verb

Word groups often come between the subject and the verb. Such word groups, usually modifying the subject, may contain a noun that at first appears to be the subject. By mentally stripping ~~~~~~ late the noun that is in

The *samples* on the t

▶ High levels of air p

respiratory tract.

The subject is *levels*, not *pollution*.

has
▶ The slaughter of pandas for their pelts have caused
∧
the panda population to decline drastically.

The subject is *slaughter*, not *pandas* or *pelts*.

hackerhandbooks.com/pocket
Ⓖ Grammar > Exercises: 10–1 to 10–4
☑ Grammar > LearningCurve: Subject-verb agreement

hackerhandbooks.com/pocket
Ⓖ Grammar > Exercises: 10–1 to 10–4
☑ Grammar > LearningCurve: Subject-verb agreement

References to additional online support appear throughout *A Pocket Style Manual*.

A Pocket Style Manual

SEVENTH EDITION

APA Version

Diana Hacker

Nancy Sommers
Harvard University

Contributing Author
Rick A. Mathews
Carthage College

Bedford/St. Martin's
A Macmillan Education Imprint
Boston ◆ New York

For Bedford/St. Martin's

*Vice President, Editorial, Macmillan Higher Education
   Humanities:* Edwin Hill
Editorial Director for English and Music: Karen S. Henry
*Publisher for Composition, Business and Technical
   Writing and Developmental Writing:* Leasa Burton
Executive Editor: Michelle Clark
Developmental Editor: Alicia Young
Production Editor: Lidia MacDonald-Carr
Production Supervisor: Lisa McDowell
Marketing Manager: Emily Rowin
Project Management: Lifland et al., Bookmakers
Director of Rights and Permissions: Hilary Newman
Senior Art Director: Anna Palchik
Text Design: Claire Seng-Niemoeller
Cover Design: William Boardman
Composition: Cenveo Publisher Services
Printing and Binding: RR Donnelley and Sons

Manufactured in the United States of America.

0   9   8   7   6   5
f   e   d   c   b   a

For information, write: Bedford/St. Martin's, 75 Arlington Street,
Boston, MA 02116   (617-399-4000)

ISBN 978-1-319-01113-0

Writing Papers in APA Style

1 Writing college papers in APA style

In most of your college courses, it's likely you will be asked to complete one or more writing assignments. Besides composition courses, a wide variety of college courses require writing. Many different types of writing—essays, laboratory reports, memos, and treatment plans, for example—are assigned in many types of courses, such as psychology, sociology, business, and nursing. Instructors in these courses typically ask their students to write in the style recommended by the American Psychological Association (APA).

APA style is a set of rules and guidelines for writers in the social sciences (psychology, sociology, criminal justice, anthropology, political science) and in business, education, and nursing. When you are assigned a paper for a particular class, you should think of that assignment as an opportunity to join a discourse community—a group of thinkers and writers in a field who share interests, ideas, and ways of communicating with one another. When you adhere to APA style, you satisfy your readers' expectations and allow them to focus attention on the substance of your writing without unnecessary distractions.

APA style may be used for many types of writing, or *genres*. The following are the most common types of papers assigned in APA style:

- research paper: literature review
- research paper: original empirical research
- laboratory report
- analytical essay
- annotated bibliography
- administrative report
- case study
- clinical paper
- professional memo
- reflective essay

Sections 1a–1j describe the requirements of these types of papers. Section 10 gives details about the typical parts of APA-style papers. And section 12 contains excerpts from several papers written in APA style.

1a Research paper: Literature review

The ideas, theories, and findings of scholars in academic journals or books contribute to what researchers call "the literature" on a topic.

A common research assignment in undergraduate classes is a literature review. When you write a literature review, you will formulate a research question and collect sources that have been written about your question. You will summarize and synthesize the sources, indicating how they relate to one another and what insights they contribute to your question. You can also suggest ways that future research might add clarity to the conversation.

For instance, you might have settled on the research question "Do cities that have high rates of poverty also experience high rates of property crime?" In answering this question, you might compare data from the U.S. Census Bureau about the incidence of poverty in a particular group of cities and data from the Uniform Crime Reports about the incidence of property crime in those cities to see if a statistically significant relationship exists.

A review of the literature may be incorporated in other types of papers, especially empirical research papers and laboratory reports. In an empirical research paper, the literature review part of the paper is typically more extensive and longer than in a laboratory report. (See also 1b and 1c.)

1b Research paper: Original empirical research

An empirical research paper is a report of an original study that you design and data that you collect, perhaps from interviews, experiments, surveys, or observations in the field. Such data are called *primary data*. A research paper may also include *secondary data*—results from studies by other researchers that are relevant to the design of your study and the analysis of your data.

In an empirical research paper, you will state a research question or a hypothesis, briefly describe the work of others on the topic, present the methods you used to collect your data, analyze the data you collected, summarize important findings, analyze others' data in light of your own, and draw conclusions.

For example, to investigate the extent of and attitudes toward cheating on your campus, you might design a survey to give to students and then follow up the survey with one-on-one interviews. The data you collect from the survey and the interviews are your primary data. You would also briefly describe other researchers' work on the topic, giving an overview of the literature before presenting your own procedures and results. And you would use previous findings in your analysis of cheating on your campus.

1c Laboratory report

In the social sciences, a laboratory report provides details of an experiment or a study that you have conducted, usually with human participants in a controlled setting. For example, you might conduct an experiment in a psychology class that investigates how people respond to stress in competitive situations. Your lab report would include the main elements found in an empirical research paper: an introduction to your hypothesis and the problem studied, a brief discussion of the literature on the topic, a description of how you conducted the study (surveys, controlled experiments, interviews, observations, and so on), the key results of the study, and a discussion of the results (see also 1b). While an empirical research paper may be up to 30 pages long, a laboratory report is typically fewer than 10 pages.

1d Analytical essay

In an analytical essay, you will formulate a thesis statement that is open to debate and then use one or more texts to build an argument around that thesis. (See also section 7.)

Analytical essays are sometimes written about only one text. For example, in a political theory course, you may be asked to write an analytical paper on Machiavelli's *The Prince*. After carefully reading the text, you will formulate a thesis statement giving your analysis of the text or some aspect of it and then identify evidence from the text that can support that thesis.

An analytical essay can also make a larger argument using more than one source. In a business course, for instance, you may be asked to analyze the management practices of a company in light of a current theory, such as stakeholder theory. In this case, you would make an argument applying the theory to the practices and use evidence to support your argument.

1e Annotated bibliography

An annotated bibliography contains two basic elements: a list of sources related to a particular topic and a brief summary and evaluation of the quality and relevance of each source. An annotated bibliography may be assigned as part of the process of writing an empirical research paper or a literature review. In that case, it is an opportunity for you to do preliminary research and to understand and describe how each source might work within your paper.

An annotated bibliography is organized and formatted like a reference list (see 11b). The annotations are typically three to seven sentences long.

1f Administrative report

An administrative report provides a brief but detailed description of a problem that is of concern to an organization, such as a corporation, school, or police department. Administrative reports are used daily by professionals in fields such as social work and criminal justice. Such reports are well researched and are accompanied by recommendations based on the research. The type of research used to write an administrative report will vary and may include internal material from documents or interviews as well as material such as articles and reports from outside sources.

Professionals working in many fields may provide administrative reports to their superiors. For example, a department head in a business may provide an expense report to the vice president for finance that explains the ways in which the department spent money. A teacher may report to an administrator about a student's progress.

1g Case study

The purpose of a case study is to gain a detailed understanding of a particular person, organization, event, or group of individuals. Case studies can vary by discipline, but most involve a deep analysis of a relatively narrow subject.

Some case studies require primary data—data that you collect. For an education class, you might study the effectiveness of particular classroom management techniques. Your study might involve observing a classroom where those techniques are used and drawing conclusions based on your observations.

Or a case study might involve a detailed description and analysis of an event, such as federal or state response to a natural disaster. A case study also can be used to study a single organization as an example of a larger issue, such as a company like Enron as an example of corporate mismanagement.

1h Clinical paper

Clinical papers are most often used by practitioners in the health professions to share information about clients. Clinical papers usually provide an overview of a client and his or her symptoms, review the relevant literature on the client's condition, and then provide details and recommendations about the course of treatment as well as actual and expected results.

1i Professional memo

Memos are widely used by members in a business or another organization to communicate with one another. Memos may identify a problem or concern within the organization, inform others about a policy or procedure, assign tasks to people, or solve a problem (or all of these things at once). Memos are often sent via e-mail.

Memos may cover a wide range of subjects and may be any length. A short memo might simply contain a task for the members of a committee. A longer memo might contain a proposal with data or ideas that are not your own.

When writing a memo, make sure that the content, language, and tone are appropriate for the intended audience (see also 2b and 2c). Memos usually provide ongoing documentation for a project and may be helpful to those doing similar projects in the future. So your audience may be broader than the initial recipients of the memo.

1j Reflective essay

A reflective essay is personal writing, usually to explore the ways in which an experience shaped your understanding of an issue or a topic in your discipline. For example, a reflective essay about your student teaching experience may include a description of how you came to view one of the theories of learning you had studied in a different light once you were teaching your own class.

2 Understanding APA conventions

Writers and researchers in the social sciences and in business, education, and nursing follow APA standards, or *conventions*, a set of agreed-upon rules. You may be asked to use these conventions to guide your own practices as you search for and evaluate sources, draft your writing, and acknowledge the contributions of others. The APA conventions that you will be expected to follow in your writing are detailed in this section.

2a Privileging current sources

While recognizing that knowledge is based on ideas and findings that have emerged over time, APA style values the currency of research. *When* a person wrote a book or an article or conducted research is as important as *what* that person wrote or researched. The date of the research you cite in your paper is an indication to your readers that you are building your own work on the most recent work of others and that you understand the connection between your work and the work that has come before.

At the same time, you will likely find older sources that are relevant to your research question. While there is nothing wrong with citing older sources, you should make clear in your paper how those findings connect to more recent research in the field. One way to determine the validity of previous research is to look for more recent articles that have cited older work. When analyzing the results of the more recent research, check whether the work supports the original findings. Doing so will help you determine whether the older research is still valid and, if so, how it aligns with your work and that of contemporary researchers.

The author's name and the date figure prominently in citations of sources within a paper and in the reference list at the end of the paper. (For more details about the use of direct quotations, see section 9. For more information on citing and documenting sources in APA style, see sections 13–15.)

IN-TEXT CITATION

Gawande (2009) noted that technology "has added yet another element of complexity to the systems we depend on and given us entirely new kinds of failure to contend with" (p. 184).

REFERENCE LIST ENTRY

Gawande, A. (2009). *The checklist manifesto: How to get things right*. New York, NY: Metropolitan Books.

2b Using appropriate tone and language

APA style calls for writing that is direct, clear, concise, engaging, objective, and formal. The active voice is more direct and concise—and therefore usually more appropriate—than the passive voice (see section 17).

INAPPROPRIATE (PASSIVE VOICE)

Support for faster female response times was found in several studies (Barber, 2010; Lee, 2009; Sumner, 2011).

The idea that social meaning is largely constructed through the interactions people have with one another has been emphasized by symbolic-interaction theorists.

APPROPRIATE (ACTIVE VOICE)

Several studies (Barber, 2010; Lee, 2009; Sumner, 2011) supported faster female response times.

Symbolic-interaction theorists have emphasized that social meaning is largely constructed through the interactions people have with one another.

In general, prefer nouns and third-person pronouns (see 27c) whenever possible. But sometimes for clarity and to avoid the passive voice, the first person (*I* or *we*) is appropriate, especially in the abstract and the method section in research papers and laboratory reports when you are describing your own procedures. Also, in reflective essays and research involving observation in the field, the first person is appropriate to describe your own experiences or to relate your experiences to a larger issue or larger body of work.

INAPPROPRIATE (THIRD PERSON, PASSIVE VOICE)

Participants were selected with a random number generator.

The children's behavior toward their peers was observed both in the classroom and on the playground.

APPROPRIATE (FIRST PERSON, ACTIVE VOICE)

I selected the participants with a random number generator.

We observed the children's behavior toward their peers both in the classroom and on the playground.

NOTE: When writing in the first person, use the plural *we* only if you have coauthors; use *I* if you are the only author.

APA style requires the past tense (*explained*) or present perfect tense (*have written*) for describing the work of others or for your own results. (See 9b.) You may use the present tense to describe the applications or effects of your results (*the data indicate*).

2c Avoiding stereotypes, bias, and offensive language

Your writing must be respectful and free of stereotypical, biased, or other offensive language. Be especially careful when describing or labeling people in terms of their race, age, disability, gender, or sexual orientation.

Labels can become dated, and it is important to recognize when their continued use is not acceptable. When naming groups of people, choose labels that the groups currently use to describe themselves. For example, *Negro* is not an acceptable label for African Americans; some people prefer the term *Native American* to *Indian,* and even better is to use the name of the specific group (*Lakota, Sioux*).

Be as specific as possible when describing age groups (*women aged 24 to 30 years*, not *young women* or *twentysomethings*), and avoid terms such as *elderly* or *senior*, which can be vague and can also carry a negative connotation.

Do not identify a person by his or her condition or disability; refer to the person first, the condition or disability second. Use *men with epilepsy* rather than *epileptics* or *epileptic men*. The term *client* is preferred to *patient* in many fields.

Use gender-neutral language (*firefighter, legislator* instead of *fireman, congressman*) and plural pronouns rather than the singular *he, him, his.* (See also 24d on avoiding sexist language.) Currently acceptable terms for describing sexual orientation are *lesbian, gay,* and *bisexual* rather than *homosexual*.

It's a good idea to check with your instructor or someone else in the discipline about the currently acceptable terms for describing and labeling people.

2d Understanding intellectual property

The term *intellectual property* refers to published works, ideas, and images that have been created by an individual or a group. When you use the intellectual property of others in your own work—by quoting, summarizing, or paraphrasing—you must give credit to the source of the information. Failure to do so is a form of academic dishonesty called *plagiarism*. (See also section 8.)

Besides summarizing, paraphrasing, or quoting another's work without proper citation, it is considered plagiarism to submit the work of someone else as your own (such as purchasing a paper or hiring someone to write a paper for you).

Consistent and proper use of the APA system of citation—in the text of the paper and in the reference list at the end of the paper—will ensure that you do not misrepresent the intellectual property of someone else as your own. (See sections 13–15 for details on the APA system of citation.)

2e Collecting and reporting data

For some types of papers, you may collect and report data yourself—from surveys you administer, from experiments you conduct, from audio or video interviews you record, from observations you make in the field, and so on. APA conventions require you to collect and report data in an ethical manner.

In collecting your data, you should be careful not to ignore groups of research participants whose responses you think may prove contrary to your research question. In reporting your findings, you must not ignore or downplay results that contradict other results or results you expected to find. If your research involves human participants, you must preserve confidentiality. And you must not falsify data or report results in a misleading way, such as by manipulating images or creating graphs with only partial data.

A standard in the social sciences is that research must be replicable—that is, other researchers must be able to use the information provided in your paper to conduct a study of their own to try to reproduce your results. If you do not collect data objectively and honestly or if you report data in a misleading way, others will not be able to come close to replicating your findings, even if they use the same method.

2f Protecting research participants

Ethics codes in the social sciences are intended to protect research participants from physical or emotional harm and to prevent falsifying data, misrepresenting research findings, and plagiarizing. Whenever you plan to collect data through interviews, surveys, experiments, or observation, you should determine whether your research project needs the review and approval of your school's institutional review board (IRB).

An IRB requires that participation in research be voluntary, that the research participants grant informed consent, and that they not be harmed (either emotionally or physically). Participants should be able to end their participation at any time without penalty. Researchers must observe confidentiality and must conduct their research with integrity and ensure that it has academic value.

Some kinds of research are exempt from IRB approval. If you analyze data that have been collected and published by someone else, those data generally are exempt from IRB review. In addition, most large data sets used in undergraduate research courses—such as the General Social Survey and the Uniform Crime Reports—are exempt, as are published data from studies conducted by organizations, commissions, government agencies, and the like.

If you are unsure whether your project needs IRB approval, ask your instructor.

3   Posing questions to start a paper

Most college assignments begin with a question worth exploring. The question might be posed in the wording of the assignment, or you might be required to come up with your own question. For a research paper, you might search for answers in books, articles, and Web sites; for a laboratory report, your answers might come from an experiment you design; for a business memo, you might conduct a customer survey. Your answers should guide your interpretation and lead to reasoned conclusions supported with valid and well-documented evidence.

Within the guidelines of your assignment, begin by asking questions that you are interested in exploring, that you feel would interest your audience, and that will contribute to an ongoing debate or to existing knowledge in the field.

For any type of assignment, you should make sure that your questions are narrow (not too broad), challenging (not too bland), and grounded (not too speculative).

3a Choosing a narrow question

If your initial question is too broad for the length you were assigned, look for ways to restrict your focus. Here, for example, is how two students narrowed their initial questions.

TOO BROAD	NARROWER
What are the hazards of fad diets?	What are the hazards of low-carbohydrate diets?
What are the benefits of stricter auto emissions standards?	How will stricter auto emissions standards create new, more competitive auto industry jobs?

3b Choosing a challenging question

Your paper will be more interesting to both you and your audience if you base it on an intellectually challenging line of inquiry. Try to draft questions that provoke thought or, if your purpose is to take a position, engage readers in a debate.

TOO BLAND	CHALLENGING
What is obsessive-compulsive disorder?	Why is obsessive-compulsive disorder so difficult to treat?
What were client S.R.'s symptoms?	How did the combined course of drug therapy and physical therapy reduce client S.R.'s symptoms?

You may need to address a bland question in the course of answering a more challenging one, but it would be a mistake to use the bland question as the focus for the whole paper.

3c Choosing a grounded question

Finally, you will want to make sure that your question is grounded, not too speculative. Although speculative questions — such as those that address morality or beliefs — are worth asking and may receive attention in some papers, they are inappropriate central questions. The central point of most papers should be grounded in facts.

TOO SPECULATIVE	GROUNDED
Is it wrong to share pornographic personal photos by cell phone?	What role should the U.S. government play in regulating mobile content?
Do students have the right to listen to music during class?	What effect does listening to music while studying have on adolescents' test performance?

4 Finding appropriate sources

Depending on your topic and your question, some sources will prove more useful than others. For example, if your question addresses whether a particular public policy has been effective, you might want to look at scholarly articles, books, reference works, and government documents. If the policy issue is the subject of current debate, you might also want to use magazines and newspaper articles, Web sites, and documents from organizations that try to influence public policy (such as think tanks).

4a Locating reference works

For some topics, you may want to begin your search by consulting general or specialized reference works. General reference works include encyclopedias, almanacs, atlases, and biographical references. Many specialized reference works are available: *Encyclopedia of Bioethics*, *The Encyclopedia of Social Work*, *Almanac of American Politics*, and *The Historical and Cultural Atlas of African Americans*, to name a few. Reference works can help you learn about a topic, but you will need to consult more in-depth sources as you write.

The reference librarians at your school are trained to assist you in finding sources and can be helpful as you conduct your research. You should take advantage of their expertise if you have questions about how to evaluate sources. Many times, they can also help you as you refine your research question or topic.

4b Locating articles

Libraries subscribe to a variety of databases (sometimes called *periodical* or *article databases*) that give students access to articles and other materials without charge. Older works that have not been digitized will not be available in databases; you may need to consult a print index as well.

What databases offer   Your library's databases can lead you to articles in newspapers, magazines, and scholarly or technical journals. General databases cover several subject areas; subject-specific databases cover one subject area in depth. Your library might subscribe to some of the following databases.

GENERAL DATABASES

Academic Search Premier. A database that indexes popular and scholarly journals.

Expanded Academic ASAP. A database that indexes the contents of magazines, newspapers, and scholarly journals.

JSTOR. A full-text archive of scholarly journals from many disciplines.

LexisNexis. A set of databases particularly strong in news, business, legal, and political topics.

ProQuest. A database of periodical articles.

SUBJECT-SPECIFIC DATABASES

Business Source Premier. An index of business abstracts and titles.

Criminal Justice Abstracts. A database for criminal justice research.

ERIC. An education database.

Health Source Nursing, Academic Version. A database for nursing topics.

PsycINFO. A database of psychology research.

PubMed. A database with abstracts of medical studies.

Many databases include the full text of at least some articles; others list only citations or citations with short summaries called *abstracts*. When the full text is not available, a citation will give you enough information to track down an article.

How to search a database   To find articles on your topic in a database, start by searching with keywords, terms related to the information you need. If the first keyword you try results in no matches, try some synonyms. If your keyword search results in too many matches, narrow it by using one of the strategies in the chart on page 16.

You can also narrow your topic by looking for repeated subjects within your search results. For example, while a search on the death penalty will yield many results, you might notice when you read through the titles of the results that multiple articles address the constitutionality of the death penalty or discuss prisoners who were wrongly convicted and put to death—in other words, two specific topics within the broader subject of the death penalty. Looking for these kinds of patterns can help you narrow your research topic.

4c Locating books

The books your library owns are listed along with other resources in its catalog. You can search the catalog by author, title, or subject.

If your search calls up too few results, try different keywords or search for books on broader topics. If your search gives you too many results, try the strategies in the chart on page 16.

Use a book's call number to find the book on the shelf. When you're retrieving the book, take time to scan other books in the area since they are likely to cover the same topic.

4d Locating other sources online

You can find a variety of reliable resources using online tools beyond those offered by your library. For example, government agencies post information on their Web sites, and the sites of many organizations are filled with information about current issues. Museums and libraries often post digital versions of primary sources, such as photographs, political speeches, and classic texts.

Although the Internet can be a rich source of information, it lacks quality control. Anyone can publish to the Web, so you'll need to evaluate online sources with special care (see 5c).

Refining keyword searches in databases and search engines

Although command terms and characters vary among databases and Web search engines, some of the most common functions are listed here.

- Use quotation marks around words that are part of a phrase: "gateway drug".

- Use AND to connect words that must appear in a document: hyperactivity AND children. Some search engines require a plus sign instead: hyperactivity+children.

- Use NOT in front of words that must not appear in a document: Persian Gulf NOT war. Some search engines require a minus sign (hyphen) instead: Persian Gulf -war.

- Use OR if only one of the terms must appear in a document: "mountain lion" OR cougar.

- Use an asterisk as a substitute for letters that might vary: "marine biolog*" (to find *marine biology* or *marine biologist*).

- Use parentheses to group a search expression and combine it with another: (standard OR student OR test*) AND reform.

NOTE: Many search engines and databases offer an advanced search option for refining your search with filters for phrases that should or should not appear, date restrictions, and so on.

This section describes the following Internet resources: search engines, directories, digital archives, government sites, news sites, blogs, and wikis.

Search engines When using a search engine, such as *Google Scholar* or *Yahoo!*, focus your search as narrowly as possible. You can sharpen your search by using the tips listed in the chart at the top of this page or by using a search engine's advanced search form.

Directories Unlike search engines, which hunt for Web pages automatically, directories are put together by information specialists who arrange reputable sites by topic: education, health, politics, and so on.

Try the following directories for scholarly research:

DMOZ: http://dmoz.org

Internet Scout Project: http://scout.wisc.edu/Archives

Librarian's Internet Index: http://lii.org

WWW Virtual Library: http://vlib.org

Digital archives Archives like the following can help you find primary resources such as the texts of books, poems, speeches, and historically significant documents; photographs; and political cartoons.

> *American Memory:* http://memory.loc.gov
>
> *Avalon Project:* http://yale.edu/lawweb/avalon/avalon.htm
>
> *Eurodocs:* http://eudocs.lib.byu.edu
>
> *Google Books:* http://books.google.com
>
> *Google Scholar:* http://scholar.google.com
>
> *Online Books Page:* http://onlinebooks.library.upenn.edu

Government sites For current topics, government sites can prove useful. Many government agencies at every level provide online information. Government-maintained sites include resources such as facts and statistics, legal texts, government reports, and searchable reference databases. Here are just a few government sites:

> *Census Bureau:* http://www.census.gov
>
> *Fedstats:* http://www.fedstats.gov
>
> *GPO Access:* http://www.gpoaccess.gov
>
> *National Criminal Justice Reference Service:* https://www.ncjrs.gov
>
> *United Nations:* http://www.un.org
>
> *University of Michigan Documents Center:* http://www.lib.umich.edu/m/moagrp

News sites Many news organizations offer up-to-date information online. Some sites require registration and charge fees for some articles. (Find out if your library subscribes to news sites that you can access at no charge.) The following news sites offer many free resources:

> *BBC:* http://www.bbc.co.uk
>
> *Google News:* http://news.google.com
>
> *Kidon Media-Link:* http://www.kidon.com/media-link
>
> *New York Times:* http://nytimes.com
>
> *Reuters:* http://www.reuters.com

Blogs A blog is a site that contains text or multimedia entries usually written and maintained by one person, with comments contributed by readers. Though some blogs are personal or devoted to partisan politics, many journalists and academics maintain blogs that cover topics of interest to researchers. The following Web sites can lead you to a wide range of blogs:

Academic Blog Portal: http://academicblogs.org

Google Blog Search: http://www.google.com/blogsearch

Science Blogs: http://scienceblogs.com

Technorati: http://technorati.com

Wikis   A wiki is a collaborative Web site with many contributors and with content that may change frequently. *Wikipedia*, a collaborative online encyclopedia, is one of the most frequently consulted wikis.

In general, *Wikipedia* may be helpful if you're checking for something that is common knowledge or looking for current information about a topic in contemporary culture. (For a discussion of common knowledge, see p. 31.) However, many scholars do not consider *Wikipedia* and wikis in general to be appropriate sources for college research. Authorship is not limited to experts; articles may be written or changed by anyone. When possible, locate and cite another, more reliable source for any useful information you find in a wiki.

5   Evaluating sources

You can often locate dozens or even hundreds of potential sources for your topic—far more than you will have time to read. Your challenge will be to determine what kinds of sources you need and to find a reasonable number of quality sources.

Later, once you have decided on sources worth consulting, your challenge will be to read them with an open mind and a critical eye.

5a Selecting sources

Determining how sources contribute to your writing How you plan to use sources affects how you evaluate them. Sources can have various functions in a paper. You can use them to

- provide background information or context for your topic
- explain terms or concepts that your readers might not understand
- provide evidence for your main idea
- lend authority to your discussion
- offer counterevidence and alternative interpretations

For examples of how student writers use sources for a variety of purposes, see section 9.

Scanning search results   The chart on page 16 shows how to refine your searches. This section explains how to scan through the results for the most useful and reliable sources.

Databases   Most article databases (see p. 14) provide at least the following information to help you decide if a source is relevant, current, scholarly, and a suitable length.

Title and brief description (How relevant?)

Date (How current?)

Name of periodical (How scholarly?)

Length (How extensive in coverage?)

Book catalogs   A book's title and date of publication are often your first clues about whether the book is worth consulting. If a title looks interesting, you can click on it for further information.

Search engines   Because anyone can publish a Web site, legitimate sources and unreliable sources live side-by-side online. Look for the following clues about the probable relevance, currency, and reliability of a site—but be aware that the clues are by no means foolproof.

Title, keywords, and lead-in text (How relevant?)

A date (How current?)

An indication of the site's sponsor or purpose (How reliable?)

The URL, especially the domain name extension: for example, .com, .edu, .gov, or .org (How relevant? How reliable?)

Determining if a source is scholarly

Many college assignments require you to use scholarly sources. Written by experts for a knowledgeable audience, these sources often go into more depth than books and articles written for a general audience. To determine if a source is scholarly, look for the following:

- Formal language and presentation
- Authors with academic or scientific credentials
- Footnotes or a bibliography documenting the works cited by the author in the source
- Original research and interpretation (rather than a summary of other people's work)
- Quotations from and analysis of primary sources
- A description of research methods or a review of related research

See pages 21–22 for a sample scholarly source and a sample popular source.

5b Reading with an open mind and a critical eye

As you begin reading the sources you have chosen, keep an open mind. Do not let your personal beliefs prevent you from considering new ideas and opposing viewpoints. Your question—not a snap judgment about the question—should guide your reading.

When you read critically, you are not necessarily judging an author's work harshly; you are simply examining its assumptions, assessing its evidence, and weighing its conclusions. For a checklist on evaluating sources, see page 23.

5c Assessing Web sources with special care

Web sources can provide valuable information, but verifying their credibility may take time. Even sites that appear to be professional and fair-minded may contain questionable information. Before using a Web source in your paper, make sure you know who created the material and for what purpose. The chart on page 24 provides a checklist for evaluating Web sources.

Common features of a scholarly source

1 Formal presentation with abstract and research methods
2 Includes review of previous research studies
3 Reports original research
4 Includes references
5 Multiple authors with academic credentials

FIRST PAGE OF ARTICLE

Cyberbullying: Using Virtual Scenarios to Educate and Raise Awareness

Vivian H. Wright, Joy J. Burnham, Christopher T. Inman, and **5**
Heather N. Ogorchock

Abstract

This study examined cyberbullying in three distinct phases to facilitate a multifaceted understanding of cyberbullying. The phases included (a) a quantitative survey, (b) a qualitative survey, and (c) development of educational scenarios/simulations (within the Second Life virtual environment). Phase III was based on adolescent feedback about cyberbullying from Phases I and II of this study. In all three phases, adolescent reactions to cyberbullying were examined and reported to raise awareness and to educate others about cyberbullying. Results from scenario development indicate that simulations created in a virtual environment are engaging and have the potential to be powerful tools in helping schools address problems such as cyberbullying education and prevention. (Keywords: cyberbullying, virtual worlds, Second Life, teacher education, counselor education)

Introduction

Cyberbullying has gained attention and recognition in recent years (Beale & Hall, 2007; Carney, 2008; Casey-Canon, Hayward, & Gowen, 2001; Kowalski & Limber, 2007; Li, 2007; Shariff, 2005). The increased interest and awareness of cyberbullying relates to such factors as the national media attention after several publicized cyberbullying tragedies (Maag, 2007; Stelter, 2008; Zifcak, 2006), the attenuation of communication boundaries via electronic devices, and computer network connectivity. The ubiquitous reality of technology use among youth. Now, with computer technology and the easy access and popularity of electronic devices among youth, presently there remains a critical need to understand cyberbullying and its possible effects during childhood and adolescents. Because cyberbullying has moved beyond established systems (i.e., home, school, and the community), we once that parents, "school professionals" (Li, 2007, p. 1778), and mental health providers must not only be made aware of cyberbullying and its consequences, but must also have access to ways to deal with this growing concern.

Two years ago, cyberbullying was considered to be a "new territory" for exploration (Li, 2007, p. 1778) because there was limited information about bullying through "electronic means" (Li, p. 1780). In contrast, today studies on cyberbullying, including some descriptions of the worst cyberbullying incidences (Maag, 2007; Stelter, 2008; Zifcak, 2006), are becoming more prevalent (Beale & Hall, 2007; Carney, 2008; Kowalski & Limber, 2007; Li, 2007). At this time, there is a need to raise awareness about the effects of cyberbullying and to create educational opportunities to serve multiple audiences (i.e., teachers, teacher educators, school administrators, school counselors, mental health professionals, students, parents) in the quest to identify and hopefully prevent cyberbullying in the future. Consequently, to facilitate a multifaceted understanding of

cyberbullying, this study sought to examine cyberbullying through three phases: (a) a quantitative survey, (b) a qualitative focus group, and (c) development of the educational scenarios/simulations (i.e., using virtual world avatars similar to those used in Linden Lab's (1993) Second Life (SL; http://secondlife.com) based on adolescent feedback from Phases I and II of this study. Adolescent reactions to cyberbullying in all three phases of this study were examined and reported with two aims in mind: (a) to raise awareness of cyberbullying, and (b) to educate others about cyberbullying.

Defining Cyberbullying

Cyberbullying has been described as a traumatic experience that can lead to physical, cognitive, emotional, and social consequences (Carney, 2008; Casey-Canon et al., 2001; Patchin & Hinduja, 2006). Cyberbullying has been defined as "bullying through the e-mail, instant messaging, in a chat room, on a website, or though digital messages or images sent to a cell phone" (Kowalski & Limber, 2007, p. 822). There are numerous methods to engage in cyberbullying, including e-mail, instant messaging, online gaming, chat rooms, and text messaging (Beale & Hall, 2007; Li, 2007). In addition, cyberbullying appears in different forms than traditional bullying. For example, Beale and Hall (2007), Mason (2007), and Willard (2008) found that at least seven different types of cyberbullying exist, including:

> Research suggests that cyberbullying has distinct gender and age differences. According to the literature, girls are more likely to be online and to cyberbully (Beale & Hall, 2007; Kowalski & Limber, 2007; Li, 2006, 2007). This finding is "opposite of what happens off-line," where boys are

- Outing or trickery: tricking a person into sharing secret or embarrassing information
- Exclusion: excluding someone purposefully

Research suggests that cyberbullying has distinct gender and age differences. According to the literature, girls are more likely to be online and to cyberbully (Beale & Hall, 2007; Kowalski & Limber, 2007; Li, 2006, 2007). This finding is "opposite of what happens off-line," where boys are more likely than girls (Beale & Hall, p. 8). Age also appears to be a factor in cyberbullying. Cyberbullying increases in the elementary years, peaks during the middle school years, and declines in the high school years (Beale & Hall). Based on the literature, cyberbullying is a growing concern among middle school-aged children (Beale & Hall; Hinduja & Patchin, 2008; Kowalski & Limber, 2007; Li, 2007; Pellegrini & Bartini, 2000; Smith, Mahdavi, Carvalho, & Tippett, 2006; Williams & Guerra, 2007). Of the middle school grades, 6th grade students are usually the

EXCERPTS FROM OTHER PAGES

3 Table 2: Percentage of Students Who Experienced Cyberbullying through Various Methods

	E-mail	Facebook	MySpace	Cell Phone	Online Video	Chat Rooms
Victim	35.3%	11.8%	52.9%	50%	14.7%	11.8%
Bully	17.6%	0%	70.6%	47.1%	11.8%	5.9%

4 ### References

Bainbridge, W. S. (2007, July). The scientific research potential of virtual worlds. *Science, 317,* 472–476.

Beale, A., & Hall, K. (2007, September/October). Cyberbullying: What *81, 8*

5 *Vivian H. Wright is an associate professor of instructional technology at the University of Alabama. In addition to teaching in the graduate program, Dr. Wright works with teacher educators on innovative ways to infuse technology in the curriculum*

Wright, V. H., Burnham, J. J., Inman, C. T., & Ogorchock, H. N. (2009). Cyberbullying: Using virtual scenarios to educate and raise awareness. *Journal of Computing in Teacher Education, 26*(1), 35-42.

Common features of a popular source

1. Eye-catching title
2. Written by a staff reporter, not an expert
3. Presents anecdotes about the topic
4. Sources are named, but no formal works cited list appears
5. Presents a summary of research but no original research

ONLINE ARTICLE

CNN Health

Home TV & Video U.S. World Politics Justice Entertainment Tech Health Living Travel Opinion iReport Money Sports

Part of complete coverage on
Bullying   SPECIAL REPORT: BULLYING

When bullying goes high-tech [1]

by **Elizabeth Landau**, CNN [2]
updated 2:12 PM EDT, Mon April 15, 2013

STORY HIGHLIGHTS
- As many as 25% of teenagers have experienced cyberbullying
- Among young people, it's rare that an online bully will be a total stranger
- Researchers are working on apps and algorithms to detect and report bullying online

(CNN) -- Brandon Turley didn't have [3] friends in sixth grade. He would often eat alone at lunch, having recently switched to his school without knowing anyone.

While browsing MySpace one day, he saw that someone from school had posted a bulletin -- a message visible to multiple people -- declaring that Turley was a "fag." Students he had never even spoken with wrote on it, too, saying they agreed.

Feeling confused and upset, Turley wrote in the comments, too, asking why his classmates would say that. The response was even worse: He was told on MySpace that a group of 12 kids wanted to beat him up, that he should stop going to school and die. On his walk from his locker to the school office to report what was happening, students yelled things like "fag" and "fatty."

"It was just crazy, and such a shock to my self-esteem that people didn't like me without even knowing me," said Turley, now 18 and a senior in high school in Oregon. "I didn't understand how that could be."

A pervasive problem
As many as 25% of teenagers have experienced cyberbullying at some point, said Justin W. Patchin, who studies the phenomenon [4] at the University of Wisconsin-Eau Claire. He and colleagues have conducted formal surveys of 15,000 middle and high school students throughout the United States, and found that about 10% [5] of teens have been victims of cyberbullying in the last 30 days.

Online bullying has a lot in common with bullying in school: Both behaviors include harassment, humiliation, teasing and aggression, Patchin said. Cyberbullying presents unique challenges in the sense that the perpetrator can attempt to be anonymous, and attacks can happen at any time of day or night.

Evaluating all sources

Checking for signs of bias

- Does the author or publisher endorse political or religious views that could affect objectivity?

- Is the author or publisher associated with a special-interest group, such as Greenpeace or the National Rifle Association, that might present a narrow view of an issue?

- How fairly does the author treat opposing views?

- Does the author's language show signs of bias?

Assessing an argument

- What is the author's central claim or thesis?

- How does the author support this claim—with relevant and sufficient evidence or with anecdotes or emotional examples?

- Are statistics accurate and used fairly? Does the author explain where the statistics come from?

- Are any of the author's assumptions questionable?

- Does the author consider opposing arguments and refute them persuasively?

6   Managing information; avoiding plagiarism

Whether you decide to record information about your sources on paper or on your computer—or both—you will need methods for managing that information: maintaining a working bibliography, keeping track of source materials, and taking notes without plagiarizing your sources. (For more on avoiding plagiarism, see section 8.)

6a   Maintaining a working bibliography

Keep a record of any sources you decide to consult. This record, called a *working bibliography*, will help you compile the list of sources at the end of your paper. (For more details about documenting sources, see section 14.)

hackerhandbooks.com/pocket
🄴 APA papers > Sample student writing (APA version)
  > Neimeyer (annotated bibliography)
  > Haddad (annotated bibliography)

Evaluating Web sources

Authorship

◾ Is there an author? You may need to do some clicking and scrolling to find the author's name. Check the home page or an "about this site" link.

◾ Can you tell whether the author is knowledgeable and credible? If the author's qualifications aren't listed on the site, look for links to the author's home page, which may provide evidence of his or her expertise.

Sponsorship

◾ Who, if anyone, sponsors the site? The sponsor of a site is often named and described on the home page.

◾ What does the URL tell you? The domain name extension often indicates the type of group hosting the site: commercial (.com), educational (.edu), nonprofit (.org), governmental (.gov), military (.mil), or network (.net). URLs may also indicate a country of origin: .uk (United Kingdom) or .jp (Japan), for instance.

Purpose and audience

◾ Why was the site created: To argue a position? To sell a product? To inform readers?

◾ Who is the site's intended audience?

Currency

◾ How current is the site? Check for the date of publication or the latest update.

◾ How current are the site's links? If many of the links no longer work, the site may be outdated for your purposes.

Once you have created a working bibliography, you can annotate it. Writing several brief sentences summarizing the key points of a source in your own words will help you identify how the source relates to your argument and to your other sources. Clarifying the source's ideas at this stage will help you separate them from your own ideas and avoid plagiarizing them later.

SAMPLE ANNOTATED BIBLIOGRAPHY ENTRY

International Monetary Fund, Western Hemisphere Department.

(2010). *United States: 2010 article IV consultation* (Country **1**
Report No. 10/249). Retrieved from http://www.imf.org
/external/pubs/ft/scr/2010/cr10249.pdf

The International Monetary Fund publishes an annual
report on each member country's economic status within the
global economy. The report outlines the country's efforts in **2**
creating international and domestic economic stability while
offering recommendations to address the country's economic
challenges. The 2010 report on the United States provides **3**
important statistics showing the United States' decrease
in imports and exports during the current economic crisis
and the effect of this contracting trade on the international
community. The report also lists specific challenges that
face the United States as it continues to recover from the
crisis. The report helps me put recent U.S. macroeconomic **4**
policy trends, as well as several of my other sources, in
context; it also gives me a basis for evaluating the effects
of these policies in both the short and the long term. I can **5**
use the report to draw conclusions about the effectiveness
of these largely Keynesian policies as well as predict future
policy revisions.

1 Use APA reference list format for each entry.
2 Summarize the source.
3 Annotations should be three to seven sentences long.
4 Evaluate the source for relevance and describe how it relates
to other sources you might use in the paper.
5 Evaluate how the source might contribute to your paper.

6b Keeping track of source materials

Save a copy of each source either electronically or in print.
Many databases will allow you to e-mail, save, or print citations, abstracts, or full texts of articles, and you can easily
download, copy, print, or take screen shots of information
from Web sites.

Working with saved files or printouts—as opposed
to relying on memory or hastily written notes—lets you
highlight key passages and make notes in the margins of

the source as you read. You also reduce the chances of unintentional plagiarism because you will be able to compare your use of a source in your paper with the actual source, not just with your notes.

NOTE: It's especially important to keep print or electronic copies of Web sources, which may change or even become inaccessible over time. Make sure that your copy includes the site's URL and your date of access.

6c Avoiding unintentional plagiarism as you take notes

When you take notes, be very careful to identify borrowed words and phrases as quotations. Even if you half-copy the author's sentences—either by mixing the author's phrases with your own without using quotation marks or by plugging your synonyms into the author's sentence structure—you are committing plagiarism, a serious academic offense.

Summarizing and paraphrasing ideas and quoting exact language are three ways of taking notes. Be sure to include exact page references for all three types of notes; you will need the page numbers later if you use the information in your paper. (See the chart on pp. 27–28 for advice about avoiding plagiarism.)

7   Supporting a thesis

For assignments that call for research—literature reviews, empirical research papers, analytical essays, annotated bibliographies, among others—you will form a research question that will lead to a thesis statement or a statement of your central idea (see section 3 on posing questions). You will usually present your thesis in the introduction, the first few paragraphs of the paper. The rest of the paper will draw on the sources you use to support your thesis.

You face three main challenges when writing a paper that draws on sources: (1) supporting a thesis, (2) citing your sources and avoiding plagiarism (see section 8), and (3) integrating quotations and other source material (see section 9).

Integrating and citing sources to avoid plagiarism

Source text

Our language is constantly changing. Like the Mississippi, it keeps forging new channels and abandoning
old ones, picking up debris, depositing unwanted silt,
and frequently bursting its banks. In every generation
there are people who deplore changes in the language
and many who wish to stop its flow. But if our language
stopped changing it would mean that American society
had ceased to be dynamic, innovative, pulsing with
life — that the great river had frozen up.
— Robert MacNeil and William Cran,
Do You Speak American? (2005), p. 1

NOTE: For details on integrating sources, see section 9. For
citing sources in the text of the paper, see section 13.

If you are using an exact sentence from a source, with no changes . . .	→ . . . put quotation marks around the sentence. Use a signal phrase and include a page number in parentheses.

MacNeil and Cran (2005) have written, "Our
language is constantly changing" (p. 1).

If you are using a few exact words from the source but not an entire sentence . . .	→ . . . put quotation marks around the exact words that you have used from the source. Use a signal phrase and include a page number in parentheses.

Some people, according to MacNeil and
Cran (2005), "deplore changes in the
language" (p. 1).

If you are using near-exact words from the source but changing some word forms (*I* to *she*, *walk* to *walked*) or adding words to clarify and make the quotation flow with your own text . . .	→ . . . put quotation marks around the quoted words and put brackets around the changes you have intro- duced. Include a signal phrase and follow the quotation with the page number in parentheses.

MacNeil and Cran (2005) compared the
English language to the Mississippi
River, which "forg[es] new channels and
abandon[s] old ones" (p. 1).

MacNeil and Cran (2005) have written,
"In every generation there are people who
deplore changes in the [English] language
and many who wish to stop its flow" (p. 1).

→

Integrating and citing sources to avoid plagiarism
(continued)

If you are para-phrasing or summarizing the source, using the author's ideas but not any of the author's exact words . . .	→ . . . introduce the ideas with a signal phrase and put the page number at the end of your sentence. Do not use quotation marks. (See 8c.) MacNeil and Cran (2005) argued that changes in the English language are natural and that they represent cultural progress (p. 1).
If you have used the source's sentence structure but substituted a few synonyms for the author's words . . .	→ STOP! This is a form of plagiarism even if you use a signal phrase and a page number. Change your sentence by using one of the techniques given in this chart or in section 9. PLAGIARIZED MacNeil and Cran (2005) claimed that, like a river, English creates new waterways and discards old ones (p. 1). INTEGRATED AND CITED CORRECTLY MacNeil and Cran (2005) claimed, "Like the Mississippi, [English] keeps forging new channels and abandoning old ones" (p. 1).

7a Forming a working thesis

Once you have read a variety of sources and considered your issue from different perspectives, you are ready to form a working thesis—a one-sentence (or occasionally a two-sentence) statement of your central idea. The thesis expresses your informed, reasoned judgment, not your opinion. Usually your thesis will appear at the end of the first paragraph.

As you learn more about your subject, your ideas may change, and your working thesis will evolve too. You can revise your working thesis as you draft.

In your research paper, your thesis will answer the central question that you pose. Here are some examples.

RESEARCH QUESTION

Is medication the right treatment for the escalating problem of childhood obesity?

POSSIBLE THESIS

Understanding the limitations of medical treatments for children highlights the complexity of the childhood obesity problem in the

United States and underscores the need for physicians, advocacy groups, and policymakers to search for other solutions.

RESEARCH QUESTION

How can a business improve employee motivation?

POSSIBLE THESIS

Setting clear expectations, sharing information in a timely fashion, and publicly offering appreciation to specific employees can help align individual motivation with corporate goals.

RESEARCH QUESTION

Why are boys diagnosed with ADHD more often than girls?

POSSIBLE THESIS

Recent studies have suggested that ADHD is diagnosed more often in boys than in girls because of personality differences between boys and girls as well as gender bias in referring adults, but an overlooked cause is that ADHD often coexists with other behavior disorders that exaggerate or mask gender differences.

Each of these thesis statements expresses a view based on the sources the writer consulted or the original research the writer conducted. The writers will need to show readers how their evidence supports their thesis.

7b Testing your thesis

When drafting and revising a thesis statement, make sure that it's suitable for your writing purpose and that you can successfully develop it with the sources available to you. Keeping the following guidelines in mind will help you develop a successful thesis statement.

- A thesis should take a position that needs to be explained and supported. It should not be a fact or description.

- A thesis should be your answer to a question, your solution to a problem, or your position on a topic or debate. It should not simply present a question, problem, or topic.

- A thesis should match the scope of the assignment. If your thesis is too broad to cover in the work assigned, for example, explore a subtopic of your original topic. If your thesis is so narrow that you don't have much to say, find out what debates surround your topic and take a position.

- A thesis should be sharply focused. Avoid vague words such as *interesting* or *good*. Use concrete language and make sure your thesis lets readers know what you plan to discuss.

- A thesis should stand up to the "So what?" question. Ask yourself why readers should be interested in your paper and care about your thesis. If your thesis matters to you, your readers are more likely to find your ideas engaging.

7c Organizing your ideas

APA encourages the use of headings to help readers follow the organization of a paper. For empirical research papers and laboratory reports, the major headings are "Method," "Results," and "Discussion." In other papers, the headings will vary, depending on the type of paper and the topic. (See also 10i.)

7d Using sources to inform and support your argument

Sources can play several different roles as you develop your points.

Providing background information or context   You can use facts and statistics to support generalizations or to establish the importance of your topic.

Explaining terms or concepts   Explain words, phrases, or ideas that might be unfamiliar to your readers. Quoting or paraphrasing a source can help you define terms and concepts in accessible language.

Supporting your claims   Back up your assertions with facts, examples, and other evidence from your research.

Lending authority to your argument   Expert opinion can give weight to your argument or discussion. But don't rely on experts to make your points for you. Express your ideas in your own words and cite authorities in the field to support your position.

Anticipating and countering other interpretations   Do not ignore sources that seem contrary to your thesis or that offer interpretations different from your own. Instead, use them to give voice to opposing ideas and interpretations before you counter them.

8 Avoiding plagiarism

A paper that relies on research is a collaboration between you and your sources. To be fair and ethical, you must acknowledge your debt to the writers of those sources. When you acknowledge your sources, you avoid plagiarism, a serious academic offense.

Three different acts are considered plagiarism: (1) failing to cite quotations and borrowed ideas, (2) failing to enclose borrowed language in quotation marks, and (3) failing to put summaries and paraphrases in your own words. (See also 2d.)

8a Citing quotations and borrowed ideas

When you cite sources, you give credit to writers from whom you've borrowed words or ideas. You also let your readers know where your information comes from, so that they can evaluate the original source.

You must cite anything you borrow from a source, including direct quotations; statistics and other specific facts; visuals such as cartoons, graphs, and diagrams; and any ideas you present in a summary or a paraphrase.

The only exception is common knowledge—information that your readers may know or could easily locate in general sources. For example, most general encyclopedias will tell readers that Sigmund Freud wrote *The Interpretation of Dreams* and that chimpanzees can learn American Sign Language. When you have seen certain information repeatedly in your reading, you don't need to cite it. However, when information has appeared in only a few sources, when it is highly specific (as with statistics or data from government agencies), or when it is controversial, you should cite the source.

APA recommends an author-date style of citations. Here, briefly, is how the author-date system usually works. See sections 13–15 for a detailed discussion of variations.

1. The source is introduced by a signal phrase that includes the last name of the author followed by the date of publication in parentheses.
2. The material being cited is followed by a page number in parentheses.

hackerhandbooks.com/pocket
APA papers > Exercises: 36–1 to 36–7
APA papers > LearningCurve: Working with sources (APA)

3. At the end of the paper, an alphabetized list of references gives publication information for the source.

IN-TEXT CITATION

As researchers Yanovski and Yanovski (2002) have explained, obesity was once considered "either a moral failing or evidence of underlying psychopathology" (p. 592).

ENTRY IN THE LIST OF REFERENCES

Yanovski, S. Z., & Yanovski, J. A. (2002). Drug therapy: Obesity.
    The New England Journal of Medicine, 346, 591-602.

8b Enclosing borrowed language in quotation marks

To show that you are using a source's exact phrases or sentences, you must enclose them in quotation marks. To omit the quotation marks is to claim—falsely—that the language is your own. Such an omission is plagiarism even if you have cited the source.

ORIGINAL SOURCE

> In an effort to seek the causes of this disturbing trend, experts have pointed to a range of important potential contributors to the rise in childhood obesity that are unrelated to media.
> —Henry J. Kaiser Family Foundation, "The Role of Media in Childhood Obesity" (2004), p. 1

PLAGIARISM

According to the Henry J. Kaiser Family Foundation (2004), experts have pointed to a range of important potential contributors to the rise in childhood obesity that are unrelated to media (p. 1).

BORROWED LANGUAGE IN QUOTATION MARKS

According to the Henry J. Kaiser Family Foundation (2004), "experts have pointed to a range of important potential contributors to the rise in childhood obesity that are unrelated to media" (p. 1).

NOTE: When quoted sentences are set off from the text by indenting, quotation marks are not used (see pp. 35–36).

8c Putting summaries and paraphrases in your own words

A summary condenses information; a paraphrase conveys information in about the same number of words as in the original source. When you summarize or paraphrase, you must name the source and restate the source's meaning in your own words. You commit plagiarism if you half-copy, or patchwrite, the author's sentences—either by mixing the author's phrases with your own without using quotation marks or by plugging your own synonyms into the author's sentence structure. The following paraphrases are plagiarized—even though the source is cited—because their language and structure are too close to those of the source.

ORIGINAL SOURCE

> In an effort to seek the causes of this disturbing trend, experts have pointed to a range of important potential contributors to the rise in childhood obesity that are unrelated to media.
> —Henry J. Kaiser Family Foundation, "The Role of Media in Childhood Obesity" (2004), p. 1

PLAGIARISM: UNACCEPTABLE BORROWING OF PHRASES

According to the Henry J. Kaiser Family Foundation (2004), experts have indicated a range of significant potential contributors to the rise in childhood obesity that are not linked to media (p. 1).

PLAGIARISM: UNACCEPTABLE BORROWING OF STRUCTURE

According to the Henry J. Kaiser Family Foundation (2004), experts have identified a variety of significant factors causing a rise in childhood obesity, factors that are not linked to media (p. 1).

To avoid plagiarizing an author's language, don't look at the source while you are summarizing or paraphrasing. After you've restated the author's ideas in your own words, return to the source and check that you haven't used the author's language or sentence structure or misrepresented the author's ideas.

ACCEPTABLE PARAPHRASE

A report by the Henry J. Kaiser Family Foundation (2004) described sources other than media for the childhood obesity crisis (p. 1).

NOTE: APA recommends using a page number after a summary or a paraphrase to help readers locate the passage in the source.

8d Avoiding self-plagiarism

You should respond to each assignment with original work. Submitting the same work (or portions of it) for two different assignments—even if the assignments are years apart or for different instructors—is usually considered self-plagiarism. Each assignment is an opportunity to explore new ideas or gain new perspective. If a new assignment benefits from writing or research you completed for an older assignment, you should cite your earlier work using proper APA style. If you are unsure about what constitutes self-plagiarism for a particular assignment or paper, you should talk to your instructor.

9 Integrating sources

Quotations, summaries, paraphrases, and facts will help you develop your ideas, but they cannot speak for you. You can use several strategies to integrate information from sources into your paper while maintaining your own voice.

9a Using quotations appropriately

Limiting your use of quotations In your writing, keep the emphasis on your own words. Do not quote excessively. It is not always necessary to quote full sentences from a source. Often you can integrate words or phrases from a source into your own sentence structure.

As researchers continue to face a number of unknowns about obesity, it may be helpful to envision treating the disorder, as Yanovski and Yanovski (2002) suggested, "in the same manner as any other chronic disease" (p. 592).

Using the ellipsis mark To condense a quoted passage, you can use the ellipsis mark (three periods, with spaces between) to indicate that you have omitted words. What remains must be grammatically complete.

hackerhandbooks.com/pocket
e APA papers > Exercises: 37–1 to 37–7
✓ APA papers > LearningCurve: Working with sources (APA)

Roman (2003) reported that "social factors are nearly as significant as individual metabolism in the formation of . . . dietary habits of adolescents" (p. 345).

The writer has omitted the words *both healthy and unhealthy* from the source.

When you want to omit a full sentence or more, use a period before the three ellipsis dots.

According to Sothern and Gordon (2003), "Environmental factors may contribute as much as 80% to the causes of childhood obesity. . . . Research suggests that obese children demonstrate decreased levels of physical activity and increased psychosocial problems" (p. 104).

Ordinarily, do not use an ellipsis mark at the beginning or at the end of a quotation. Readers will understand that you have taken the quoted material from a longer passage. The only exception occurs when you feel it necessary, for clarity, to indicate that your quotation begins or ends in the middle of a sentence.

Make sure that omissions and ellipsis marks do not distort the meaning of your source.

Using brackets   Brackets allow you to insert your own words into quoted material to clarify a confusing reference or to make the quoted words fit grammatically into the context of your writing.

The cost of treating obesity currently totals $117 billion per year—a price, according to the surgeon general, "second only to the cost of [treating] tobacco use" (Carmona, 2004).

To indicate an error such as a misspelling in a quotation, insert [*sic*], italicized and with brackets around it, right after the error.

NOTE: It is not necessary to use brackets in a quotation to indicate that you have changed a lowercase letter to a capital or vice versa to fit the sense of your sentence.

Setting off long quotations   When you quote 40 or more words, set off the quotation by indenting it one-half inch from the left margin. Use the normal right margin and double-space the quotation.

Long quotations should be introduced by an informative sentence, usually followed by a colon. Quotation marks are unnecessary because the indented format tells readers that the passage is taken from the source.

Yanovski and Yanovski (2002) have traced the history of treatments for obesity:

> For many years, obesity was approached as if it were either a moral failing or evidence of underlying psychopathology. With the advent of behavioral treatments for obesity in the 1960s, hope arose that modification of maladaptive eating and exercise habits would lead to sustained weight loss, and that time-limited programs would produce permanent changes in weight. (p. 592)

At the end of the indented quotation, the parenthetical citation goes outside the final punctuation mark.

9b Using signal phrases to integrate sources

Whenever you include a direct quotation, a paraphrase, or a summary in your paper, prepare readers for it with a signal phrase. A signal phrase usually names the author of the source, gives the publication date in parentheses, and often provides some context. It is acceptable in APA style to call authors by their last name only, even on first mention. If your paper refers to two authors with the same last name, use their initials as well.

See the chart on page 37 for a list of verbs commonly used in signal phrases.

NOTE: Use the past tense or present perfect tense to introduce quotations, other source material, and your own results: *Davis (2009) noted . . . , Manning (2010) has claimed . . . , men performed better than women. . . .* Use the present tense to discuss the applications or effects of your own results or knowledge that has clearly been established: *the data suggest . . . , researchers agree. . . .*

Marking boundaries Avoid dropping quotations into your text without warning. Provide clear signal phrases, including at least the author's name and the date of publication. Signal phrases mark the boundaries between source material and your own words and ideas.

DROPPED QUOTATION

Obesity was once considered in a very different light. "For many years, obesity was approached as if it were either a moral failing or evidence of underlying psychopathology" (Yanovski & Yanovski, 2002, p. 592).

QUOTATION WITH SIGNAL PHRASE

As researchers Yanovski and Yanovski (2002) have explained, obesity was once considered "either a moral failing or evidence of underlying psychopathology" (p. 592).

Using signal phrases in APA papers

To avoid monotony, try to vary both the language and the placement of your signal phrases.

Model signal phrases

In the words of Carmona (2004), ". . ."

As Yanovski and Yanovski (2002) have noted, ". . ."

Hoppin and Taveras (2004), medical researchers, pointed out that ". . ."

". . . ," claimed Critser (2003).

". . . ," wrote Duenwald (2004), ". . ."

Researchers McDuffie et al. (2003) have offered a compelling argument for this view: ". . ."

Hilts (2002) answered these objections with the following analysis: ". . ."

Verbs in signal phrases

Are you providing background, explaining a concept, supporting a claim, lending authority, or refuting a belief? Choose a verb that is appropriate for the way you are using the source.

admitted	contended	reasoned
agreed	declared	refuted
argued	denied	rejected
asserted	emphasized	reported
believed	insisted	responded
claimed	noted	suggested
compared	observed	thought
confirmed	pointed out	wrote

Integrating statistics and other facts   When you are citing a statistic or another specific fact, a signal phrase is often not necessary. In most cases, readers will understand that the citation refers to the statistic or fact (not the whole paragraph).

In purely financial terms, the drugs cost more than $3 a day on average (Duenwald, 2004).

There is nothing wrong, however, with using a signal phrase.

Duenwald (2004) pointed out that in purely financial terms, the drugs cost more than $3 a day on average.

Putting source material in context   Provide context for any source material that appears in your paper. A signal phrase can help you connect your own ideas with those of another writer by clarifying how the source will contribute to your paper. It's a good idea to embed source material, especially long quotations, between sentences of your own that interpret the source and link the source to your own ideas.

QUOTATION WITH EFFECTIVE CONTEXT
A report by the Henry J. Kaiser Family Foundation (2004) outlined trends that may have contributed to the childhood obesity crisis, including food advertising for children as well as

> a reduction in physical education classes . . . , an increase
> in the availability of sodas and snacks in public schools,
> the growth in the number of fast-food outlets . . . , and the
> increasing number of highly processed high-calorie and high-
> fat grocery products. (p. 1)

Addressing each of these areas requires more than a doctor armed with a prescription pad; it requires a broad mobilization not just of doctors and concerned parents but of educators, food industry executives, advertisers, and media representatives.

9c Synthesizing sources

When you synthesize multiple sources in a research or an analytical paper (or any other paper that involves sources), you create a conversation about your topic. You show readers how the ideas of one source relate to those of another by connecting and analyzing the ideas in the context of your argument or discussion. Keep the emphasis on your own writing. The thread of your ideas should be easy to identify and to understand, with or without your sources.

In the following sample synthesis, Luisa Mirano uses her own analysis to shape the conversation among her sources. She does not simply string quotations together or allow sources to overwhelm her writing. In the final sentence, she explains to readers how her sources support and extend her argument.

SAMPLE SYNTHESIS (DRAFT)

1   Medical treatments have clear costs for individual patients, including unpleasant side effects, little information about long-term use, and uncertainty that they will yield significant weight loss. The financial burden is heavy as well; the drugs cost more than $3 a day on average (Duenwald, 2004). In each of the clinical trials, use of medication was accompanied by expensive behavioral therapies, including counseling, nutrition education, fitness

2   advising, and monitoring. As Critser (2003) noted in his book *Fat Land*, use of weight-loss drugs is unlikely to have an effect without the proper "support system"—one that includes doctors, facilities, time,

3   and money (p. 3). For many families, this level of care is prohibitively expensive.

Both medical experts and policymakers recognize that solutions might come not only from a laboratory but also from policy, education, and advocacy. A handbook designed to educate doctors on obesity called for "major changes in some aspects of western culture" (Hoppin & Taveras, 2004, Conclusion section, para. 1). Solving the childhood obesity problem will require broad mobilization of doctors and concerned parents and also of educators, food industry executives, advertisers, and media representatives.

(Margin labels: Student writer | Source 1 | Student writer | Source 2 | Student writer | Source 3 | Student writer)

1 Student writer Luisa Mirano begins with a claim that needs support.

2 Signal phrases indicate how sources contribute to Mirano's paper and show that the ideas that follow are not her own.

3 Mirano interprets and connects sources. Each paragraph ends with her own thoughts.

Formatting Papers in APA Style

10   Parts of a paper in APA style

This section describes the different parts of papers typically written in APA style. Not all of the parts described in this section are used in every genre, or type of paper. For example, method and results sections are used in research papers but not in annotated bibliographies, professional memos, or reflective essays.

The chart on page 43 provides a quick overview of the parts that are typically used in each genre. If you have any doubt about which parts to include in a particular paper, check your assignment or ask your instructor.

10a   Title page

A title page is used in nearly all types of APA-style papers. It is always the first page and generally includes a running head, the title of the paper, the name of the author, and an author's note.

The title should briefly and accurately describe the purpose of the paper. The title should be concise yet specific and should not include unnecessary words such as "A Report on" or "A Paper About." Abbreviations should not be used in titles.

Effective titles indicate to the reader the main ideas, theories, or variables used in a paper. For example, the title for the lab report on page 81—"Reaction Times for Detection of Objects in Two Visual Search Tasks"—includes information about the variables in the study (visual reaction times) as well as the methodology (visual search tasks). The title of the annotated bibliography on page 79—"Keynesian Policy: Implications for the Current U.S. Economic Crisis"—alerts the reader to the bibliography's theoretical perspective (Keynesian economic theory) and its subject (the current economic crisis).

For papers submitted for coursework, the author's note may include a few sentences that contain the title of the course, the name of the professor teaching the course, and any acknowledgments or thanks for assistance. Papers submitted for publication or for presentation at professional meetings may include additional information such as sources of grant money used to support the research and contact information for the author.

▶ Formatting the title page: **p. 47**

▶ Sample title pages: **12a–12d, 12f–12j**

10b Abstract

An abstract is a short (150-to-250-word) summary of the content of the paper; it is generally used in literature reviews, empirical research papers, laboratory reports, and case studies. An abstract is always on the second page by itself. The purpose of the abstract is to provide an overview of the most important ideas of the paper, including the research question or hypothesis, methods, and key findings. In a paper prepared for publication, it is helpful to include key terms at the end of the abstract so that readers can find the paper online or in a database using a keyword search.

Even though it appears at the beginning of the paper, some writers find it effective to write the abstract after an entire draft is finished rather than before they begin writing. One way to approach writing the abstract is to ask yourself, "If someone read only the abstract of my paper, would the reader have a good understanding of the purpose of my paper and my most important findings and ideas?"

▶ Formatting the abstract: **p. 51**

▶ Sample abstracts: **pp. 56**, **62**, **68**, **82**, **99**

10c Introduction

Most genres using APA style have an introduction, which begins on a new page following the abstract (or the title page for a paper without an abstract). The introduction is the first few paragraphs of the paper and typically contains a thesis statement or research question. In most papers, the introduction answers the questions "What is my paper about?" and "Why is it important?"

The introduction can frame the research question or thesis statement in relation to the work of others, in which case it answers the question "What have others written about my topic?" In an empirical research paper, the introduction briefly describes how you conducted your study. Finally, the introduction lays the foundation for the rest of the paper by giving readers a sense of what to expect and what conclusions you will draw. You should reserve a full discussion of the implications of your research for the discussion section (see 10f).

As with abstracts, some writers prefer to write the introduction after drafting the entire paper.

▶ Formatting the introduction: **p. 51**

▶ Sample introductions: **pp. 57**, **63**, **83**, **90**, **100**, **102**

10d Method

The method section is used in empirical research papers, laboratory reports, and case studies and sometimes in clinical papers. It describes the details of the research design—how you conducted your study. Each discipline has its own methods of investigation, so the particular contents of the method section will vary depending on the discipline in which you are writing.

Required sections in different types of papers

Type of paper	Title page	Abstract	Introduction	Method	Results	Discussion (Conclusion)	References	Footnotes	Headings	Appendices	Visuals
Literature review	●	●	●			●	●	◗	●		◗
Empirical research	●	●	●	●	●	●	●	◗	●	◗	●
Analytical essay	●	◗	●			◗	●	◗	◗	◗	◗
Annotated bibliography	◗						◗				
Laboratory report	●	●	●	●	●	●	●	◗	●	◗	●
Administrative report	◗	◗	●			◗	◗	◗	●	◗	◗
Clinical practice paper	●	◗	●	◗	◗	◗	◗	◗	●	◗	◗
Reflective essay	●		●			◗	◗	◗	◗		
Professional memo			●			◗	◗	◗	◗		◗
Case study	●	●	●	●	●	●	●	◗	●	◗	◗

● required in most papers   ◗ required in some papers

Anyone interested in replicating your study will rely on the method section to conduct his or her own research, so it is important that you include all relevant details of the research design. A good method section fully answers the question "How did I design my research and conduct my investigation?"

Writers often use subsections, labeled with subheadings, to organize the information in the method section. Subsections might include the procedures used to generate a sample of a population and specific information about participants or materials.

Some details should not be included in the method section. If you collected data using a survey, for example, you might discuss general characteristics of the survey in the method section and include the survey questions as an appendix (see 10j).

▶ Formatting the method section: **p. 51**

▶ Sample method sections: **pp. 64, 69, 84**

10e Results

Empirical research papers, laboratory reports, and case studies must include a results section, which contains an analysis of the data. Clinical papers sometimes include a results section. The method used in the study will determine the type of analysis you present in the results section.

Studies that have generated numerical data frequently use statistical analysis to determine whether statistically significant relationships exist between independent and dependent variables. Social and behavioral scientists refer to this type of study as *quantitative*. Observational field studies in sociology, anthropology, and education are examples of *qualitative* research. The nature of the research question will determine whether quantitative or qualitative methods are preferred.

The results section answers the question "What significant relationships exist between the important variables in my study?" The results section focuses on the data and on any statistical or other analysis you have performed. You should present the results as clearly and succinctly as possible; tables or other visuals can be a helpful way to display results. Interpretation of the findings should be saved for the discussion section (see 10f).

Like the method section, the results section may include subsections to describe the data, the procedures used to analyze the data, and important findings. The section often includes charts, tables, figures, or other visuals that concisely present important data (see 10k). In the results section, you must acknowledge all relevant findings, even those that do not support your hypothesis, your research question, or the results you expected to find (see 2e).

▶ Formatting the results section: **p. 51**
▶ Sample results sections: **pp. 66, 84**

10f Discussion

A discussion section is used in empirical research papers, laboratory reports, and case studies. It is frequently used in literature reviews, clinical papers, memos, reflective essays, and administrative reports; in these genres, it may be labeled "Conclusion."

In a paper involving research or an experiment, the purpose of the discussion section is to interpret the results in light of your research question or hypothesis. The discussion section attempts to answer the question "What do the findings or the data in my study mean?" In answering this question, you should reflect critically on the study as a whole, making connections between your study and previous studies and noting any ways in which your study may be improved. You should also discuss any unanticipated findings and, where appropriate, offer explanations for them. The following are other questions commonly addressed in the discussion section: "Was my sample adequate?" "Were my measures precise and appropriate?" "Were there any problems in my research design? If so, how might someone design a better study?" "Can the results of my study be generalized to larger (or other) populations?" "Given the findings of my study and the relevant literature, do any important questions remain unanswered?"

In other genres, the discussion section or conclusion is used to highlight important points, to summarize key ideas, or to make connections. In a literature review, the discussion or conclusion section provides an opportunity to critically assess the findings of other studies and to draw conclusions in relation to your research question.

▶ Formatting the discussion section: **p. 51**
▶ Sample discussion (conclusion) section: **p. 85**

10g References

The reference section provides full bibliographic information for each source used in the paper so that an interested
reader can locate the source. The reference section begins
on a new page following the end of the body of the paper.
Any paper that uses outside sources must include a reference list.

▶ Formatting the reference list: **p. 53**

▶ Sample reference lists: **pp. 60, 78, 88**

10h Footnotes

Footnotes are used for additional information that is too
long or complicated to include in the main text (see 15a).
Footnotes should be used sparingly; in-text citations are
the primary method of citing source material (see section
13). Footnotes are also used in tables and figures (see 15b).

▶ Formatting footnotes: **p. 51**

▶ Sample footnotes in text: **pp. 57, 75**

▶ Sample footnotes in tables: **pp. 59, 64, 91, 95**

10i Headings

Headings are used in APA papers to provide structure and
organization. Headings can be used in any genre. Like
an outline, the heading structure of a paper gives readers a sense of how the ideas of the paper are organized.
In empirical research papers and laboratory reports, three
first-level headings in the body of the paper remain constant: "Method," "Results," and "Discussion." Each of
these first-level headings may have second- or third-level
subheadings.

▶ Formatting headings: **p. 51**

▶ Sample headings: **12a–12b, 12f–12h, 12j–12k**

10j Appendices

In almost any genre using APA style, some information
may be important but too distracting to include in the
main text of the paper and too long for a footnote. Such
material can be placed in an appendix at the end of the
paper following the reference list. For example, if you
developed a long survey to collect the data used in your

study, you could include a copy of the survey questions, without any responses, as an appendix.

▶ Formatting the appendices: **p. 72**

▶ Sample appendices: **pp. 72, 73**

10k Visuals

Visuals include tables, figures, graphs, charts, images, or any other nontext content found in a paper. While visuals are not required in any genre, they are often a good way to summarize data or other results. For example, it is common to create tables that display the results of statistical analysis such as correlation and multiple regression. Other commonly used visuals in some fields are diagrams that show the anticipated and actual relationships between independent and dependent variables. The chart on pages 48–49 shows various types of visuals and suggests how they might be used in a paper.

While visuals provide a snapshot of important information, you should include a written description or interpretation of the information contained in any visual.

▶ Formatting visuals: **p. 52**

▶ Sample visuals: **pp. 59, 64, 66, 86, 91, 95, 101**

11   APA paper format

The American Psychological Association makes a number of recommendations for formatting a paper and preparing a list of references. The guidelines in this section are consistent with advice given in the *Publication Manual of the American Psychological Association*, 6th ed. (Washington, DC: APA, 2010).

The explanations and examples in 11a and 11b for formatting the text and the reference list are consistent with APA's guidelines for papers prepared for publication and with typical requirements for undergraduate papers in the social sciences, business, education, and nursing.

11a Formatting the paper

Title page   Begin at the top left with the words "Running head," followed by a colon and the title of your

Choosing visuals to suit your purpose

Pie chart

Pie charts compare a part or parts to the whole. Segments of the pie represent percentages of the whole (and always total 100 percent).

Health insurance coverage in the United States (2007)

Bar graph (or line graph)

Bar graphs highlight trends over a period of time or compare numerical data. Line graphs display the same data as bar graphs; the data are graphed as points, and the points are connected with lines.

THE PURSUIT OF PROPERTY
Home ownership rates in the United States

Infographic

An infographic presents data in a visually engaging form. The data are usually numerical, as in bar graphs or line graphs, but they are represented by a graphic element instead of by bars or lines.

Just 8% of kids growing up in low-income communities graduate from college by age 24.

Table

Tables display numbers and words in columns and rows. They can be used to organize complicated numerical information into an easily understood format.

Sources [top to bottom]: Kaiser Foundation; US Census Bureau; Data provided courtesy of www.postsecondary.org; UNAIDS.

Prices of daily doses of AIDS drugs
($US)

Drug	Brazil	Uganda	Côte d'Ivoire	US
3TC (Lamivudine)	1.66	3.26	2.95	8.70
ddC (Zalcitabine)	0.24	4.17	3.75	8.80
Didanosine	2.04	5.26	3.48	7.25
Efavirenz	6.96	n/a	6.41	13.13
Indinavir	10.32	12.79	9.07	14.93
Nelfinavir	4.14	4.45	4.39	6.47
Nevirapine	5.04	n/a	n/a	8.48
Saquinavir	6.24	7.37	5.52	6.50
Stavudine	0.56	6.19	4.10	9.07
ZDV/3TC	1.44	7.34	n/a	18.78
Zidovudine	1.08	4.34	2.43	10.12

Source: UNAIDS, 2000

Diagram

Diagrams, useful in scientific and technical writing, concisely illustrate processes, structures, or interactions.

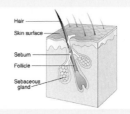

Flowchart

Flowcharts show structures or steps in a process and their relation to one another.

Photograph

Photographs can be used to vividly depict people, scenes, or objects discussed in a text.

Map

Maps illustrate geographic, historical, or political information. They can pinpoint the features of a place, emphasize a relation-ship among regions, or describe a situation or an event. Symbols and varied colors show significant features and points of interest.

Sources [top to bottom]:
NIAMS; Arizona Board of Regents;
Behrouz Mehri/Getty Images; *Economist*.

paper (shortened to no more than 50 characters) in all capital letters. Put the page number 1 flush with the right margin.

About halfway down the page, on separate lines, center the full title of your paper, your name, and your school's name. At the bottom of the page, you may add the heading "Author Note," centered, followed by a brief paragraph that lists specific information about the course or department or provides acknowledgments or contact information. (See section 12 for sample title pages.)

Font If your instructor does not require a specific font, choose one that is standard and easy to read (such as 12-point Times New Roman).

Page numbers and running head Number all pages with arabic numerals (1, 2, 3, and so on) in the upper right corner about one-half inch from the top of the page. Flush with the left margin and on the same line as the page number, type a running head consisting of the title of the paper (shortened to no more than 50 characters) in all capital letters. On the title page only, include the words "Running head" followed by a colon before the title. (See section 12 for examples of running heads and page numbers.)

Margins, line spacing, and paragraph indents Use margins of one inch on all sides of the page. Left-align the text. Double-space throughout the paper. Indent the first line of each paragraph and footnote one-half inch.

Capitalization, italics, and quotation marks Capitalize all words of four letters or more (and all nouns, pronouns, verbs, adjectives, and adverbs of any length) in titles of works in the text of the paper. Capitalize the first word following a colon in a title or a heading. Capitalize the first word after a colon if the word begins a complete sentence.

Italicize the titles of books, periodicals, and other long works, such as Web sites. Use quotation marks for titles of periodical articles, short stories, and other short works.

NOTE: APA has different requirements for titles in the reference list. See page 53.

Long quotations When a quotation is 40 or more words, set it off from the text by indenting it one-half inch from the left margin. Double-space the quotation. Do not use quotation marks around it. (See p. 77 for an example. See also pp. 35–36 for more information about integrating long quotations.)

Footnotes If you insert a footnote number in the text of your paper, place the number immediately following any mark of punctuation except a dash. At the bottom of the page, begin the note with a one-half-inch indent and the superscript number corresponding to the number in the text. Insert an extra double-spaced line between the last line of text on the page and the footnote. Double-space the footnote. (See p. 57 for an example. See also section 15 for more details about footnotes.)

Abstract If your paper requires one, include an abstract after the title page. Center the word "Abstract" (in regular font, not boldface) one inch from the top of the page. Double-space the abstract and do not indent the first line.

For a paper prepared for publication, a list of keywords follows the abstract. Leave one line of space after the abstract and begin with the word "Keywords," indented and italicized, followed by a colon. Then list important words related to your paper. Check with your instructor for requirements in your course. (See section 12 for sample abstract pages.)

Introduction On a new page following the abstract, center the complete title of the paper one inch below the top of the page. The introduction immediately follows the title, with no heading. Begin the first paragraph of the introduction with a one-half-inch indent. (See also 10c.)

Headings Major (first-level) headings are centered and boldface. In research papers and laboratory reports, the major headings are "Method," "Results," and "Discussion." In other types of papers, the major headings should be informative and concise, conveying the structure of the paper. Second-level headings are flush left and boldface. Third-level headings are indented and boldface, followed by a period and the text on the same line.

In first- and second-level headings, capitalize the first and last words and all words of four or more letters (and nouns, pronouns, verbs, adjectives, and adverbs of any length). In third-level headings, capitalize only the first word, any proper nouns, and the first word after a colon.

First-Level Heading Centered

Second-Level Heading Flush Left

   Third-level heading indented. Text immediately follows.

NOTE: Always type the title of the paper, the headings "Abstract" and "References," and appendix titles in regular font, not boldface.

Visuals   APA classifies visuals as tables and figures (figures include graphs, charts, drawings, and photographs).

Tables   Label each table with an arabic numeral (Table 1, Table 2) and provide a clear title. The label and title should appear on separate lines above the table, flush left and double-spaced. Type the table number in regular font; italicize the table title.

Table 2

Effect of Nifedipine (Procardia) on Blood Pressure in Women

   If you have used data from an outside source or have taken or adapted the table from a source, give the source information in a note below the table. Begin with the word "Note," italicized and followed by a period. If you use lettered footnotes to explain specific data in the table, those footnotes begin on a new line after the source information. Begin each footnote with the superscript letter corresponding to the letter in the table; do not indent the first line. (See also 15b. See pp. 59, 64, and 91 for examples of tables in papers.)

Figures   Place the figure number and a caption below the figure, flush left and double-spaced. Begin with the word "Figure" and an arabic numeral, both italicized, followed by a period. Place the caption, not italicized, on the same line. If you have taken or adapted the figure from an outside source, give the source information immediately following the caption. Use the term "From" or "Adapted from" before the source information. (See also 15b. See pp. 66 and 86 for examples of figures in papers.)

11b Preparing the list of references

Begin your list of references on a new page at the end of the paper. Center the title "References" one inch from the top of the page. Double-space throughout. (See section 12 for sample reference lists.)

Indenting entries Type the first line of each entry flush left and indent any additional lines one-half inch.

Alphabetizing the list Alphabetize the reference list by the last names of the authors (or editors); when a work has no author or editor, alphabetize by the first word of the title other than *A*, *An*, or *The*.

If you list two or more works by the same author, arrange the entries by year, the earliest first. If you include two or more works by the same author in the same year, arrange them alphabetically by title. Add the letters "a," "b," and so on in the parentheses after the year. For journal articles, use only the year and the letter: (2015a). For articles in magazines and newspapers, use the full date and the letter in the reference list: (2015a, July 17); use only the year and the letter in in-text citations.

Authors' names Invert all authors' names and use initials instead of first names. Separate the names with commas. For two to seven authors, use an ampersand (&) before the last author's name (see item 2, p. 114). For eight or more authors, give the first six authors, three ellipsis dots, and the last author (see item 3, p. 115).

Titles of books and articles Italicize the titles and subtitles of books. Do not italicize or use quotation marks around the titles of articles. Capitalize only the first word of the title and subtitle (and all proper nouns). Capitalize names of periodicals as you would capitalize them normally (see 37c).

Abbreviations for page numbers Abbreviations for "page" and "pages" ("p." and "pp.") are used before page numbers of newspaper articles and articles in edited books (see item 15a on p. 122 and item 31b on p. 126) but not before page numbers of articles in magazines and scholarly journals (see items 13–14 on pp. 117–18).

Breaking a URL or DOI When a URL or a DOI (digital object identifier) must be divided, break it after a double slash or before any other mark of punctuation. Do not insert a hyphen, and do not add a period at the end.

12 Sample pages from papers in APA style

This section contains pages from 11 student papers from a range of social science and related disciplines—psychology, sociology, economics, criminology, nursing, education, and business. The pages show typical APA style for organization and formatting as well as proper APA style for in-text citations and the reference list. The samples may be helpful as you write different types of papers for your courses.

12a Research paper: Literature review (psychology)

Luisa Mirano, a student in an introductory psychology course, wrote a research paper reviewing the literature on treatments for childhood obesity. Her paper describes what researchers have written about effective treatments; she also draws conclusions based on her reading of the literature.

hackerhandbooks.com/pocket

🄴 APA papers > Sample student writing
> Mirano (literature review)
> Riss (nursing practice paper)
> Ratajczak (business proposal)

🄴 APA papers > Sample student writing (APA version)
> Conderman (research paper)
> Elwell (analytical essay)
> Gibson (reflective essay)
> Johnson (laboratory report)
> Niemeyer (annotated bibliography)
> Spencer (business report)
> Thompson (administrative report)
> Zopf (research paper)

[1]   Running head: CAN MEDICATION CURE OBESITY IN CHILDREN?   1   [2]

Can Medication Cure Obesity in Children?   [3]

A Review of the Literature

Luisa Mirano

Northwest-Shoals Community College

Author Note   [4]

This paper was prepared for Psychology 108, Section B, taught by

Professor Kang.

[1] Short title, no more than 50 characters, in all capital letters on all pages; words "Running head" and colon on title page only.
[2] Arabic page number on all pages. [3] Full title and writer's name and affiliation, centered. [4] Author's note (optional) for extra information.

(Annotations indicate APA-style formatting and effective writing.)

1 CAN MEDICATION CURE OBESITY IN CHILDREN? 2 **2**

3 Abstract

In recent years, policymakers and medical experts have expressed alarm about the growing problem of childhood obesity in the United States. While most agree that the issue deserves attention, consensus dissolves around how to respond to the problem. This literature review **4** examines one approach to treating childhood obesity: medication. The paper compares the effectiveness for adolescents of the only two drugs approved by the Food and Drug Administration (FDA) for long-term treatment of obesity, sibutramine and orlistat. This examination of pharmacological treatments for obesity points out the limitations of medication and suggests the need for a comprehensive solution that combines medical, social, behavioral, and political approaches to this complex problem.

5 *Keywords:* obesity, childhood, adolescence, medication, public policy

1 Short title, no more than 50 characters, flush left. **2** Page number, flush right. **3** Abstract appears on separate page; heading centered and not boldface. **4** Abstract is 150-to-250-word overview of paper. **5** Keywords (optional) help readers search for a paper online or in a database.

CAN MEDICATION CURE OBESITY IN CHILDREN?   3

Can Medication Cure Obesity in Children?   [1]
A Review of the Literature

In March 2004, U.S. Surgeon General Richard Carmona called
attention to a health problem in the United States that, until
recently, has been overlooked: childhood obesity. Carmona said that   [2]
the "astounding" 15% child obesity rate constitutes an "epidemic."
Since the early 1980s, that rate has "doubled in children and tripled
in adolescents." Now more than nine million children are classified as
obese.[1] This literature review considers whether the use of medication
is a promising approach for solving the childhood obesity problem by
responding to the following questions:

1. What are the implications of childhood obesity?   [3]
2. Is medication effective at treating childhood obesity?
3. Is medication safe for children?
4. Is medication the best solution?

Understanding the limitations of medical treatments for children   [4]
highlights the complexity of the childhood obesity problem in the
United States and underscores the need for physicians, advocacy
groups, and policymakers to search for other solutions.

What Are the Implications of Childhood Obesity?   [5]

Obesity can be a devastating problem from both an individual
and a societal perspective. Obesity puts children at risk for a number
of medical complications, including Type 2 diabetes, hypertension,
sleep apnea, and orthopedic problems (Henry J. Kaiser Family

[1]Obesity is measured in terms of body-mass index (BMI): weight   [6]
in kilograms divided by square of height in meters. An adolescent with
a BMI in the 95th percentile for his or her age and gender is considered
obese.

[1] Full title, centered and not boldface. [2] Introduction provides
background on writer's topic. [3] Questions provide organization
and are repeated as main headings of paper. [4] Paper's thesis.
[5] First-level heading, centered and boldface. [6] Footnote defines
essential term without interrupting text.

CAN MEDICATION CURE OBESITY IN CHILDREN?   4

Foundation, 2004, p. 1). Researchers Hoppin and Taveras (2004)
have noted that obesity is often associated with psychological issues
1 such as depression, anxiety, and binge eating (Complications section,
Table 4).

Obesity also poses serious problems for a society struggling to
cope with rising health care costs. The cost of treating obesity currently
totals $117 billion per year—a price, according to the surgeon general,
2 "second only to the cost of [treating] tobacco use" (Carmona, 2004).
And as the number of children who suffer from obesity grows, long-term
costs will only increase.

3   **Is Medication Effective at Treating Childhood Obesity?**

The widening scope of the obesity problem has prompted medical
professionals to rethink old conceptions of the disorder and its causes.
4 As researchers Yanovski and Yanovski (2002) have explained, obesity
was once considered "either a moral failing or evidence of underlying
psychopathology" (p. 592). But this view has shifted: Many medical
professionals now consider obesity a biomedical rather than a moral
condition, influenced by both genetic and environmental factors.
Yanovski and Yanovski have further noted that the development of
weight-loss medications in the early 1990s showed that "obesity
should be treated in the same manner as any other chronic
5 disease . . . through the long-term use of medication" (p. 592).

The search for the right long-term medication has been
complicated. Many of the drugs authorized by the Food and Drug
Administration (FDA) in the early 1990s proved to be a disappointment.
Two of the medications—fenfluramine and dexfenfluramine—were
withdrawn from the market because of severe side effects (Yanovski &
Yanovski, 2002, p. 592), and several others were classified by the Drug
Enforcement Administration as having the "potential for abuse" (Hoppin

1 Section title and table number in parentheses help readers
locate information in online source with no page numbers.
2 Author (Carmona) is not named in signal phrase, so name
and date appear in parentheses after quotation. **3** First-level
heading, centered and boldface. **4** In signal phrase, "and" links
names of two authors; date is given in parentheses; page number
is given at end of quotation, before final period. **5** Ellipsis mark
indicates omitted words in middle of sentence.

Research paper: Literature review   Table

CAN MEDICATION CURE OBESITY IN CHILDREN?   6

Table 1   **1**

Effectiveness of Sibutramine and Orlistat in Adolescents   **2**

Medication	Subjects	Treatment[a]	Side effects	Average weight loss/gain	
Sibutramine	Control	0-6 months: placebo 6-12 months: sibutramine	Months 6-12: increased blood pressure; increased pulse rate	After 6 months: loss of 3.2 kg (7 lb) After 12 months: loss of 4.5 kg (9.9 lb)	**3**
	Medicated	0-12 months: sibutramine	Increased blood pressure; increased pulse rate	After 6 months: loss of 7.8 kg (17.2 lb) After 12 months: loss of 7.0 kg (15.4 lb)	
Orlistat	Control	0-12 months: placebo	None	Gain of 0.67 kg (1.5 lb)	
	Medicated	0-12 months: orlistat	Oily spotting; flatulence; abdominal discomfort	Loss of 1.3 kg (2.9 lb)	

Note. The data on sibutramine are adapted from "Behavior Therapy and   **4**
Sibutramine for the Treatment of Adolescent Obesity," by R. I.
Berkowitz, T. A. Wadden, A. M. Tershakovec, & J. L. Cronquist, 2003,
Journal of the American Medical Association, 289, pp. 1807-1809. The
data on orlistat are adapted from *Xenical (Orlistat) Capsules: Complete
Product Information*, by Roche Laboratories, December 2003, retrieved
from http://www.rocheusa.com/products/xenical/pi.pdf
[a]The medication and/or placebo were combined with behavioral therapy   **5**
in all groups over all time periods.

1 Table summarizes findings from two sources. **2** Table number
and title on separate lines; title italic. **3** Abbreviations and
numerals used throughout table to save space. **4** Note gives
sources of data used in table. Format of note differs from format
of reference list. **5** Content note explains data common to all
subjects.

CAN MEDICATION CURE OBESITY IN CHILDREN? 9

1 References

2 Berkowitz, R. I., Wadden, T. A., Tershakovec, A. M., & Cronquist, J. L.
(2003). Behavior therapy and sibutramine for the treatment of
adolescent obesity. *Journal of the American Medical Association,
289,* 1805-1812.

3 Carmona, R. H. (2004, March 2). *The growing epidemic of childhood
obesity.* Testimony before the Subcommittee on Competition,
Foreign Commerce, and Infrastructure of the U.S. Senate
Committee on Commerce, Science, and Transportation.
Retrieved from http://www.hhs.gov/asl/testify/t040302.html

Critser, G. (2003). *Fat land.* Boston, MA: Houghton Mifflin.

4 Duenwald, M. (2004, January 6). Slim pickings: Looking beyond ephedra.
The New York Times, p. F1. Retrieved from http://nytimes.com/

5 Henry J. Kaiser Family Foundation. (2004, February). *The role of
media in childhood obesity.* Retrieved from http://www.kff.org
/entmedia/7030.cfm

Hilts, P. J. (2002, March 20). Petition asks for removal of diet drug
from market. *The New York Times,* p. A26. Retrieved from http://
nytimes.com/

Hoppin, A. G., & Taveras, E. M. (2004, June 25). Assessment and
management of childhood and adolescent obesity. *Clinical
Update.* Retrieved from http://www.medscape.com/viewarticle
/481633

6 McDuffie, J. R., Calis, K. A., Uwaifo, G. I., Sebring, N. G., Fallon,
E. M., Hubbard, V. S., & Yanovski, J. A. (2002). Three-month
tolerability of orlistat in adolescents with obesity-related
comorbid conditions. *Obesity Research, 10,* 642-650.

Roche Laboratories. (2003, December). *Xenical (orlistat) capsules:
Complete product information.* Retrieved from http://www

1 List of references on new page; heading centered and not
boldface. **2** List alphabetized by authors' last names, corporate
names, or titles (for works with no authors). **3** Authors' names
inverted, with initial(s) for first name(s). **4** Double-spaced
throughout. **5** First line of each entry flush left; subsequent lines
indented ½". **6** For a work with up to seven authors, all authors'
names are listed; ampersand (&) precedes last author's name.

12b Research paper: Empirical research (psychology)

In a research methods course, Jessica Conderman conducted an experiment on taste sensitivity. Her paper reviews the literature on the topic and then reports on and analyzes her own results. Because her study involved human participants, she received approval from her school's institutional review board (IRB; see 2f).

Research paper: Empirical research   Title page

1 Running head: INFLUENCES ON TASTE SENSITIVITY   1 **2**

The Influence of Sex and Learning on Taste Sensitivity   **3**

Jessica S. Conderman

Carthage College

Author Note   **4**

Jessica S. Conderman, PSYC 471-01 Advanced Research Methods,

Dr. Leslie Cameron, Department of Psychology, Carthage College.

Thank you to the Department of Psychology and Quality of Life

Committee for funding support.

---

1 Short title, no more than 50 characters, in all capital letters on all pages; words "Running head" and colon on title page only. **2** Arabic page number on all pages. **3** Full title and writer's name and affiliation, centered. **4** Author's note (optional) for extra information.

(Annotations indicate APA-style formatting and effective writing.)

Research paper: Empirical research **Abstract**

1 INFLUENCES ON TASTE SENSITIVITY 2

2 Abstract

Perceptual learning enhances a person's ability to detect specific stimuli after the person experiences exposure to the stimuli.

3 Perceptual learning has been observed in taste aversion, but it has not been extensively investigated in taste sensitivity. The current study examined the effect of perceptual learning in taste thresholds of females and males. I studied taste sensitivity longitudinally, testing

4 every other day for 1 month, in 6 young adults (3 males, 3 females) between 19 and 21 years of age. Taste thresholds were determined using an electrogustometer at 4 tongue locations (front-left, front-right, back-left, back-right) corresponding to the chorda tympani and glossopharyngeal nerves. Results indicate that males and females demonstrated a perceptual learning effect—thresholds decreased with practice—and were consistent with previous research that females' thresholds were lower than males' for all tongue locations. In contrast to previous research in olfaction (Dalton, Doolittle, & Breslin, 2002), both males and females "learned." However, females overall performed better in the task, which is consistent with the previous literature on the chemical senses.

5 *Keywords:* perceptual learning, taste aversion, taste sensitivity, sex differences

1 Short title, no more than 50 characters, flush left; page number flush right. **2** Abstract appears on separate page; heading centered and not boldface. **3** Abstract is 150-to-250-word overview of paper. **4** Numerals used for all numbers in abstract, even those under 10. **5** Keywords (optional) help readers search for a paper online or in a database.

Research paper: Empirical research   First text page

INFLUENCES ON TASTE SENSITIVITY   3

The Influence of Sex and Learning on Taste Sensitivity **1**

The development of taste involves changes in taste preferences
and aversions that are influenced by personal experiences. These can
vary among cultures, age groups, and sexes (Nakazato, Endo, Yoshimura, **2**
& Tomita, 2002; Tomita & Ikeda, 2002). Through various experiences
with different taste stimuli, people develop taste acuity (Scahill &
Mackintosh, 2004). Taste acuity allows people to distinguish between
different flavors and determine their taste preferences and aversions
(Tomita & Ikeda, 2002). Taste sensitivity allows people to detect the
differences between various stimuli, such as electric or hot and cold,
through the nerves in the tongue (Nakazato et al., 2002). The detection **3**
and differentiation of taste stimuli determine how people perceive food
and develop dietary habits.

The main purpose of this study was to determine if perceptual **4**
learning occurs in taste sensitivity by measuring taste thresholds in the
tongue. An electrogustometer delivered electric stimuli to participants'
tongues. (The threshold is the minimum amount of current required to
discriminate between two short pulses of current.) Perceptual learning
has been found in taste aversion research but, to my knowledge, has
not been examined directly in taste sensitivity measured through
electrogustometry. But Lobb, Elliffe, and Stillman (2000) did suspect
learning when taste thresholds continued to decrease as testing
progressed after the initial 10 sessions were omitted. Taste aversion
studies have shown that participants demonstrated a learning effect as
they gained exposure to electric stimuli (Bennett & Mackintosh, 1999;
Blair & Hall, 2003; Dwyer, Hodder, & Honey, 2004). **5**

[Introduction continues with the writer's hypothesis and a review of
the literature on various aspects of the writer's research.]

---

1 Full title, repeated and centered, not boldface. **2** First part of
introduction provides background on writer's topic. **3** Second
and subsequent citations to work with three to five authors use
"et al." after first author's name. **4** Writer explains her purpose
and establishes importance of her research in context of previous
research. **5** Two or more sources in one parenthetical citation
listed alphabetically and separated by semicolons.

INFLUENCES ON TASTE SENSITIVITY   7

model and determined that the electrogustometer had high test-retest reliability, but Lobb et al. (2000) found that electrogustometry test-retest reliability was questionable.

1
Method

2
Participants

Participants were recruited through the college resident assistant program. Each participant provided written consent prior to testing.

3
Taste sensitivity was studied in six young adults (three males, three females), ranging from 19 to 21 years of age, for one month with no more than one day separating sessions. There were a total of 15 testing sessions per participant. All participants were screened prior to testing and reported being nonsmokers with no current medication intake.

Materials

4
The Rion TR-06 electrogustometer with a 5-mm diameter stainless steel anode administered an electric stimulus directly to the tongue. The levels of electric current are listed in Table 1.

5
Table 1

6
Electrogustometry Currents for Testing Taste Sensitivity

dB	−6	−4	−2	0	2	4	6	8	10	12	14	16	18	20	22	24	26
µA	4	5	6.4	8	10	13	16	20	25	32	44	50	64	80	100	136	170

Note. The electrogustometry currents are shown in dB on the dial of the Rion TR-06 electrogustometer. The corresponding µA levels are as given in Kuga, Ikeda, Suzuki, & Takeuchi (2002).

7
Procedure

Participants were instructed not to eat or drink anything besides water at least one hour prior to testing. During each trial, two low-level electric pulses were presented in quick succession to the same location

1 Method section begins with main heading, centered and boldface. **2** Second-level headings flush left and boldface. **3** All numbers under 10, including number of participants, spelled out. **4** Numbers for precise increments expressed in numerals with abbreviated units of measure. **5** Short table appears immediately following its mention in the text. **6** Table number and title appear above table; title italic. **7** Procedure section explains in detail how writer conducted the experiment.

INFLUENCES ON TASTE SENSITIVITY 8

on the tongue. One stimulus was a standard stimulus that remained constant at 4 μA, a very low current. The other stimulus was a test stimulus, which varied in intensity. All testing began with pulses at 4 μA and 13 μA. Participants responded by reporting which of the stimuli seemed stronger, generally through finger taps. Participants' tongues were tested on the four locations corresponding to the chorda tympani and glossopharyngeal nerves (front-left, front-right, back-left, back-right). Tongue locations were tested in the same sequence for every session, starting at the back-left and ending at the front-right. Stimulus duration was set at 0.5 s (Lobb et al., 2000). Sessions were held at approximately the same time of day for each participant throughout the study.

After participants reported five consecutive correct responses (identifying which stimulus seemed stronger), a "reversal" occurred— the test stimulus became higher or lower than the previous test stimulus. For all reversals after the first, the strength of the test stimulus increased after one inaccurate response and decreased after two accurate responses (Frank, Hettinger, Barry, Gent, & Doty, 2003; Miller, Mirza, & Doty, 2002). Electric stimulation continued until seven [1] reversals occurred per location (Miller et al., 2002). [2]

Statistical Analysis

Taste thresholds were calculated for each participant using the geometric mean of the last four reversals in each session (Ajdukovic, 1991). Two analyses of variance (ANOVA) for repeated measures were used. The first 2 $\times$ 2 $\times$ 15 design was used to determine the effect [3] and interactions of tongue location (back-front), sex (male-female), and number of sessions. The second 2 $\times$ 2 $\times$ 15 design was used to determine the effect and interaction of tongue location (back left-right), sex, and number of sessions.

[1] For first reference to sources with three to five authors, all authors' names are given. [2] For subsequent references to sources with three to five authors, the first author's name is followed by "et al." [3] Writer uses familiar terminology in the field and standard notation (2 $\times$ 2 $\times$ 15) to describe experiment design.

Research paper: Empirical research   Text page

INFLUENCES ON TASTE SENSITIVITY   9

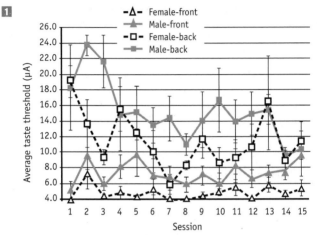

Figure 1. Perceptual learning in taste sensitivity in males and females, for front and back tongue locations. Error bars represent standard errors.

Results

The taste thresholds across trials for males and females in the back and front tongue locations are shown in Figure 1. Across sessions, taste thresholds (that is, the minimum current required to determine the difference between two pulses) decreased for males and females in the back tongue locations. A repeated-measures ANOVA revealed a main effect of session, $F(1, 14) = 4.603$, $p = 0.000$, and location, $F(1, 1) = 22.843$, $p = 0.009$. There was also an interaction between session and

[Paper continues with the discussion section, which interprets the results of the experiment in the context of previous research, and ends with a reference list.]

■ Figure presents data graphically for part of experiment.
■ Figure number and caption appear below figure. ■ Results section analyzes the data and uses figures to present the data graphically. ■ Writer uses standard notation to analyze data.

12c Research paper: Qualitative methodology (sociology)

Bradley Zopf undertook a qualitative study for a sociology seminar. His methods included observing young African American males and interviewing them about their clothing choices. Because his research involved human participants, he received approval from his school's institutional review board (IRB; see 2f).

Research paper: Qualitative methodology   Title page

[1] Running head: AFRICAN AMERICAN MALES' PERCEPTIONS OF DRESS   1 [2]

African American Males' Perceptions of Urban   [3]
and Hip-Hop Styles of Dress
Bradley J. Zopf
University of Chicago

Author Note   [4]
Bradley Zopf, SOCI 31600, Seminar: Social Stratification, Professor
Edward Laumann, Department of Sociology, University of Chicago.
Faculty adviser: Edward Laumann; preceptor: Kim Babon.

[1] Short title, no more than 50 characters, in all capital letters on all pages; words "Running head" and colon on title page only. [2] Arabic page number on all pages. [3] Full title and writer's name and affiliation, centered. [4] Author's note (optional) for extra information.

(Annotations indicate APA-style formatting and effective writing.)

1 AFRICAN AMERICAN MALES' PERCEPTIONS OF DRESS   2

2   Abstract

African American males are often stereotyped as rebellious because of
the clothing they wear. Because these stereotypes are often held by
authority figures (teachers, parents, police), there is little research
about how African American males perceive their choice of clothing
3 styles. Therefore, the question "Is the urban wear or hip-hop style of
clothing a result of an African American oppositional culture or a result
of purchasing choices?" has yet to be answered from the perspective of
African American males themselves. Research suggesting that African
Americans form a distinct collective identity, or oppositional culture,
has argued that African Americans formulate a conscious resistance
to conforming to white standards of conduct, dress, and behavior.
However, in interviews with 20 African American males, I found that
respondents reported that their clothing styles are a matter of personal
preference, a desire to look presentable, and a way to express their
unique sense of style.

4   *Keywords:* African American males, clothing, stereotypes,
oppositional culture, urban culture, hip-hop style

1 Short title, no more than 50 characters, flush left; page number
flush right. **2** Abstract appears on separate page; heading
centered and not boldface. **3** Abstract is 150-to-250-word
overview of paper. **4** Keywords (optional) help readers search for
a paper online or in a database.

Research paper: Qualitative methodology   Method

[The paper begins with a review of the literature, followed by the method section.]

Method

For this research, I conducted 20 interviews with African American **1**
males between the ages of 18 and 35, with the average age being 27,
in downtown Chicago, IL. I asked African American males about their
views on clothing styles, specifically if they considered themselves
to have a style and how they perceive hip-hop or urban wear styles.
Questions concerning their clothing styles during their teenage years
were a means to understand if, how, and why older males changed their
preferred clothing styles. Since the focus of the research was to analyze
how hip-hop and urban styles are or are not forms of oppositional
behavior, African American males were the target group. Because
this group is the most likely demographic to wear such clothing and
therefore experience the stereotypes that are attached to these styles,
it was important to understand how African American males themselves
thought of their own styles, the hip-hop and urban styles in general,
and the stereotypes.

I conducted the interviews in person on State Street in downtown **2**
and tape-recorded 19 of 20 to ensure accuracy. I selected subjects
through an informal screening process attempting to diversify the
subjects' styles. In other words, I attempted to interview both those
I perceived as wearing hip-hop or urban-style clothing as well as
those wearing conventional business casual and business formal attire.
The sample, therefore, was a convenience sample purposely biased to **3**
select subjects wearing a wide range of dress styles. While this type
of sampling does not yield a random sample, the goal was to find
exploratory information that will allow for a future project concerning
consumption, clothing styles, and African Americans.

---

1 Method section describes writer's research design—the sample
and the setting where interviews took place. **2** First person and
active voice (*I conducted*) used when appropriate rather than
third person and passive (*Subjects were selected*). **3** Writer uses
terminology from the discipline (such as *convenience sample*)
and explains his choice of method.

Research paper: Qualitative methodology   Method

All interviews were conducted between April and June of 2006 in downtown Chicago. Most interviews lasted around 10 minutes, but a few were longer. I approached potential participants and identified myself as a student at the University of Chicago completing a study on clothing styles and fashion. Informed consent was obtained verbally and recorded on tape.

1   With the convenience sample, a few problems did arise. Specifically, most interviews were conducted on weekdays because the streets on the weekends were so busy and crowded that few people were willing to stop and talk. Most interviews took place between 9:00 a.m. and 6:00 p.m.; therefore, the late evening and night crowds were not interviewed. Location was also somewhat problematic as South State Street is dominated by DePaul University, so an overrepresentation of DePaul students and workers may have confounded my sample. I attempted to correct for this by conducting several interviews on North State Street, but most of the interviews did come from the southern location.

Other potential issues were that I often did not approach people in groups, people wearing headphones, and people using cell phones. These people, when approached, were less likely to consent to being interviewed. Other self-selection biases were also present because potential participants could choose to participate or not.

Also, the memory of older participants about what they wore in high school could have been affected by the passage of time. Many of the older participants may have suffered from memory bias; however, most of the 20 respondents provided clear and descriptive information about their high school clothing styles and why they chose them.

Finally, the interviewer himself being a Caucasian male might have caused some respondents to withhold certain comments directed at

---

1 Writer acknowledges limitations of his method.

Research paper: Qualitative methodology   Method

white society or white people in general. While this did not seem to
be the case, as most participants seemed to talk freely, there is the
possibility that respondents chose not to characterize their style as
oppositional because the interviewer was white.

The face-to-face interview method, however, was most appropriate   **1**
for this type of research. It gave me the ability to draw out answers
from participants as well as to ask them to describe their answers in
greater detail. For example, when participants talked about casual
clothing, hip-hop clothing, or urban wear, I could ask them to further
describe what they meant by their answers as well as why they gave
those answers. This research focused on the African American males'
perspective on clothing styles, and the interview technique was most
appropriate because it allowed the participants to explain responses at
a broader and more descriptive level.

**[The paper continues with a results section, a discussion section,
and a reference list, ending with the two appendices shown on
pages 72–73.]**

1 After discussing limitations of his method, writer explains why
method was appropriate and effective.

AFRICAN AMERICAN MALES' PERCEPTIONS OF DRESS 18

1

Appendix A

2

Interview Questions

1. Do you consider yourself to have a particular style of clothing? Please describe.

2. When you were in high school, did you have a similar or different style?

3. Why do you think it has changed or not changed?

4. Are you familiar with urban wear or hip-hop styles of clothing?

5. Do you consider the two styles to be similar or different? Why?

6. Could you please describe what the urban wear style is? Hip-hop style?

7. What types of clothes are they?

8. Who typically wears these types of clothing?

9. Do you think that people who wear these types of clothing are stereotyped? If so, how and why?

10. What is the most important aspect of a person's style? Why is it important to have a style, or is it not important?

Additional follow-up questions were asked on the basis of interviewee responses.

1 Appendices provide information relevant to the study that is not appropriate in body of paper. **2** Each appendix starts on new page. The letters "A," "B," and so on are used to label appendices. Label and title centered, not boldface.

AFRICAN AMERICAN MALES' PERCEPTIONS OF DRESS　　　　　　19

Appendix B

Participant Characteristics

Number of respondents: 20

Range of ages of respondents: 18-35

Average age of respondents: 27

Descriptions of Interviews　　　　　　　　

Interview 1, April 5, 2006

African American male, 25

Wearing fitted jeans, dark khaki jacket, polo shirt, casual black dress
shoes, earring in left ear, and no sunglasses or hat

Interview 2, April 5, 2006

African American male, 18

Wearing oversized red and black Sean John jacket, zipped and visible
gold chain, fitted NY Yankees hat, black Timberland boots, and black
baggy jeans

Interview 3, April 12, 2006

African American male, 30

Wearing white long-sleeve cotton shirt, baggy jeans, and white tennis
shoes

Interview 4, April 12, 2006

African American male, 34

Wearing saggy jeans, baseball cap, gold necklace, Bulls jacket, and
multiple T-shirts

Interview 5, April 21, 2006

African American male, 22

Wearing casual dress shoes, fitted jeans, and a white T-shirt

Interview 6, April 21, 2006

African American male, 35

Wearing long-sleeve white T-shirt, jeans, and Timberland construction boots

1 Appendix presents relevant observations about each
participant.

12d Analytical essay (sociology)

For a course in sociological theory, Hannah Elwell's assignment was to write an essay using several of Karl Marx's concepts and ideas to explain Walmart's economic success. Elwell's analysis draws on Marx's theories of exploitation of waged labor and fetishism of commodities.

Analytical essay   **Title page**

1 Running head: SECRET OF WALMART'S SUCCESS: A MARXIAN ANALYSIS   1 **2**

3   The Secret of Walmart's Success: A Marxian Analysis

Hannah Elwell

University of Southern Maine

4   Author Note

This paper was prepared for SOC 300, Sociological Theory, taught by Professor Cheryl Laz.

---

1 Short title, no more than 50 characters, in all capital letters on all pages; words "Running head" and colon on title page only. **2** Arabic page number on all pages. **3** Full title and writer's name and affiliation, centered. **4** Author's note (optional) for extra information.

(Annotations indicate APA-style formatting and effective writing.)

Analytical essay   First text page

SECRET OF WALMART'S SUCCESS: A MARXIAN ANALYSIS   2   **1**

The Secret of Walmart's Success: A Marxian Analysis   **2**

What do big-screen TVs, bar soap, plastic building blocks, and   **3**
strawberry toaster pastries have in common? All of these seemingly
disparate items—along with many more—can be found on the shelves   **4**
of your local Walmart. The retail chain offers a stunning variety of
consumer goods and groceries all under one roof, from electronics to
apparel to cleaning supplies to frozen food. Walmart also offers certain
services along with its products. A number of stores contain their own
hair salons, photography studios, auto centers, or pharmacies, and some
even provide health care, boasting walk-in clinics and vision centers
where customers can receive eye examinations and other routine clinical
services from independent health care professionals.

In every sense, Walmart is a massive corporation. The buildings
that house the shelves full of consumer goods are colossal, with the
average Walmart Supercenter measuring 185,000 square feet ("About
Us," n.d.). Walmart stores are large not just in size but also in number: **5**
There are more than nine thousand stores across 15 different countries,
and they collectively employ 2.1 million people ("Walmart Stores,"
2011). As the world's largest company, Walmart is enormously successful
and powerful. Writer Charles Fishman (2007) noted in his article "The
Wal-Mart You Don't Know"[1] that the retailer "does more business than
Target, Sears, Kmart, J.C. Penney, Safeway, and Kroger combined."

So what is the secret to its economic success? Although Walmart
is a modern phenomenon, the answer to this question can be found in
the nineteenth-century teachings of one of modern economics' most
influential thinkers, Karl Marx. From a Marxian perspective, Walmart can
be seen as the epitome of capitalism. Its success is born from the

---

[1]In 2008, Wal-Mart changed the name of its stores to Walmart.   **6**

1 Short title, no more than 50 characters, flush left; page number
flush right. **2** Full title, repeated and centered, not boldface.
3 Short analytical essay often does not require an abstract or
headings. **4** Writer begins with engaging description. **5** Source
with no author cited in text with first word or two of title; "n.d." for
source with no date. **6** Footnote provides important explanation
without interrupting text.

SECRET OF WALMART'S SUCCESS: A MARXIAN ANALYSIS   3

1 exploitation of waged labor and the fetishism of commodities—two
defining aspects of our modern capitalist, consumer culture.

The capitalist system is marked by a concentration of wealth
and resources—instead of being equally divided among all members
of society, wealth and resources end up in the hands of a select few
(the bourgeoisie), who then gain control over those with little or no
resources (the proletariat), thus creating class antagonism between
2 the two. In *The Communist Manifesto*, Marx (1848/2011) noted that
industrial society was characterized by a "distinct feature: it has
simplified class antagonisms: Society as a whole is more and more
splitting up into two great hostile camps, into two great classes
directly facing each other: bourgeoisie and proletariat" (p. 53).

It is important to note that as a corporation and not a group of
people, Walmart does not have any actual class interests of its own.
However, those who stand to make a profit from Walmart's capitalist
enterprises are certainly members of the bourgeoisie and thus are
representatives of that class. Similarly, those who work for Walmart are
members of the proletariat. Thus, Walmart becomes a perfect example of
the class antagonism that Marx described in *The Communist Manifesto*.

3   An examination of the ways in which these two classes work
against each other is key to understanding how Walmart is so profitable.
In *Capital*, Marx (1867/2011) explained the difference between the
ways in which the owners (the bourgeoisie) and the workers (the
proletariat) relate to capital when he noted that "the circulation of
commodities is the starting-point of capital" (p. 73). However, for the
bourgeoisie and the proletariat, the form that this circulation takes
is markedly different. For the proletariat, it can be illustrated by the
formula C-M-C: exchanging a commodity (C) for money (M) and then
exchanging that money for another commodity (C). For the bourgeoisie,

---

1 Thesis sets up organization around two Marxian concepts.
2 For republished work, date of original publication is given
before date of publication of current source. **3** Topic sentence
provides transition to fuller explanation of "class antagonism."

SECRET OF WALMART'S SUCCESS: A MARXIAN ANALYSIS   4

the formula changes to M-C-M', or exchanging money for a commodity
that is then exchanged for more money (M'). Marx elaborated on this
distinction:

> The circuit C-M-C starts with one commodity, and finishes with   **1**
> another, which falls out of circulation and into consumption.
> Consumption, the satisfaction of wants, in one word, use-value,
> is its end and aim. The circuit M-C-M, on the contrary, commences
> with money and ends with money. Its leading motive, and the
> goal that attracts it, is therefore mere exchange-value. (p. 74)   **2**

Of course, the bourgeoisie is not simply exchanging one sum of money
for the same sum of money, but rather for a greater sum. In the case
of the M-C-M' circuit, in Marx's words, "More money is withdrawn from
circulation at the finish than was thrown into it at the start. . . .
The . . . process is therefore M-C-M' . . . the original sum advanced,   **3**
plus an increment. This increment or excess over the original value
I call 'surplus-value'" (p. 74).

This surplus-value is how Walmart makes its profit—spending
money to get commodities and then selling the commodities for a
higher price. The secret to this formula is production. Producers, or
suppliers, do not simply buy a commodity and then somehow sell that
same commodity back at a higher price. Rather, they buy commodities—
for example, cloth, thread, and cotton stuffing—and with them produce
a new commodity—perhaps a throw pillow—that they can then sell
for a new, higher price. As a retailer, Walmart does not produce its own
commodities, so it does in fact buy and then sell the same commodities
(the throw pillows, for example) at a profit. It counts on its suppliers
for the actual production work. Walmart also counts on its suppliers
(or rather, pressures them very strongly) to keep the cost of their
production work low so that Walmart can make a profit from the

---

1 Quotation of 40 or more words indented without quotation
marks. **2** Page number in parentheses after the final period.
3 Ellipsis mark indicates words omitted from source.

Analytical essay   Reference list

SECRET OF WALMART'S SUCCESS: A MARXIAN ANALYSIS   8

1   References

2 About us. (n.d.). *Walmart corporate*. Retrieved from http://
   walmartstores.com/AboutUs/7606.aspx

3 Fishman, C. (2007, December 19). The Wal-Mart you don't know.
   Fast Company. Retrieved from http://www.fastcompany.com
   /magazine/77/walmart.html

4 Marx, K. (2011). *Capital*. In S. Appelrouth & L. D. Edles, *Classical
   and contemporary sociological theory* (pp. 63-76). Los Angeles,
   CA: Pine Forge Press. (Original work published 1867)

5 Marx, K. (2011). *The Communist manifesto*. In S. Appelrouth &
   L. D. Edles, *Classical and contemporary sociological theory*
   (pp. 50-63). Los Angeles, CA: Pine Forge Press. (Original work
   published 1848)

6 Marx, K. (2011). *Economic and philosophic manuscripts of 1844*. In
   S. Appelrouth & L. D. Edles, *Classical and contemporary
   sociological theory* (pp. 41-50). Los Angeles, CA: Pine Forge
   Press. (Original work published 1844)

Walmart Stores, Inc. data sheet: Worldwide unit details. (2011, April).
   Walmart corporate. Retrieved from http://walmartstores
   .com/pressroom/news/10594.aspx

1 List of references on new page; heading centered and not boldface. **2** Abbreviation "n.d." used for source with no date of publication or update. **3** List alphabetized by authors' last names or titles (for works with no authors). First line of each entry flush left; subsequent lines indented ½". Double-spaced throughout. **4** Authors' names inverted, with initial(s) for first name(s). **5** For older work contained in recent work, date of original publication given in parentheses at end of entry. **6** Two or more works by one author in same year alphabetized by title.

12e Annotated bibliography (economics)

Katie Niemeyer, a student in an intermediate macroeconomics course, prepared a reference list for a paper on the implications of Keynesian policy for the U.S. economy. She annotated each reference list entry by summarizing the source and then evaluating how it would apply to the topic of her paper.

Annotated bibliography   **First page**

---

[1] Running head: KEYNESIAN POLICY: IMPLICATIONS FOR U.S. CRISIS   1   [2]

Katie Niemeyer   [3]

Professor Brent McClintock

2520 Intermediate Macroeconomics

   Keynesian Policy: Implications for the Current U.S. Economic Crisis   [4]

Auerbach, A. J., Gale, W. G., & Harris, B. H. (2010). Activist fiscal   [5]

   policy. *Journal of Economic Perspectives, 24*(4), 141-164.

         This article provides a historical review of U.S. fiscal policy   [6]

   in the last 30 years, including the activist policy decisions made

   by the Obama administration in the economic crisis starting

   in 2008. The authors chart the government's economic tactics

   through time—from previous government policies of fiscal

   restraint to the current activist policy that supports the private

   sector. The article provides specific information about President

   Obama's American Recovery and Restoration Act and the Making

   Work Pay Credit. It addresses the concerns and support for such

   policy decisions by fiscally conservative classical economists as

   well as proponents of Keynesian activist policies.

Bergsten, C. F. (2005). *The United States and the world economy*.

   Washington, DC: Institute for International Economics.

---

[1] Short title, no more than 50 characters, in all capital letters on all pages; words "Running head" and colon on first page only.
[2] Arabic page number on all pages. [3] Writer's name, instructor, and course title, flush left. [4] Full title, centered and not boldface.
[5] Each entry begins at left margin; subsequent lines indented ½".
[6] Entire annotation indented ½"; first line indented additional ½".

(Annotations indicate APA-style formatting and effective writing.)

1 KEYNESIAN POLICY: IMPLICATIONS FOR U.S. CRISIS 2

2 Bergsten's book offers figures and graphs that will support my points about the productivity boom of the 1990s and the expansion of U.S. participation in the world economy. Figure 2 demonstrates the positive role the microprocessor played in U.S. economic expansion in the 1990s by showing the contribution of information technology to GDP. Figure 3 demonstrates the incredible increase in U.S. trade since 1960 owing to productivity growth and economic deregulation of the global market. It graphically shows that the U.S. trade/GDP ratio tripled from the 1960s to 2003.

Courtois, R. (2009, April). *What we do and don't know about discretionary fiscal policy* (Report No. EB09-04). Retrieved from the Federal Reserve Bank of Richmond website: http://www .richmondfed.org/publications/research/economic_brief/2009 /pdf/eb_09-04.pdf

3 This economic brief published by the Federal Reserve Bank of Richmond outlines the United States' expansive use of discretionary fiscal policy in the current economic crisis, while at the same time explaining why classical economists disagree with such measures. Supporting the nondiscretionary tendencies of classical theorists, **4** Courtois (2009) wrote, "The current recession was not identified as such by the National Bureau of Economic Research until December 2008, a full year after it began" (p. 3). The discussion of specific concerns with the Obama administration's stimulus packages and discretionary fiscal policy, in both the long and the short run, can help me present multiple viewpoints in my paper.

[Writer continues with five more annotated sources.]

1 Short title, no more than 50 characters, flush left; page number flush right on all pages. **2** Writer assesses how source will be useful in her paper. **3** Double-spaced throughout. **4** Quotation captures major point of report; writer includes page number for direct quotation.

12f Laboratory report (psychology)

Allison Leigh Johnson conducted a cognition experiment for a laboratory assignment in a psychology course. Her experiment focused on participants' reaction times in detecting objects in a variety of situations. Because this experiment was conducted in a classroom setting, Johnson did not have to seek approval from an institutional review board (IRB; see 2f).

Laboratory report   **Title page**

1 Running head: REACTION TIMES IN TWO VISUAL SEARCH TASKS   1   **2**

Reaction Times for Detection of Objects in Two Visual Search Tasks   **3**
Allison Leigh Johnson
Carthage College

Author Note   **4**
Allison Leigh Johnson, Department of Psychology, Carthage
College. This research was conducted for Psychology 2300, Cognition:
Theories and Application, taught by Professor Leslie Cameron.

1 Short title, no more than 50 characters, in all capital letters on all pages; words "Running head" and colon on title page only.
2 Arabic page number on all pages. **3** Full title and writer's name and affiliation, centered. **4** Author's note (optional) for extra information.

(Annotations indicate APA-style formatting and effective writing.)

1 REACTION TIMES IN TWO VISUAL SEARCH TASKS   2

2   Abstract

Visual detection of an object can be automatic or can require attention.
The reaction time varies depending on the type of search task being
3 performed. In this visual search experiment, 3 independent variables
were tested: type of search, number of distracters, and presence or
absence of a target. A feature search contains distracters notably
different from the target, while a conjunctive search contains
4 distracters with features similar to the target. For this experiment,
14 Carthage College students participated in a setting of their choice.
A green circle was the target. During the feature search, reaction
times were similar regardless of the number of distracters and the
presence or absence of the target. In the conjunctive search, the
number of distracters and the presence or absence of the target
affected reaction times. This visual search experiment supports the idea
that feature searches are automatic and conjunctive searches require
attention from the viewer.

5   *Keywords:* visual search, cognition, feature search, conjunctive
search

1 Short title, no more than 50 characters, flush left; page number
flush right. **2** Abstract appears on separate page; heading
centered and not boldface. **3** Numerals used for all numbers in
abstract, even those under 10. **4** Abstract is 150-to-250-word
overview of paper. **5** Keywords (optional) help readers search for
a paper online or in a database.

REACTION TIMES IN TWO VISUAL SEARCH TASKS   3

Reaction Times for Detection of Objects in Two Visual Search Tasks **1**

Vision is one of the five senses, and it is the sense trusted most by **2**
humans (Reisberg, 2010). We use our vision for everything. We are always
looking for things, whether it is where we are going or finding a friend at
a party. Our vision detects the object(s) we are looking for. Some objects
are easier to detect than others. Spotting your sister wearing a purple **3**
shirt in a crowd of boring white shirts is automatic and can be done with
ease. However, if your sister was also wearing a white shirt, it would take
much time and attention to spot her in that same crowd.

The "pop out effect" describes the quick identification of an object
being searched for because of its salient features (Reeves, 2007). When you
look for your sister wearing a purple shirt, for example, you use the pop
out effect for quick identification. The pop out effect works when attention
is drawn to a specific object that is different from the surrounding objects.

Two types of searches are used to scan an environment, the
feature search and the conjunctive search (Reeves, 2007). The feature
search is simply scanning the environment for the feature or features
of a target. The conjunctive search is scanning for a combination of
features (Reeves, 2007). Other objects that possess one of the features
being searched for are called *distracters*. Distracters, as the name
suggests, draw one's attention away from the target. When one object
is being searched for in a sea of repetitious different objects, the target
is easily found because it is unique. As more distracters are added, the
time to detect the target increases (Wolfe, 1998).

Treisman's (1986) feature integration theory explained that
single-feature searches are easy because they are automatic and that
attention is required when more features are added because these items
must be mentally constructed. This is demonstrated in visual

1 Full title, repeated and centered, not boldface. **2** Introduction
briefly describes previous research on topic and provides
background on writer's experiment. **3** Writer uses second-
person pronouns (*you*, *your*) in an everyday example to explain
a complex concept.

REACTION TIMES IN TWO VISUAL SEARCH TASKS   4

search experiments. The purpose of a visual search experiment is for the participant to identify the target as fast as possible. In my visual **1** search experiment, the target was a green circle. The hypothesis of the experiment was that the green circle would be easier to detect in a feature search than in a conjunctive search because, according to Treisman's theory, attention is needed for the latter task.

2 **Method**

3 **Participants**

     Fourteen Carthage College undergraduates participated. Four were male. All were 19 to 21 years old.

4 **Materials**

     The experiment was conducted in an environment of each participant's choice, typically in a classroom or library, using the ZAPS online psychology laboratory (2004).

Procedure

     In the feature search, orange squares were the distracters, and a green circle was the target. The conjunctive search contained distracters of orange circles, green squares, and orange squares, with the green circle as the target. For every trial under both searches, **5** either four, 16, or 64 stimuli were present on the screen. If the green circle was present, the participant pressed the *M* key, and if it was not present the *C* key. There were 24 trials for each search, and feedback was given by the online program after each.

Variables

     The three independent variables were number of distracters present, type of search, and presence or absence of the target. The dependent variable was the reaction time.

6 **Results**

     The reaction times in the feature search were constant regardless

1 Hypothesis at end of introduction. **2** Method heading (first-level heading) centered and boldface. **3** Method section presents details about how writer conducted her experiment. **4** Second-level headings flush left and boldface. **5** Numerals (except when used to begin a sentence) for all numbers greater than 10; numbers below 10 spelled out. **6** Results section describes data writer collected.

Laboratory report   **Text page**

REACTION TIMES IN TWO VISUAL SEARCH TASKS   5

of the presence of the target and the number of distracters. The
reaction times varied in the conjunctive search depending on the
presence of the target and the number of distracters. Reaction times
increased as the number of distracters increased, and reaction times
were longer when the target was not present. Figure 1 shows the   **1**
reaction times based on the three independent variables.

Discussion   **2**

The way the three variables interacted greatly affected the
times needed by participants to find the target. The data in Figure 1
show similar reaction times for the feature search and varying reaction
times for the conjunctive search. In the feature search, the reaction
times, regardless of the two variables, were constant. In the conjunctive
search, the reaction times were higher when there were more distracters
and even higher when the target was not present. Without the target,
participants scanned most of the screen to try to detect the green
circle, which is more time-consuming than when the target is present.
Reaction times also increased as the number of distracters increased.

The results were primarily as expected. In Wolfe's (1998) study of   **3**
visual search, the slope of the feature search graph was significantly
lower than the slopes of the conjunctive search graphs. The slower
reaction time shown in Figure 1 for the conjunctive search is consistent
with Wolfe's findings. The results of this visual search experiment   **4**
provide more evidence of the difference between the two types of
searches found in previous studies. The results support Treisman's
(1986) feature integration theory. Detecting a target among distracters
in the feature search is automatic—attention is not necessary. Treisman
also stated that to detect a target among two or more distracters,
attention is needed to piece together all of the features. This "mental

1 Writer explains results in text and presents numerical results
graphically in figure. **2** Discussion section analyzes and
interprets results of experiment. **3** Writer analyzes data in
context of her hypothesis and other researchers' results. **4** When
author is cited two (or more) times in text of one paragraph, date
is not included in parentheses in subsequent citations.

REACTION TIMES IN TWO VISUAL SEARCH TASKS   6

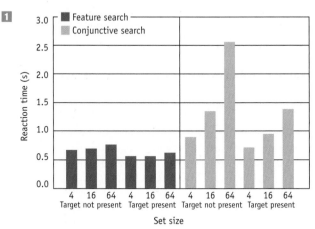

Figure 1. Reaction time based on the type of search, number of distracters (set size), and presence or absence of the target. Total experiments: 14; collected trials: 702.

gluing" of features requires attention, which in turn takes time. This is also shown in Figure 1. The reaction times, as predicted by Treisman's theory, increased when the number of distracters increased. Visual search explains why searching for clothes, people, cars, and so on takes various amounts of time depending on the target. It takes less time, because of automaticity, to detect a target with a single, standout feature than it would to detect a target with a number of features.

My study, however, does not account for the position of the target and the distracters on the screen. The position of the target could alter the reaction times if, for example, the target was always near the top where a person would most likely start scanning the environment. More

---

1 Figure presents experiment data in bar graph. **2** Figure title and caption below figure. **3** Figure caption includes brief description of source of data. **4** Writer discusses limitations of her experiment and suggests other variables that might be investigated.

Laboratory report   **Text page**

REACTION TIMES IN TWO VISUAL SEARCH TASKS   7

visual search experiments could include more distracters or even change
distracters to see how the reaction times differ. This experiment covered
only two varying objects and shapes, a fairly simple environment.
More complex visual search experiments could further investigate the   **1**
theory Treisman (1986) believed applies to all searches. My experiment
did not account for the difference between eye movement and head
movement to search for the stimulus, a factor that could change the
reaction times. Future experiments could explore these factors to test
whether Treisman's theory applies in all situations.

1 Writer suggests directions for future research.

REACTION TIMES IN TWO VISUAL SEARCH TASKS   8

[1]   References

[2] Reeves, R. (2007). *The Norton psychology labs workbook*. New York,
        NY: Norton.

     Reisberg, D. (2010). *Cognition: Exploring the science of the mind*. New
        York, NY: Norton.

[3] Treisman, A. (1986). Features and objects in visual processing.
        Scientific American, 255, 114-125.

[4] Wolfe, J. M. (1998). What do 1,000,000 trials tell us about visual
        search? *Psychological Science, 9*, 33-39.

[5] *ZAPS: The Norton psychology labs*. (2004). Retrieved from
        http://wwnorton.com/ZAPS/

[1] List of references on new page; heading centered and not
boldface. **[2]** List alphabetized by authors' last names, corporate
names, or titles (for works with no authors). **[3]** Authors' names
inverted, with initial(s) for first name(s). **[4]** First line of each entry
flush left; subsequent lines indented ½". **[5]** Double-spaced
throughout.

12g Administrative report (criminology/ criminal justice)

For a course on crime and crime policy, Chris Thompson was asked to write a report on crime in his hometown, as if he were briefing a new chief of police. Thompson's report presents and analyzes local crime statistics and compares the town's data to federal crime statistics.

Administrative report	Title page

1 Running head: CRIME IN LEESBURG, VIRGINIA   1 **2**

Crime in Leesburg, Virginia   **3**
Chris Thompson
George Mason University

Author Note   **4**
This paper was prepared for Administration of Justice 305: Crime Policy, taught by Professor Devon Johnson.

1 Short title, no more than 50 characters, in all capital letters on all pages; words "Running head" and colon on title page only. **2** Arabic page number on all pages. **3** Full title and writer's name and affiliation, centered. **4** Author's note (optional) for extra information.

(Annotations indicate APA-style formatting and effective writing.)

1 CRIME IN LEESBURG, VIRGINIA 2

2 Crime in Leesburg, Virginia

3 This report reviews crime statistics in Leesburg, Virginia, to familiarize the new police chief with the town and offer some suggestions about where to focus law enforcement resources. It analyzes local and national statistics from the FBI's Uniform Crime Reports (UCR) for the United States and for Leesburg and offers a basic assessment of the town's needs to provide a useful snapshot for the chief of police.

4 **Description of Leesburg, Virginia**

Leesburg, Virginia, is a suburb of Washington, DC, 40 miles to the northwest. In 2008, its population was 39,899 (U.S. Department of Justice, 2009, Table 8). Like many northern Virginia and southern Maryland communities, it serves as a suburban bedroom community to those employed in the nation's capital. The town has grown significantly in the last three decades.

5 Leesburg's population is predominantly middle and upper middle class, with a median household income 75% higher than the national average (Town of Leesburg, Virginia, 2009a). Leesburg is populated by young (median age 32.3), well-educated (about 50% with a bachelor's degree, about 17% with an advanced degree) citizens; half are white-collar professionals (Town of Leesburg, Virginia, 2009a).

The Leesburg Police Department has 77 sworn officers, operates 24 hours a day, and uses numerous special teams and modern law enforcement techniques. The department has divided the city into three patrol areas to address the specific needs of each zone (Town of Leesburg, Virginia, 2009b).

Nature and Extent of Crime in Leesburg, Virginia

6 Tables 1 and 2 show the FBI's UCR statistics for 2008. Table 1 contains statistics for Leesburg and the United States, and Table 2

---

1 Short title, no more than 50 characters, flush left; page number flush right. **2** Full title, repeated and centered, not boldface. **3** Introduction gives purpose of report and acknowledges audience. **4** Main headings (first-level headings), centered and boldface, define major sections of report. **5** Demographic information provides background for statistics in next section. **6** Writer refers in text to data tables.

Administrative report   **Text page**

Table 1

Crime Rates, by Crime, in Leesburg, Virginia, and in the United States, 2008

Offense type	Leesburg		United States		
	No. reported offenses	Rate per 100,000 inhabitants	No. reported offenses	Rate per 100,000 inhabitants	
Violent crime					
Forcible rape	7	17.5	89,000	29.3	
Murder and nonnegligent manslaughter	1	2.5	16,272	5.4	
Robbery	22	55.1	441,855	145.3	
Aggravated assault	29	72.7	834,885	274.6	
Total violent crime	59	147.8	1,382,012	454.5	
Property crime					
Larceny theft	715	1,792	6,588,873	2,167	
Burglary	62	155.4	2,222,196	730.8	
Vehicle theft	25	62.7	956,846	314.7	
Total property crime	802	2,010	9,767,915	3,212.5	

Note. The data for Leesburg, Virginia, are from U.S. Department of Justice (2009), Table 8. The data for the United States are from U.S. Department of Justice (2009), Table 1.

presents the crime rate in Leesburg as a percentage of the national average. A discussion of the accuracy of the UCR is on page 5.

Crime Rates in Leesburg Compared With the National Average

The following list of index crimes compares their rates in Leesburg, Virginia (first value), with the national average (second value). In general, the crime rate in Leesburg is lower than it is across the country. This may be due in part to the demographics of the town's residents and the commuter-oriented suburban nature of the community.

1 Table number and title above table; table title italic. **2** Clearly labeled data categories reinforce writer's purpose. **3** Main section of report analyzes details from tables. Section is divided into subsections, with second-level headings (not shown), that discuss the specific crime statistics listed in Table 1.

12h Clinical practice paper (nursing)

Julie Riss, a student in a nursing class focused on clinical experience, wrote a practice paper in which she provides a detailed client history, her assessment of the client's condition, nursing diagnoses of the client's health issues, her own recommendations for interventions, and her rationales for the interventions.

Nursing practice paper   **Title page**

[1] Running head: ALL AND HTN IN ONE CLIENT   1 [2]

[3]   Acute Lymphoblastic Leukemia and Hypertension in One Client:

A Nursing Practice Paper

Julie Riss

George Mason University

[4]   Author Note

This paper was prepared for Nursing 451, taught by Professor Durham. The author wishes to thank the nursing staff of Milltown General Hospital for help in understanding client care and diagnosis.

---

[1] Short title, no more than 50 characters, in all capital letters on all pages; words "Running head" and colon on title page only. [2] Arabic page number on all pages. [3] Full title and writer's name and affiliation, centered. [4] Author's note (optional) for extra information.

(Annotations indicate APA-style formatting and effective writing.)

ALL AND HTN IN ONE CLIENT   2 **1**

Acute Lymphoblastic Leukemia and Hypertension in One Client: **2**
A Nursing Practice Paper

Historical and Physical Assessment **3**

Physical History **4**

E.B. is a 16-year-old white male 5'10" tall weighing 190 lb. He
was admitted to the hospital on April 14, 2006, due to decreased
platelets and a need for a PRBC transfusion. He was diagnosed in
October 2005 with T-cell acute lymphoblastic leukemia (ALL), after
a 2-week period of decreased energy, decreased oral intake, easy **5**
bruising, and petechia. The client had experienced a 20-lb weight loss
in the previous 6 months. At the time of diagnosis, his CBC showed a
WBC count of 32, an H & H of 13/38, and a platelet count of 34,000.
He began induction chemotherapy on October 12, 2005, receiving
vincristine, 6-mercaptopurine, doxorubicin, intrathecal methotrexate,
and then high-dose methotrexate per protocol. During his hospital stay
he required packed red cells and platelets on two different occasions. He
was diagnosed with hypertension (HTN) due to systolic blood pressure
readings consistently ranging between 130s and 150s and was started
on nifedipine. E.B. has a history of mild ADHD, migraines, and deep
vein thrombosis (DVT). He has tolerated the induction and consolidation
phases of chemotherapy well and is now in the maintenance phase.

Psychosocial History **6**

There is a possibility of a depressive episode a year previously
when he would not attend school. He got into serious trouble and was
sent to a shelter for 1 month. He currently lives with his mother, father,
and 14-year-old sister.

Family History

Paternal: prostate cancer and hypertension in grandfather

Maternal: breast cancer and heart disease

---

1 Short title, no more than 50 characters, flush left; page number
flush right. **2** Full title, repeated and centered, not boldface.
3 First-level heading, boldface and centered. **4** Second-level
heading, boldface and flush left. **5** Writer's summary of client's
medical history. **6** Headings guide readers and define sections.

ALL AND HTN IN ONE CLIENT   3

1 **Current Assessment**

Client's physical exam reveals him to be alert and oriented to person, place, and time. He communicates, though not readily. His speech and vision are intact. He has an equal grip bilaterally and can

2 move all extremities, though he is generally weak. Capillary refill is less than 2 s. His peripheral pulses are strong and equal, and he is positive for posterior tibial and dorsalis pedis bilaterally. His lungs are clear to auscultation, his respiratory rate is 16, and his oxygen saturation is 99% on room air. He has positive bowel sounds in all quadrants, and his abdomen is soft, round, and nontender. He is on a regular diet, but his appetite has been poor. Client is voiding appropriately, and his urine is clear and yellow. He appears pale and is unkempt. His skin is warm, dry, and intact. He has alopecia as a result of chemotherapy. His mediport site has no redness or inflammation. He appears somber and is slow to comply with nursing instructions.

[The writer includes two sections, not shown, describing the client's diagnoses.]

Rationale for Orders

3 Vital signs are monitored every four hours per unit standard. In addition, the client's hypertension is an indication for close monitoring of blood pressure. He has generalized weakness, so fall precautions should be implemented. Though he is weak, ambulation is important, especially considering the client's history of DVT. A regular diet is ordered—I'm not sure why the client is not on a low-sodium diet, given his hypertension. Intake and output monitoring is standard on the unit. His hematological status needs to be carefully monitored due to his anemia and thrombocytopenia; therefore he has a CBC with manual differential done each morning. In addition, his hematological status is checked posttransfusion to see if the blood and platelets he receives

1 Detailed assessment of client. **2** Writer uses neutral tone and appropriate medical terminology. **3** Physiology, prescribed treatments, and nursing practices are applied in this section.

ALL AND HTN IN ONE CLIENT   6

Pharmacological Interventions and Goals ▣1

Medications and Effects ▣2

ondansetron hydrochloride (Zofran) 8 mg PO PRN	serotonin receptor antagonist, antiemetic—prevention of nausea and vomiting associated with chemotherapy ▣3
famotidine (Pepcid) 10 mg PO ac	H2 receptor antagonist, antiulcer agent—prevention of heartburn
nifedipine (Procardia) 30 mg PO bid	calcium channel blocker, antihypertensive—prevention of hypertension
enoxaparin sodium (Lovenox) 60 mg SQ bid	low-molecular-weight heparin derivative, anticoagulant— prevention of DVT
mercaptopurine (Purinethol) 100 mg PO qhs	antimetabolite, antineoplastic— treatment of ALL
PRBCs—2 units leukoreduced, irradiated[a]	to increase RBC count

[a]Because these products are dispensed by pharmacy, they are considered pharmacological interventions, even though technically not medications.

Laboratory Tests and Significance ▣4

Complete Blood Count (CBC)[a]

Result name	Result	Abnormal	Normal range
WBC	3.0	*	4.5–13.0
RBC	3.73	*	4.20–5.40
Hgb	11.5		11.1–15.7
Hct	32.4	*	34.0–46.0
MCV	86.8		78.0–95.0
MCH	30.7		26.0–32.0
MCHC	35.4		32.0–36.0
RDW	14.6		11.5–15.5
Platelet	98	*	140–400
MPV	8.3		7.4–10.4

[a]*Rationale:* Client's ALL diagnosis and treatment necessitate frequent monitoring of his hematological status. WBC count, RBC, and hematocrit are decreased due to chemotherapy. The platelet count is low.

▣1 Main section heading, centered and boldface. ▣2 Short tables placed within text of paper; no table number necessary. ▣3 Two columns display client's medications and possible side effects. ▣4 Table presents client's lab reports.

12i Reflective essay (education)

For a service learning course exploring issues of diversity, power, and opportunity in school settings, Onnalee Gibson wrote about her experiences working with an 11th-grade student. She used professional sources to inform her ideas, but the essay is focused on her own reflections on the experience.

Reflective essay   **Title page**

1 Running head: SERVICE LEARNING: ERIC   1 **2**

3   A Reflection on Service Learning:
                              Working With Eric
                              Onnalee L. Gibson
                          Michigan State University

4   Author Note
         This paper was prepared for Teacher Education 250, taught by
    Professor Carter. The author wishes to thank the guidance staff of
    Waverly High School for advice and assistance.

---

1 Short title, no more than 50 characters, in all capital letters on all pages; words "Running head" and colon on title page only. **2** Arabic page number on all pages. **3** Full title and writer's name and affiliation, centered. **4** Author's note (optional) for extra information.

(Annotations indicate APA-style formatting and effective writing.)

SERVICE LEARNING: ERIC   2 **1**

A Reflection on Service Learning: **2**
Working With Eric

The first time I saw the beautiful yet simple architecture of   **3**
Waverly High School, I was enchanted. I remember driving by while
exploring my new surroundings as a transfer student to Michigan State
University and marveling at the long front wall of reflective windows,
the shapely bushes, and the general cleanliness of the school grounds.
When I was assigned to do a service learning project in a local school
district, I hoped for the opportunity to find out what it would be like
to work at a school like Waverly—a school where the attention to its
students' needs was evident from the outside in.

Waverly High School, which currently enrolls about 1,100 students   **4**
in grades nine through 12 and has a teaching staff of 63, is extremely
diverse in several ways. Economically, students range from poverty level
to affluent. Numerous ethnic and racial groups are represented. And in
terms of achievement, the student body boasts an assortment of talents
and abilities.

The school provides a curriculum that strives to meet the needs
of each student and uses a unique grade reporting system that itemizes
each aspect of a student's grade. The system allows both teachers and
parents to see where academic achievement and academic problems
surface. Unlike most schools, which evaluate students on subjects in one
number or letter grade, Waverly has a report card that lists individual
grades for tests, homework, exams, papers, projects, participation,
community service, and attendance. Thus, if a student is doing every
homework assignment and is still failing tests, this breakdown of the
grades may effectively highlight how the student can be helped.

It was this unique way of evaluating students that led to my   **5**

---

1 Short title, no more than 50 characters, flush left; page number
flush right. **2** Full title, repeated and centered, not boldface.
3 Writer begins with descriptive passages. **4** Background about
school sets scene for personal experiences. **5** Transition from
background to personal experiences.

12j Business report

Brian Spencer, a student in an introductory business course, wrote an investigative report on the problem of employee motivation at a small company. His report combines research from outside sources, facts about the company's situation, and information from interviews with employees and management. It concludes with his recommendations.

Business report   **Title page**

1

2

3   Positively Affecting Employee Motivation

                          Prepared by Brian Spencer

                        Report Distributed March 9, 2006

4   Prepared for OAISYS

---

1 Formatting of all pages of report consistent with typical style in business. **2** Title page counted in numbering, but no page number appears. **3** Title, writer's name, and date centered. **4** Company name centered at bottom of page.

(Annotations indicate business-style formatting **and** effective writing.**)**

Employee Motivation 2   **1**

Abstract   **2**

Corporate goals, such as sales quotas or increases in market share, do not always take into account employee motivation. Motivating employees is thus a challenge and an opportunity for firms that want to outperform their competitors. For a firm to achieve its goals, its employees must be motivated to perform effectively.

Empirical research conducted with employees of a subject firm, OAISYS,   **3** echoed theories published by leading authorities in journals, books, and online reports. These theories argue that monetary incentives are not the primary drivers for employee motivation. Clear expectations, communication of progress toward goals, accountability, and public appreciation are common primary drivers. A firm aiming to achieve superior performance should focus on these activities.

1 Page formatted in typical business style. Short title and page number flush right. **2** Abstract on separate page; heading flush left and boldface. **3** Paragraphs separated by extra line of space; first line of paragraph not indented.

Employee Motivation 3

1 Introduction

All firms strive to maximize performance. Such performance is typically defined by one or more tangible measurements such as total sales, earnings per share, return on assets, and so on. The performance of a firm is created and delivered by its employees. Employees, however, are not necessarily motivated to do their part to maximize a firm's performance. Factors that motivate employees can be much more complex than corporate goals. This report will define the problem of employee motivation in one company and examine potential solutions.

OAISYS is a small business based in Tempe, Arizona, that manufactures business call recording products. Currently OAISYS employs 27 people. The business has been notably successful, generating annual compound sales growth of over 20% during the last three years. The company's management and board of directors expect revenue growth to accelerate over the coming three years to an annual compound rate of over 35%. This ambitious corporate goal will require maximum productivity and effectiveness from all employees, both current and prospective. OAISYS's management requested an analysis of its current personnel structure focused on the alignment of individual employee motivation with its corporate goal.

2 Background on Current Human Resources Program

OAISYS is currently structured departmentally by function. It has teams for research and development, sales, marketing, operations, and administration. Every employee has access to the same employment

[The writer uses the next section to present evidence from research studies and from interviews with employees.]

1 Introduction presents problem to be discussed and establishes scope of report. **2** Heading announces purpose of section.

Employee Motivation 5

Doug Ames, manager of operations for OAISYS, noted that some of
these issues keep the company from outperforming expectations:
"Communication is not timely or uniform, expectations are not clear
and consistent, and some employees do not contribute significantly yet
nothing is done" (personal communication, February 28, 2006).

Recommendations   **1**

It appears that a combination of steps can be used to unlock greater
performance for OAISYS. Most important, steps can be taken to
strengthen the corporate culture in key areas such as communication,
accountability, and appreciation. Employee feedback indicates that
these are areas of weakness or motivators that can be improved. This
feedback is summarized in Figure 1.   **2**

A plan to use communication effectively to set expectations, share
results in a timely fashion, and publicly offer appreciation to specific
contributors will likely go a long way toward aligning individual
motivation with corporate goals. Additionally, holding individuals
accountable for results will bring parity to the workplace.

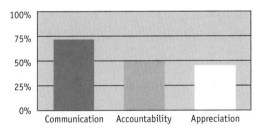

3

Figure 1. Areas of greatest need for improvements in motivation.   **4**

---

1 Writer presents recommendations based on his research and
interviews. **2** Figure summarizes research findings. **3** Figure
graphically illustrates support for key recommendation. **4** Figure
number and caption appear below figure.

12k Professional memo (business)

For a course in business writing, Kelly Ratajczak wrote a proposal, in the form of a memorandum. Her purpose was to persuade her supervisor of the benefits of a well-ness program for employees at the medium-size company where she was an intern.

1   MEMORANDUM

2 To: Jay Crosson, Senior Vice President, Human Resources

From: Kelly Ratajczak, Intern, Purchasing Department

Subject: Proposal to Add a Wellness Program

Date: April 24, 2011

3 Health care costs are rising. In the long run, implementing a wellness program in our corporate culture will decrease the company's health care costs.

4

5 Research indicates that nearly 70% of health care costs are from common illnesses related to high blood pressure, overweight, lack of exercise, high cholesterol, stress, poor nutrition, and other preventable health issues (Hall, 2006). Health care costs are a major expense for most businesses, and they do not reflect costs due to the loss of productivity or absenteeism. A wellness program would address most, if not all, of these health care issues and related costs.

6 **Benefits of Healthier Employees**

Not only would a wellness program substantially reduce costs associated with employee health care, but our company would prosper through

---

1 Formatting consistent with typical style for business memo.
2 First page counted in numbering, but no page number appears.
3 Clear point in first paragraph. **4** Paragraphs separated by extra line of space; first line of paragraph not indented.
5 Introduction provides background information. **6** Headings, flush left and boldface, define sections.

(Annotations indicate business-style formatting and effective writing.)

Documenting Sources in APA Style

The APA system for documenting sources is set forth in the *Publication Manual of the American Psychological Association,* 6th ed. (Washington, DC: APA, 2010).

13 APA in-text citations

APA's in-text citations provide the author's last name and the year of publication, usually before the cited material, and a page number in parentheses directly after the cited material. In the following models, the elements of the in-text citation are highlighted.

NOTE: APA style requires the use of the past tense or the present perfect tense in signal phrases introducing cited material: *Smith (2012) reported, Smith (2012) has argued.* See also page 36.

hackerhandbooks.com/pocket
APA papers > Exercises: 38–1 to 38–3 and 38–9 to 38–11

■ **1. Basic format for a quotation**   Ordinarily, introduce the quotation with a signal phrase that includes the author's last name followed by the year of publication in parentheses. Put the page number (preceded by "p.") in parentheses after the quotation. For sources from the Web without page numbers, see item 12a on page 108.

Critser (2003) noted that many health care providers still "remain either in ignorance or outright denial about the health danger to the poor and the young" (p. 5).

If the author is not named in the signal phrase, place the author's name, the year, and the page number in parentheses after the quotation: (Critser, 2003, p. 5). (See items 6 and 12 for citing sources that lack authors; item 12 also explains how to handle sources without dates or page numbers.)

NOTE: Do not include a month in an in-text citation, even if the entry in the reference list includes the month.

■ **2. Basic format for a summary or a paraphrase**   As for a quotation (see item 1), include the author's last name and the year either in a signal phrase introducing the material or in parentheses following it. Use a page number, if one is available, following the cited material. For sources from the Web without page numbers, see item 12a on page 108.

Yanovski and Yanovski (2002) explained that sibutramine suppresses appetite by blocking the reuptake of the neurotransmitters serotonin and norepinephrine in the brain (p. 594).

Sibutramine suppresses appetite by blocking the reuptake of the neurotransmitters serotonin and norepinephrine in the brain (Yanovski & Yanovski, 2002, p. 594).

■ **3. Work with two authors**   Name both authors in the signal phrase or in parentheses each time you cite the work. In the parentheses, use "&" between the authors' names; in the signal phrase, use "and."

According to Sothern and Gordon (2003), "Environmental factors may contribute as much as 80% to the causes of childhood obesity" (p. 104).

Obese children often engage in limited physical activity (Sothern & Gordon, 2003, p. 104).

■ **4. Work with three to five authors**   Identify all authors in the signal phrase or in parentheses the first time you cite the source.

In 2003, Berkowitz, Wadden, Tershakovec, and Cronquist concluded, "Sibutramine . . . must be carefully monitored in adolescents, as in adults, to control increases in [blood pressure] and pulse rate" (p. 1811).

In subsequent citations, use the first author's name followed by "et al." in either the signal phrase or the parentheses.

As Berkowitz et al. (2003) advised, "Until more extensive safety and efficacy data are available, . . . weight-loss medications should be used only on an experimental basis for adolescents" (p. 1811).

■ **5. Work with six or more authors**   Use the first author's name followed by "et al." in the signal phrase or in parentheses.

McDuffie et al. (2002) found that orlistat, combined with behavioral therapy, produced an average weight loss of 4.4 kg, or 9.7 pounds (p. 646).

■ **6. Work with unknown author**   If the author is unknown, mention the work's title in the signal phrase or give the first word or two of the title in parentheses. Titles of short works such as articles are put in quotation marks; titles of long works such as books and reports are italicized.

Children struggling to control their weight must also struggle with the pressures of television advertising that, on the one hand, encourages the consumption of junk food and, on the other, celebrates thin celebrities ("Television," 2002).

NOTE: In the rare case when "Anonymous" is specified as the author, treat it as if it were a real name: (Anonymous, 2001). In the list of references, also use the name Anonymous as author.

■ **7. Organization as author**   Name the organization in the signal phrase or in the parentheses the first time you cite the source.

Obesity puts children at risk for a number of medical complications, including Type 2 diabetes, hypertension, sleep apnea, and orthopedic problems (Henry J. Kaiser Family Foundation, 2004, p. 1).

If the organization has a familiar abbreviation, you may include it in brackets the first time you cite the source and use the abbreviation alone in later citations.

FIRST CITATION   (Centers for Disease Control and Prevention [CDC], 2012)

LATER CITATIONS   (CDC, 2012)

■ **8. Authors with the same last name**   If your reference list includes two or more authors with the same last name, use initials with the last names in your in-text citations.

Research by E. Smith (1989) revealed that. . . .

One 2012 study contradicted . . . (R. Smith, p. 234).

■ **9. Two or more works by the same author in the same year**   In the reference list, you will use lowercase letters ("a," "b," and so on) with the year to order the entries. (See item 8 on p. 116.) Use those same letters with the year in the in-text citation.

Research by Durgin (2003b) has yielded new findings about the role of counseling in treating childhood obesity.

■ **10. Two or more works in the same parentheses**   Put the works in parentheses in the same order that they appear in the reference list, separated with semicolons.

Researchers have indicated that studies of pharmacological treatments for childhood obesity are inconclusive (Berkowitz et al., 2003; McDuffie et al., 2002).

■ **11. Multiple citations to the same work in one paragraph**   If you give the author's name in the text of your paper (not in parentheses) and you mention that source again in the text of the same paragraph, give only the author's name, not the date, in the later citation. If any subsequent reference in the same paragraph is in parentheses, include both the author and the date in the parentheses.

Principal Jean Patrice said, "You have to be able to reach students where they are instead of making them come to you. If you don't, you'll lose them" (personal communication, April 10, 2006). Patrice expressed her desire to see all students get something out of their educational experience. This feeling is common among members of Waverly's faculty. With such a positive view of student potential, it is no wonder that 97% of Waverly High School graduates go on to a four-year university (Patrice, 2006).

■ **12. Web source** Cite sources from the Web as you would cite any other source, giving the author and the year when they are available.

Atkinson (2001) found that children who spent at least four hours a day watching TV were less likely to engage in adequate physical activity during the week.

Usually a page number is not available; occasionally a Web source will lack an author or a date (see items 12a, 12b, and 12c).

a. No page numbers If the source has numbered paragraphs, use the paragraph number preceded by the abbreviation "para.": (Hall, 2012, para. 5). If the source has no numbered paragraphs but contains headings, cite the appropriate heading in parentheses; you may also indicate which paragraph under the heading you are referring to, even if the paragraphs are not numbered.

Hoppin and Taveras (2004) pointed out that several other medications were classified by the Drug Enforcement Administration as having the "potential for abuse" (Weight-Loss Drugs section, para. 6).

NOTE: Some PDF documents have stable page numbers; when that is the case, you can give the page number in the parenthetical citation.

b. Unknown author Mention the title of the source in a signal phrase or give the first word or two of the title in parentheses (see also item 6). (If an organization serves as the author, see item 7.)

The body's basal metabolic rate, or BMR, is a measure of its at-rest energy requirement ("Exercise," 2003).

c. Unknown date Use the abbreviation "n.d." (for "no date").

Attempts to establish a definitive link between television programming and children's eating habits have been problematic (Magnus, n.d.).

■ **13. An entire Web site** If you are citing an entire Web site, not an internal page or a section, give the URL in the text of your paper but do not include it in the reference list.

The U.S. Center for Nutrition Policy and Promotion website (http://www.cnpp.usda.gov/) provides useful information about diet and nutrition for children and adults.

■ **14. Multivolume work** Add the volume number in parentheses with the page number.

Banford (2009) has demonstrated stable weight loss over time from a combination of psychological counseling, exercise, and nutritional planning (Volume 2, p. 135).

■ **15. Personal communication** Interviews that you conduct, memos, letters, e-mail messages, social media posts, and similar communications should be cited in the text only, not in the reference list. (Use the first initial with the last name in parentheses.)

One of Atkinson's colleagues, who has studied the effect of the media on children's eating habits, has suggested that advertisers need to design ads responsibly for their younger viewers (F. Johnson, personal communication, October 20, 2013).

■ **16. Course materials** Cite lecture notes from your instructor or your own class notes as personal communication (see item 15). If your instructor distributes or posts material that contains publication information, cite as you would the appropriate source. See also item 65 on page 135.

■ **17. Part of a source (chapter, figure)** To cite a specific part of a source, such as a whole chapter or a figure or table, identify the element in parentheses. Don't abbreviate terms such as "Figure," "Chapter," and "Section"; "page" is always abbreviated "p." (or "pp." for more than one page).

The data support the finding that weight loss stabilizes with consistent therapy and ongoing monitoring (Hanniman, 2010, Figure 8-3, p. 345).

■ **18. Indirect source** When a writer's or a speaker's quoted words appear in a source written by someone else, begin the parenthetical citation with the words "as cited in." In the following example, Critser is the author of the source given in the reference list; that source contains a quotation by Satcher.

Former surgeon general Dr. David Satcher described "a nation of young people seriously at risk of starting out obese and dooming themselves to the difficult task of overcoming a tough illness" (as cited in Critser, 2003, p. 4).

■ **19. Sacred or classical text** Identify the text, the version or edition, and the chapter, verse, or line. It is not necessary to include the source in the reference list.

Peace activists have long cited the biblical prophet's vision of a world without war: "And they shall beat their swords into plowshares, and their spears into pruning hooks" (Isaiah 2:4, Revised Standard Version).

14 APA list of references

The information you will need for the reference list at the end of your paper will differ slightly for some sources, but the main principles apply to all sources: You should identify an author, a creator, or a producer whenever possible; give a title; and provide the date on which the source was produced. Some sources will require page numbers; some will require a publisher; and some will require retrieval information.

▶ General guidelines for the reference list, **p. 113**

14a General guidelines for listing authors (print and online)

The formatting of authors' names in items 1–12 applies to all sources in print and on the Web—books, articles, Web sites, and so on. For more models of specific source types, see items 13–69.

Directory to APA reference list models

General guidelines for the reference list

In the list of references, include only sources that you have quoted, summarized, or paraphrased in your paper.

Authors and dates

- Alphabetize entries by authors' last names; if a work has no author, alphabetize it by its title.

- For all authors' names, put the last name first, followed by a comma; use initials for the first and middle names.

- With two or more authors, use an ampersand (&) before the last author's name. Separate the names with commas. Include names for the first seven authors; if there are eight or more authors, give the first six authors, three ellipsis dots, and the last author.

- If the author is a company or an organization, give the name in normal order.

- Put the date of publication in parentheses immediately after the first element of the citation.

- For books, give the year of publication. For magazines, newspapers, and newsletters, give the year and month or the year, month, and day. For Web sources, give the date of posting, if available. Use the season if a publication gives only a season, not a month.

Titles

- Italicize the titles and subtitles of books, journals, and other long works.

- Use no italics or quotation marks for the titles of articles.

- For books and articles, capitalize only the first word of the title and subtitle and all proper nouns.

- For the titles of journals, magazines, and newspapers, capitalize all words of four letters or more (and all nouns, pronouns, verbs, adjectives, and adverbs of any length).

Place of publication and publisher

- Take the information about a book from its title page and copyright page. If more than one place of publication is listed, use only the first.

- Give the city and state for all US cities. Use postal abbreviations for all states.

- Give the city and country for all non-US cities; include the province for Canadian cities. Do not abbreviate the country or province.

- Do not give a state if the publisher's name includes it (Ann Arbor: University of Michigan Press, for example).

→

General guidelines for the reference list *(continued)*

- In publishers' names, omit terms such as "Company" (or "Co.") and "Inc." but keep "Books" and "Press." Omit first names or initials (Norton, not W. W. Norton).

- If the publisher is the same as the author, use the word "Author" in the publisher position.

Volume, issue, and page numbers

- For a journal or a magazine, give only the volume number if the publication is paginated continuously through each volume; give the volume and issue numbers if each issue begins on page 1.

- Italicize the volume number and put the issue number, not italicized, in parentheses.

- When an article appears on consecutive pages, provide the range of pages. When an article does not appear on consecutive pages, give all page numbers: A1, A17.

- For daily and weekly newspapers, use "p." or "pp." before page numbers (if any). For journals and magazines, do not use "p." or "pp."

URLs, DOIs, and other retrieval information

- For articles and books from the Web, use the DOI (digital object identifier) if the source has one, and do not give a URL. If a source does not have a DOI, give the URL.

- Use a retrieval date for a Web source only if the content is likely to change. Most of the examples in 14b do not show a retrieval date because the content of the sources is stable. If you are unsure about whether to use a date, include it or consult your instructor.

■ **1. Single author**

author: last   year
name + initial(s) (book)   title (book)

Rosenberg, T. (2011). *Join the club: How peer pressure can transform the world.*

       place of
      publication   publisher

      New York, NY: Norton.

■ **2. Two to seven authors** List up to seven authors by last names followed by initials. Use an ampersand (&) before the name of the last author. (See items 3–5 on pp. 105–06 for citing works with multiple authors in the text of your paper.)

all authors:
last name + initial(s)

Ludwig, J., Duncan, G. J., Gennetian, L. A., Katz, L. F., Kessler, R. C., Kling,

year
(journal)   title (article)

J. R., & Sanbonmatsu, L. (2012). Neighborhood effects on the long-

journal
title   volume   page(s)

term well-being of low-income adults. *Science, 337,* 1505-1510.

DOI

doi:10.1126/science.1224648

■ **3. Eight or more authors**   List the names of the first six authors followed by three ellipsis dots and the last author's name.

Tøttrup, A. P., Klaassen, R. H. G., Kristensen, M. W., Strandberg, R.,
    Vardanis, Y., Lindström, Å., . . . Thorup, K. (2012). Drought in
    Africa caused delayed arrival of European songbirds. *Science,*
    338, 1307. doi:10.1126/science.1227548

■ **4. Organization as author**

author:
organization name   year   title (book)

American Psychiatric Association. (2013). *Diagnostic and statistical manual of*

organization
place   as author
edition   of publication   and publisher

mental disorders (5th ed.). Washington, DC: Author.

■ **5. Unknown author**

year + month + day
title (article)   (weekly publication)   journal title

The rise of the sharing economy. (2013, March 9). *The Economist,*

volume,
issue   page(s)

406(8826), 14.

place of
title (book)   year   publication   publisher

New concise world atlas. (2010). New York, NY: Oxford University Press.

■ **6. Author using a pseudonym (pen name) or screen name**   Use the author's real name, if known, and give the pseudonym or screen name in brackets exactly as it appears in the source. If only the screen name is known, begin with that name and do not use brackets. (See also items 47 and 68 on citing screen names in social media.)

screen name | year + month + day (daily publication) | title of original article

littlebigman. (2012, December 13). Re: Who's watching? Privacy concerns

| label | title of publication

persist as smart meters roll out [Comment]. *National Geographic Daily News*.

URL for Web publication

Retrieved from http://news.nationalgeographic.com/

■ **7. Two or more works by the same author** Use the author's name for all entries. List the entries by year, the earliest first.

Heinrich, B. (2009). *Summer world: A season of bounty*. New York, NY: Ecco.

Heinrich, B. (2012). *Life everlasting: The animal way of death*. New

York, NY: Houghton Mifflin Harcourt.

■ **8. Two or more works by the same author in the same year** List the works alphabetically by title. In the parentheses, following the year add "a," "b," and so on. Use these same letters when giving the year in the in-text citation. (See also p. 53 and item 9 on p. 107.)

Bower, B. (2012a, December 15). Families in flux. *Science News,*

182(12), 16.

Bower, B. (2012b, November 3). Human-Neandertal mating gets a new

date. *Science News, 182*(9), 8.

■ **9. Editor** Use the abbreviation "Ed." for one editor, "Eds." for more than one editor.

all editors: last name + initial(s) | year | title (book)

Carr, S. C., MacLachlan, M., & Furnham, A. (Eds.). (2012). *Humanitarian work*

place of publication | publisher

psychology. New York, NY: Palgrave.

■ **10. Author and editor** Begin with the name of the author, followed by the name of the editor and the abbreviation "Ed." For an author with two or more editors, use the abbreviation "Ed." after each editor's name: Gray, W., & Jones, P. (Ed.), & Smith, A. (Ed.).

author | editor | year | title (book)

James, W., & Pelikan, J. (Ed.). (2009). *The varieties of religious experience*.

place of publication | publisher | original publication information

New York, NY: Library of America. (Original work published 1902)

■ **11. Translator** Begin with the name of the author. After the title, in parentheses place the name of the translator and the abbreviation "Trans." (for "Translator"). Add the original date of publication at the end of the entry.

author   year   title (book)   translator   place of publication

Scheffer, P. (2011). *Immigrant nations* (L. Waters, Trans.). Cambridge, England:

publisher   original publication information

Polity Press. (Original work published 2007)

■ **12. Editor and translator** If the editor and translator are the same person, the same name appears in both the editor position and the translator position.

Girard, R., & Williams, J. G. (Ed.). (2012). *Resurrection from the*
underground (J. G. Williams, Trans.). East Lansing: Michigan
State University Press. (Original work published 1996)

14b Articles and other short works

▶ Citation at a glance: Article in a journal or magazine,
pp. 119–20

▶ Citation at a glance: Article from a database, **p. 121**

■ **13. Article in a journal** If an article from the Web or a database has no DOI, include the URL for the journal's home page.

a. Print

all authors: last name + initial(s)   year   article title

Bippus, A. M., Dunbar, N. E., & Liu, S.-J. (2012). Humorous responses to

interpersonal complaints: Effects of humor style and nonverbal expression.

journal title   volume page(s)

The Journal of Psychology, 146, 437-453.

b. Web

all authors: last name + initial(s)   year   article title

Vargas, N., & Schafer, M. H. (2013). Diversity in action: Interpersonal networks

journal title   volume, issue page(s)

and the distribution of advice. *Social Science Research, 42*(1), 46-58.

DOI

doi:10.1016/j.ssresearch.2012.08.013

author   year   article title

Brenton, S. (2011). When the personal becomes political: Mitigating damage

                              journal title (no volume available)

  following scandals. *Current Research in Social Psychology*. Retrieved from

                    URL for journal home page

  http://www.uiowa.edu/~grpproc/crisp/crisp.html

c. Database

    year
author   (journal)   article title

Sohn, K. (2012). The social class origins of U.S. teachers, 1860-1920.

              volume,
     journal title issue page(s)   DOI

  Journal of Social History, 45(4), 908-935. doi:10.1093/jsh/shr121

■ **14. Article in a magazine** If an article from the Web or a database has no DOI, include the URL for the journal's home page.

a. Print

      year + month
author (monthly magazine) article title magazine title

Comstock, J. (2012, December). The underrated sense. *Psychology Today,*

 volume,
 issue page(s)

 45(6), 46-47.

b. Web

    date of posting
author (when available) article title magazine title

Burns, J. (2012, December 3). The measure of all things. *The American Prospect.*

     URL for home page

  Retrieved from http://prospect.org/

c. Database

    year + month   volume,
author (monthly magazine) article title magazine title issue page(s)

Tucker, A. (2012, November). Primal instinct. *Smithsonian, 43*(7), 54-63.

     URL for magazine home page

  Retrieved from http://www.smithsonianmag.com/

Citation at a glance
Article in a journal or magazine `APA`

To cite an article in a print journal or magazine in APA style, include the following elements:

1. Author(s)
2. Year of publication for journal; complete date for magazine
3. Title and subtitle of article
4. Name of journal or magazine
5. Volume number; issue number, if required (see p. 114)
6. Page number(s) of article

JOURNAL TABLE OF CONTENTS

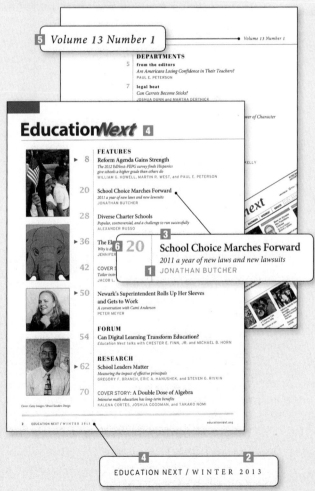

5 Volume 13 Number 1

Volume 13 Number 1

DEPARTMENTS

5 from the editors
Are Americans Losing Confidence in Their Teachers?
PAUL E. PETERSON

7 legal beat
Can Carrots Become Sticks?
JOSHUA DUNN and MARTHA DERTHICK

Education*Next* **4**

...ower of Character

FEATURES

▶ 8 Reform Agenda Gains Strength
The 2012 EdNext-PEPG survey finds Hispanics give schools a higher grade than others do
WILLIAM G. HOWELL, MARTIN R. WEST, and PAUL E. PETERSON

20 School Choice Marches Forward
2011 a year of new laws and new lawsuits
JONATHAN BUTCHER

28 Diverse Charter Schools
Popular, controversial, and a challenge to run successfully
ALEXANDER RUSSO

▶ 36 The El...
Why is d...
JENNIFER...

3

6 20 School Choice Marches Forward
2011 a year of new laws and new lawsuits
1 JONATHAN BUTCHER

42 COVER S...
Tailor instr...
JACOB L...

▶ 50 Newark's Superintendent Rolls Up Her Sleeves and Gets to Work
A conversation with Cami Anderson
PETER MEYER

FORUM

54 Can Digital Learning Transform Education?
Education Next talks with CHESTER E. FINN, JR. and MICHAEL B. HORN

RESEARCH

▶ 62 School Leaders Matter
Measuring the impact of effective principals
GREGORY F. BRANCH, ERIC A. HANUSHEK, and STEVEN G. RIVKIN

70 COVER STORY: A Double Dose of Algebra
Intensive math education has long-term benefits
KALENA CORTES, JOSHUA GOODMAN, and TAKAKO NOMI

Cover: Getty Images / Bruce Sanders Design

2 EDUCATION NEXT / WINTER 2013

educationnext.org

4 EDUCATION NEXT / WINTER 2013 **2**

FIRST PAGE OF ARTICLE

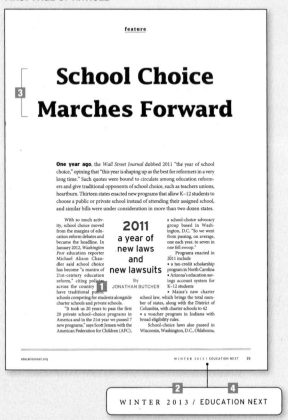

feature

School Choice Marches Forward

One year ago, the *Wall Street Journal* dubbed 2011 "the year of school choice," opining that "this year is shaping up as the best for reformers in a very long time." Such quotes were bound to circulate among education reformers and give traditional opponents of school choice, such as teachers unions, heartburn. Thirteen states enacted new programs that allow K–12 students to choose a public or private school instead of attending their assigned school, and similar bills were under consideration in more than two dozen states.

With so much activity, school choice moved from the margins of education reform debates and became the headline. In January 2012, *Washington Post* education reporter Michael Alison Chandler said school choice has become "a mantra of 21st-century education reform," citing policies across the country **1** have traditional public schools competing for students alongside charter schools and private schools.

"It took us 20 years to pass the first 20 private school-choice programs in America and in the 21st year we passed 7 new programs," says Scott Jensen with the American Federation for Children (AFC),

2011
a year of new laws and new lawsuits
By
JONATHAN BUTCHER

a school-choice advocacy group based in Washington, D.C. "So we went from passing, on average, one each year, to seven in one fell swoop."

Programs enacted in 2011 include
• a tax-credit scholarship program in North Carolina
• Arizona's education savings account system for K–12 students
• Maine's new charter school law, which brings the total number of states, along with the District of Columbia, with charter schools to 42
• a voucher program in Indiana with broad eligibility rules.

School-choice laws also passed in Wisconsin, Washington, D.C., Oklahoma,

REFERENCE LIST ENTRY FOR AN ARTICLE IN A PRINT JOURNAL OR MAGAZINE

1   **2**   **3**   **4**

Butcher, J. (2013). School choice marches forward. *Education Next,*

5   **6**

13(1), 20-27.

For more on citing articles in APA style, see items 13–15.

120

Citation at a glance
Article from a database APA

To cite an article from a database in APA style, include the following elements:

1. Author(s)
2. Year of publication for journal; complete date for magazine or newspaper
3. Title and subtitle of article
4. Name of periodical
5. Volume number; issue number, if required (see p. 114)
6. Page number(s)
7. DOI (digital object identifier)
8. URL for periodical's home page (if there is no DOI)

DATABASE RECORD

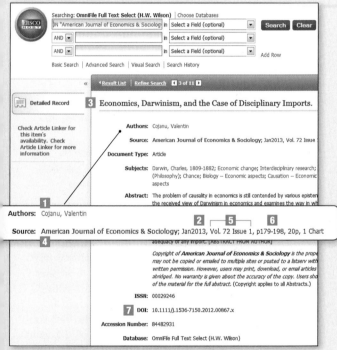

Reprinted by permission of EBSCO Publishing.

REFERENCE LIST ENTRY FOR AN ARTICLE FROM A DATABASE

```
    1      2                    3
Cojanu, V. (2013). Economics, Darwinism, and the case of

                            4
    disciplinary imports. American Journal of Economics & Sociology,

    5     6              7
    72, 179-198. doi:10.1111/j.1536-7150.2012.00867.x
```

For more on citing articles from a database in APA style, see items 13–15.

■ 15. Article in a newspaper

a. Print

author year + month + day   article title

Swarns, R. L. (2012, December 9). A family, for a few days a year. *The*

  newspaper title   page(s)

  New York Times, pp. 1, 20.

b. Web

author: last
name + initial(s) year + month + day   article title

Villanueva-Whitman, E. (2012, November 27). Working to stimulate

      newspaper title

  memory function. *Des Moines Register*. Retrieved from http://www

     URL for
     home page

  .desmoinesregister.com/

■ 16. Abstract

a. Abstract of a journal article

Morales, J., Calvo, A., & Bialystok, E. (2013). Working memory
  development in monolingual and bilingual children [Abstract].
  Journal of Experimental Child Psychology, 114, 187-202.
  Retrieved from http://www.sciencedirect.com/

b. Abstract of a paper

Denham, B. (2012). Diffusing deviant behavior: A communication
  perspective on the construction of moral panics [Abstract]. Paper
  presented at the AEJMC 2012 Conference, Chicago, IL. Retrieved
  from http://www.aejmc.org/home/2012/04/ctm-2012-abstracts/

■ 17. Supplemental material
If an article on the Web contains supplemental material that is not part of the main article, cite the material as you would an article and add the label "Supplemental material" in brackets following the title.

Reis, S., Grennfelt, P., Klimont, Z., Amann, M., ApSimon, H., Hettelingh,
  J.-P., . . . Williams, M. (2012). From acid rain to climate change
  [Supplemental material]. *Science 338*(6111), 1153-1154.
  doi:10.1126/science.1226514

■ 18. Article with a title in its title
If an article title contains another article title or a term usually placed in quotation marks, use quotation marks around the internal title or the term.

Easterling, D., & Millesen, J. L. (2012, Summer). Diversifying civic leadership: What it takes to move from "new faces" to adaptive problem solving. *National Civic Review*, 20-27. doi:10.1002/ncr.21073

◼ 19. Letter to the editor
If the letter has no title, use the bracketed words as the title, as in the following example.

Lim, C. (2012, November-December). [Letter to the editor]. *Sierra*. Retrieved from http://www.sierraclub.org/sierra/

◼ 20. Editorial or other unsigned article

The business case for transit dollars [Editorial]. (2012, December 9). *Star Tribune*. Retrieved from http://www.startribune.com/

◼ 21. Newsletter article

Scrivener, L. (n.d.). Why is the minimum wage issue important for food justice advocates? *Food Workers — Food Justice, 15*. Retrieved from http://www.thedatabank.com/dpg/199 /pm.asp?nav=1&ID=41429

◼ 22. Review
In brackets, give the type of work reviewed, the title, and the author for a book or the year for a film. If the review has no author or title, use the material in brackets as the title.

Aviram, R. B. (2012). [Review of the book *What do I say? The therapist's guide to answering client questions*, by L. N. Edelstein & C. A. Waehler]. *Psychotherapy, 49*(4), 570-571. doi:10.1037/a0029815

Bradley, A., & Olufs, E. (2012). Family dynamics and school violence [Review of the motion picture *We need to talk about Kevin*, 2011]. *PsycCRITIQUES, 57*(49). doi:10.1037/a0030982

◼ 23. Published interview

Githongo, J. (2012, November 20). A conversation with John Githongo [Interview by Baobab]. *The Economist*. Retrieved from http://www.economist.com/

◼ 24. Article in a reference work (encyclopedia, dictionary, wiki)
a. Print
Konijn, E. A. (2008). Affects and media exposure. In W. Donsbach (Ed.), *The international encyclopedia of communication* (Vol. 1, pp. 123-129). Malden, MA: Blackwell.

b. Web

Ethnomethodology. (2006). In *STS wiki*. Retrieved December 15,
    2012, from http://www.stswiki.org/index.php?title
    =Ethnomethodology

■ **25. Comment on an online article**   If the writer's real
name and screen name are both given, put the real name
first, followed by the screen name in brackets.

Danboy125. (2012, November 9). Re: No flowers on the psych ward
    [Comment]. *The Atlantic*. Retrieved from http://www.theatlantic.com/

■ **26. Testimony before a legislative body**

Carmona, R. H. (2004, March 2). *The growing epidemic of childhood
    obesity*. Testimony before the Subcommittee on Competition,
    Foreign Commerce, and Infrastructure of the U.S. Senate
    Committee on Commerce, Science, and Transportation. Retrieved
    from http://www.hhs.gov/asl/testify/t040302.html

■ **27. Paper presented at a meeting or symposium (unpublished)**

Karimi, S., Key, G., & Tat, D. (2011, April 22). *Complex predicates in
    focus*. Paper presented at the West Coast Conference on Formal
    Linguistics, Tucson, AZ.

■ **28. Poster session at a conference**

Lacara, N. (2011, April 24). *Predicate which appositives*. Poster session
    presented at the West Coast Conference on Formal Linguistics,
    Tucson, AZ.

14c Books and other long works

▶ Citation at a glance: Book, **p. 125**

■ **29. Basic format for a book**

a. Print

author(s):
last name
+ initial(s)   year   book title

Child, B. J. (2012). *Holding our world together: Ojibwe women and the*

                              place of
                              publication   publisher

survival of community. New York, NY: Viking.

Citation at a glance
Book APA

To cite a print book in APA style, include the following elements:

1. Author(s)
2. Year of publication
3. Title and subtitle
4. Place of publication
5. Publisher

TITLE PAGE

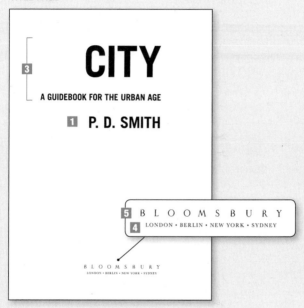

FROM COPYRIGHT PAGE

First published in Great Britain and the USA in 2012 **2**

Bloomsbury Publishing Plc, 50 Bedford Square, London WC1B 3DP
Bloomsbury USA, 175 Fifth Avenue, New York, NY 10010

Copyright © 2012 by P. D. Smith

© P.D. Smith, 2012, City: A Guidebook for the Urban Age, and Bloomsbury Publishing Plc.

REFERENCE LIST ENTRY FOR A PRINT BOOK

   1   2   3   4

Smith, P. D. (2012). *City: A guidebook for the urban age.* London,

           5

England: Bloomsbury.

For more on citing books in APA style, see items 29–37.

■ **29. Basic format for a book** (*cont.*)

b. Web (or online library)   Give the URL for the home page of the Web site or the online library.

author(s)   year   book title
Amponsah, N. A., & Falola, T. (2012). *Women's roles in sub-Saharan Africa.*

URL
Retrieved from http://books.google.com/

c. E-book   Give the version in brackets after the title ("Kindle version," "Nook version," and so on). Include the DOI or, if a DOI is not available, the URL for the home page of the site from which you downloaded the book.

Wolf, D. A., & Folbre, N. (Eds.). (2012). *Universal coverage of long-term care in the United States* [Adobe Digital Editions version]. Retrieved from https://www.russellsage.org/

d. Database   Give the URL for the database.

Beasley, M. H. (2012). *Women of the Washington press: Politics, prejudice, and persistence.* Retrieved from http://muse.jhu.edu/

■ **30. Edition other than the first**

Harvey, P. (2013). *An introduction to Buddhism: Teachings, history, and practices* (2nd ed.). Cambridge, England: Cambridge University Press.

■ **31. Selection in an anthology or a collection**

a. Entire anthology

editor(s)   year
Warren, A. E. A., Lerner, R. M., & Phelps, E. (Eds.). (2011). *Thriving and*

title of anthology
spirituality among youth: Research perspectives and future possibilities.

place of
publication publisher
Hoboken, NJ: Wiley.

b. Selection in an anthology

author of
selection   year   title of selection
Lazar, S. W. (2012). Neural correlates of positive youth development.

editors of anthology
In A. E. A. Warren, R. M. Lerner, & E. Phelps (Eds.), *Thriving and*

title of anthology
spirituality among youth: Research perspectives and future possibilities

page numbers   place of
of selection   publication publisher
(pp. 77-90). Hoboken, NJ: Wiley.

■ 32. Multivolume work

a. All volumes

Khalakdina, M. (2008-2011). *Human development in the Indian context: A socio-cultural focus* (Vols. 1-2). New Delhi, India: Sage.

b. One volume, with title

Jensen, R. E. (Ed.). (2012). *Voices of the American West: Vol. 1. The Indian interviews of Eli S. Ricker, 1903-1919*. Lincoln: University of Nebraska Press.

■ 33. Introduction, preface, foreword, or afterword

Zachary, L. J. (2012). Foreword. In L. A. Daloz, *Mentor: Guiding the journey of adult learners* (pp. v-vii). San Francisco, CA: Jossey-Bass.

■ 34. Dictionary or other reference work

Leong, F. T. L. (Ed.). (2008). *Encyclopedia of counseling* (Vols. 1-4). Thousand Oaks, CA: Sage.

Nichols, J. D., & Nyholm, E. (2012). *A concise dictionary of Minnesota Ojibwe*. Minneapolis: University of Minnesota Press.

■ 35. Republished book

Mailer, N. (2008). *Miami and the siege of Chicago: An informal history of the Republican and Democratic conventions of 1968*. New York, NY: New York Review Books. (Original work published 1968)

■ 36. Book with a title in its title   If the book title contains another book title or an article title, do not italicize the internal title and do not put quotation marks around it.

Marcus, L. (Ed.). (1999). *Sigmund Freud's* The interpretation of dreams: *New interdisciplinary essays*. Manchester, England: Manchester University Press.

■ 37. Book in a language other than English   Place the English translation, not italicized, in brackets.

Carminati, G. G., & Méndez, A. (2012). *Étapes de vie, étapes de soins* [Stages of life, stages of care]. Chêne-Bourg, Switzerland: Médecine & Hygiène.

■ 38. Dissertation

a. Published

Hymel, K. M. (2009). *Essays in urban economics* (Doctoral dissertation). Available from ProQuest Dissertations and Theses database. (AAT 3355930)

b. Unpublished

Mitchell, R. D. (2007). *The Wesleyan Quadrilateral: Relocating the conversation* (Unpublished doctoral dissertation). Claremont School of Theology, Claremont, CA.

■ 39. Conference proceedings

Yu, F.-Y., Hirashima, T., Supnithi, T., & Biswas, G. (2011). *Proceedings of the 19th International Conference on Computers in Education: ICCE 2011.* Retrieved from http://www.apsce.net:8080 /icce2011/program/proceedings/

■ 40. Government document If the document has a number, place the number in parentheses after the title.

U.S. Transportation Department, Pipeline and Hazardous Materials Safety Administration. (2012). *Emergency response guidebook 2012.* Washington, DC: Author.

U.S. Census Bureau, Bureau of Economic Analysis. (2012, December). *U.S. international trade in goods and services, October 2012* (Report No. CB12-232, BEA12-55, FT-900 [12-10]). Retrieved from http://www.census.gov/foreign-trade /Press-Release/2012pr/10/

■ 41. Report from a private organization If the publisher and the author are the same for a print source, see item 4 on page 115.

Ford Foundation. (2012, November). *Eastern Africa.* Retrieved from http://www.fordfoundation.org/pdfs/library/Eastern-Africa -brochure-2012.pdf

Atwood, B., Beam, M., Hindman, D. B., Hindman, E. B., Pintak, L., & Shors, B. (2012, May 25). *The Murrow Rural Information Initiative: Final report.* Pullman: Murrow College of Communication, Washington State University.

■ **42. Legal source**   The title of a court case is italicized in an in-text citation, but it is not italicized in the reference list.

Sweatt v. Painter, 339 U.S. 629 (1950). Retrieved from Cornell
University Law School, Legal Information Institute
website: http://www.law.cornell.edu/supct/html/historics
/USSC_CR_0339_0629_ZS.html

■ **43. Sacred or classical text**   It is not necessary to list sacred works such as the Bible or the Qur'an or classical Greek and Roman works (such as the *Odyssey*) in your reference list. See item 19 on page 110 for how to cite these sources in the text of your paper.

14d Web sites and parts of Web sites

▶ Citation at a glance: Section in a Web document, **pp. 130–31**

NOTE: In an APA paper or an APA reference list entry, the word "website" is spelled all lowercase, as one word.

■ **44. Entire Web site**   Do not include an entire Web site in the reference list. Give the URL in parentheses when you mention it in the text of your paper. (See item 13 on p. 109.)

■ **45. Document from a Web site**   If the publisher is known and is not named as the author, include the publisher in your retrieval statement.

Wagner, D. A., Murphy, K. M., & De Korne, H. (2012, December).
*Learning first: A research agenda for improving learning in
low-income countries*. Retrieved from Brookings Institution
website: http://www.brookings.edu/research/papers/2012/12
/learning-first-wagner-murphy-de-korne

Gerber, A. S., & Green, D. P. (2012). *Field experiments: Design, analysis,
and interpretation*. Retrieved from Yale Institution for Social and
Policy Studies website: http://isps.yale.edu/research/data/d081#
.UUy2HFdPL5w

Centers for Disease Control and Prevention. (2012, December 10).
Concussion in winter sports. Retrieved from http://www.cdc.gov
/Features/HockeyConcussions/index.html

Citation at a glance

Section in a Web document APA

To cite a section in a Web document in APA style, include the following elements:

1. Author(s)
2. Date of publication or most recent update ("n.d." if there is no date)
3. Title of section
4. Title of document
5. URL of section

WEB DOCUMENT CONTENTS PAGE

ON-SCREEN VIEW OF DOCUMENT

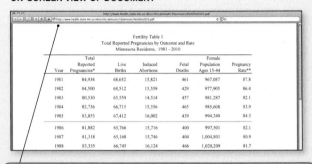

REFERENCE LIST ENTRY FOR A SECTION IN A WEB DOCUMENT

1   2   3   4

Minnesota Department of Health. (n.d.). Fertility. In *2010*

Minnesota health statistics annual summary. Retrieved from

5

http://www.health.state.mn.us/divs/chs/annsum/10annsum

/Fertility2010.pdf

For more on citing documents from Web sites in APA style, see items 45 and 46.

■ **46. Section in a Web document** Cite as a chapter in a book or a selection in an anthology (see item 31b).

Pew Research Center. (2012, December 12). About the 2012 Pew global attitudes survey. In *Social networking popular across globe*. Retrieved from http://www.pewglobal.org/2012/12/12 /social-networking-popular-across-globe

Chang, W.-Y., & Milan, L. M. (2012, October). Relationship between degree field and emigration. In *International mobility and employment characteristics among recent recipients of U.S. doctorates*. Retrieved from National Science Foundation website: http://www.nsf.gov/statistics /infbrief/nsf13300

■ **47. Blog post** If the writer's real name and screen name are both given, put the real name first, followed by the screen name in brackets. End with the URL for the post.

Kerssen, T. (2012, October 5). Hunger is political: Food Sovereignty Prize honors social movements [Blog post]. Retrieved from http://www.foodfirst.org/en/node/4020

■ **48. Blog comment**

Studebakerhawk_14611. (2012, December 5). Re: A people's history of MOOCs [Blog comment]. Retrieved from http://www.insidehighered .com/blogs/library-babel-fish/people's-history-moocs

14e Audio, visual, and multimedia sources

■ 49. Podcast

Schulz, K. (2011, March). *Kathryn Schulz: On being wrong* [Video podcast]. Retrieved from TED on http://itunes.apple.com/

Taylor, A., & Parfitt, G. (2011, January 13). *Physical activity and mental health: What's the evidence?* [Audio podcast]. Retrieved from Open University on http://itunes.apple.com/

■ 50. Video or audio on the Web

Kurzen, B. (2012, April 5). *Going beyond Muslim-Christian conflict in Nigeria* [Video file]. Retrieved from http://www.youtube.com/watch?v=JD8MIJOA050

Bever, T., Piattelli-Palmarini, M., Hammond, M., Barss, A., & Bergesen, A. (2012, February 2). *A basic introduction to Chomsky's linguistics* [Audio file]. Retrieved from University of Arizona, College of Social & Behavioral Sciences, Department of Linguistics website: http://linguistics.arizona.edu/node/711

■ 51. Transcript of an audio or a video file

Malone, T. W. *Collective intelligence* [Transcript of video file]. Retrieved from http://edge.org/conversation/collective-intelligence

■ 52. Film (DVD, BD, or other format)   In brackets following the title, add a description of the medium. Use "Motion picture" if you viewed the film in a theater; "Video file" if you downloaded the film from the Web or through a streaming service; "DVD" or "BD" if you viewed the film on DVD or Blu-ray Disc. For a motion picture or a DVD or BD, add the location and name of the studio. If you retrieved the film from the Web or used a streaming service, give the URL for the home page.

Affleck, B. (Director). (2012). *Argo* [Motion picture]. Burbank, CA: Warner Bros.

Ross, G. (Director and Writer), & Collins, S. (Writer). (2012). *The hunger games* [Video file]. Retrieved from http://netflix.com/

■ 53. Television or radio program

a. Series

Hager, M. (Executive producer), & Schieffer, B. (Moderator). (2012). *Face the nation* [Television series]. Washington, DC: CBS News.

b. Episode on the air

Harleston, R. (Host). (2012, December 1). Federal role in support
of autism [Television series episode]. In *Washington journal*.
Washington, DC: C-SPAN.

c. Episode on the Web

Morton, D. (Producer). (2012). Fast times at West Philly High
[Television series episode]. In M. Hager (Executive producer),
Frontline. Retrieved from http://www.wgbh.org/

■ **54. Music recording**

Chibalonza, A. (2012). Jubilee. On *African voices* [CD]. Merenberg,
Germany: ZYX Music.

African voices [CD]. (2012). Merenberg, Germany: ZYX Music.

■ **55. Lecture, speech, or address**

Verghese, A. (2012, December 6). *Colonialism and patterns of ethnic
conflict in contemporary India*. Address at the Freeman Spogli
Institute, Stanford University, Stanford, CA.

Donovan, S. (2012, June 12). *Assisted housing mobility in challenging
times* [Video file]. Address at the 5th National Conference on
Assisted Housing Mobility, Urban Institute, Washington, DC.

■ **56. Data set or graphic representation of data (graph,
chart, table)**   If the item is numbered in the source, indicate the number in parentheses after the title. If the graphic
appears within a larger document, do not italicize the title
of the graphic.

U.S. Department of Agriculture, Economic Research Service. (2011).
Daily intake of nutrients by food source: 2005-08 [Data set].
Retrieved from http://www.ers.usda.gov/data-products
/food-consumption-and-nutrient-intakes.aspx

Gallup. (2012, December 5). *In U.S., more cite obesity as most urgent
health problem* [Graphs]. Retrieved from http://www.gallup.com
/poll/159083/cite-obesity-urgent-health-problem.aspx

■ **57. Mobile application software (app)**   Begin with the
developer of the app, if known (as in the second example).

MindNode Touch 2.3 [Mobile application software]. (2012). Retrieved
from http://itunes.apple.com/

Source Tree Solutions. mojoPortal [Mobile application software].
(2012). Retrieved from http://www.microsoft.com/web/gallery/

■ **58. Video game**   If the game can be played on the Web or was downloaded from the Web, give the URL instead of publication information.

Firaxis Games. (2010). Sid Meier's Civilization V [Video game]. New York, NY: Take-Two Interactive. Xbox 360.

Atom Entertainment. (2012). Edgeworld [Video game]. Retrieved from http://www.addictinggames.com/

■ **59. Map**

Ukraine [Map]. (2008). Retrieved from the University of Texas at Austin Perry-Castañeda Library Map Collection website: http://www.lib.utexas.edu/maps/cia08/ukraine_sm_2008.gif

Syrian uprising map [Map]. (2012, October). Retrieved from http://www.polgeonow.com/2012/10/syria-uprising-map-october-2012-7.html

■ **60. Advertisement**

VMware [Advertisement]. (2012, September). *Harvard Business Review, 90*(9), 27.

■ **61. Work of art or photograph**

Olson, A. (2011). *Short story* [Painting]. Museum of Contemporary Art, Chicago, IL.

Crowner, S. (2012). *Kurtyna fragments* [Painting]. Retrieved from http://www.walkerart.org/

Weber, J. (1992). *Toward freedom* [Outdoor mural]. Sherman Oaks, CA.

■ **62. Brochure or fact sheet**

National Council of State Boards of Nursing. (2011). *A nurse's guide to professional boundaries* [Brochure]. Retrieved from https://www.ncsbn.org/

World Health Organization. (2012, September). *Road traffic injuries* (No. 358) [Fact sheet]. Retrieved from http://www.who.int/mediacentre/factsheets/fs358/en/index.html

■ **63. Press release**

Urban Institute. (2012, October 11). Two studies address health policy on campaign trail [Press release]. Retrieved from http://www.urban.org/publications/901537.html

■ 64. Presentation slides

Boeninger, C. F. (2008, August). *Web 2.0 tools for reference and instructional services* [Presentation slides]. Retrieved from http://libraryvoice.com /archives/2008/08/04/opal-20-conference-presentation-slides

■ **65. Lecture notes or other course materials** Cite materials that your instructor has posted on the Web as you would a Web document or a section in a Web document (see item 45 or 46). If the materials are handouts or printouts, cite whatever information is available in the source. Cite the instructor's personal notes or material that is not posted (such as slides) as personal communication in the text of your paper (see items 15 and 16 on p. 109).

Blum, R. (2011). Neurodevelopment in the first decade of life [Lecture notes and audio file]. In R. Blum & L. M. Blum, *Child health and development*. Retrieved from http://ocw.jhsph.edu /index.cfm/go/viewCourse/course/childhealth/coursePage /lectureNotes/

14f Personal communication and social media

■ **66. E-mail** E-mail messages, letters, and other personal communication are not included in the list of references. (See item 15 on p. 109 for citing these sources in the text of your paper.)

■ **67. Online posting** If an online posting is not archived, cite it as a personal communication in the text of your paper and do not include it in the list of references. If the posting is archived, give the URL and the name of the discussion list if it is not part of the URL.

McKinney, J. (2006, December 19). Adult education-healthcare partnerships [Electronic mailing list message]. Retrieved from http://www.nifl.gov/pipermail/healthliteracy/2006/000524 .html

■ **68. Twitter post (tweet)** If the writer's real name and screen name are both given, put the real name first, followed by the screen name in brackets. If only the screen name is known, do not put it in brackets. Include the entire text of the tweet as the title; end with the URL.

CQ Researcher. (2012, December 5). Up to 80 percent of the
600,000 processed foods sold in America have sugar
added to their recipes. See http://bit.ly/UmfA4L [Tweet].
Retrieved from https://twitter.com/cqresearcher/status
/276449095521038336

■ **69. Facebook post** If the writer's real name and screen
name are both given, put the real name first, followed by the
screen name in brackets. If only the screen name is known,
do not put it in brackets. Give a few words of the post as a
title. Include the URL for the poster's Facebook page. If you
are citing a personal Facebook page that will not be accessible to your readers, cite it as personal communication in
your text, not in the reference list (see item 15 on p. 109).

U.S. Department of Education. (2012, October 9). They are resilient
[Facebook post]. Retrieved October 15, 2012, from http://www
.facebook.com/ED.gov

15 APA notes

15a Footnotes in the text

Occasionally, you may use footnotes to provide additional
material that is important but that might interrupt the
flow of the paper. Notes should be brief and focused. Use
notes sparingly; if the material will take more than a few
sentences, you should consider integrating the information in the text or placing it in an appendix (see 10j).

In the text of your paper, use a superscript arabic
numeral to indicate a note. At the bottom of the page,
place the same superscript numeral and the text of the
note. Number the notes consecutively throughout the
paper. (See also "Footnotes" in 11a for more details.)

TEXT

Now more than nine million children are classified as obese.[1]

FOOTNOTE

   [1]Obesity is measured in terms of body-mass index (BMI):
weight in kilograms divided by square of height in meters. An
adolescent with a BMI in the 95th percentile for his or her age and
gender is considered obese.

15b Notes in tables and figures

Notes in tables A note at the bottom of a table can provide an explanation of terms used in the table, such as abbreviations and symbols. If your table contains data from an outside source or if you have taken or adapted the table from a source, give the source information directly following any explanation of terms.

If you need to explain specific information within the table, use lettered footnotes within the table and corresponding letters in the footnotes following the source information. (See also "Visuals" in 11a.)

TABLE NOTE

Note. The data on sibutramine are adapted from "Behavior Therapy and Sibutramine for the Treatment of Adolescent Obesity," by R. I. Berkowitz, T. A. Wadden, A. M. Tershakovec, & J. L. Cronquist, 2003, *Journal of the American Medical Association, 289*, pp. 1807-1809. The data on orlistat are adapted from *Xenical (Orlistat) Capsules: Complete Product Information*, by Roche Laboratories, December 2003, retrieved from http://www.rocheusa.com/products /xenical/pi.pdf

[a]The medication and/or placebo were combined with behavioral therapy in all groups over all time periods.

Notes in figures Each figure should have a number and a caption, a brief explanation of the content of the figure, at the bottom of the figure. If you have taken or adapted the figure from an outside source, give the source information immediately following the caption. (See also "Visuals" in 11a.)

FIGURE NOTE

Figure 1. As countries engage in a currency war, the exchange rates against the dollar can fluctuate widely. Adapted from "Currencies Against the Dollar," September 30, 2011, *The Economist*, retrieved from http://www.economist.com/blogs/dailychart/2011/09 /emerging-market-currencies

Clarity

16 Tighten wordy sentences.

Long sentences are not necessarily wordy, nor are short sentences always concise. A sentence is wordy if it can be tightened without loss of meaning.

16a Redundancies

Redundancies such as *cooperate together*, *yellow in color*, and *basic essentials* are a common source of wordiness. There is no need to say the same thing twice.

▶ Daniel ~~is employed~~ at a private rehabilitation center
  works

  ~~working~~ as a physical therapist.

Modifiers are redundant when their meanings are suggested by other words in the sentence.

▶ Sylvia ~~very hurriedly~~ scribbled her name and

  phone number on the back of a greasy napkin.

16b Empty or inflated phrases

An empty word or phrase can be cut with little or no loss of meaning. An inflated phrase can be reduced to a word or two.

▶ ~~In my opinion,~~ Our current immigration policy is
                    O

  misguided.

▶ Funds are limited ~~at this point in time.~~
                     now.

INFLATED	CONCISE
along the lines of	like
at the present time	now, currently
because of the fact that	because
by means of	by
due to the fact that	because
for the reason that	because
in order to	to
in spite of the fact that	although, though

hackerhandbooks.com/pocket
e Clarity > Exercises: 1–1 to 1–4
✓ Clarity > LearningCurve: Word choice and appropriate language

INFLATED	CONCISE
in the event that	if
until such time as	until

16c Needlessly complex structures

In a rough draft, sentence structures are often more complex than they need to be.

▶ Researchers ~~were involved in examining~~ *examined* the effect
  of classical music on unborn babies.

▶ ~~It is imperative that~~ _A_ll night managers _must_ follow strict
  procedures when locking the safe.

▶ The analyst claimed that because of volatile market
  conditions she could not ~~make an~~ estimate ~~of~~ the
  company's future profits.

17 Prefer active verbs.

As a rule, active verbs express meaning more vigorously than their weaker counterparts — forms of the verb *be* or verbs in the passive voice. Forms of *be* (*be, am, is, are, was, were, being, been*) lack vigor because they convey no action. Passive verbs lack strength because their subjects receive the action instead of doing it.

Forms of *be* and passive verbs have legitimate uses, but choose an active verb whenever possible.

***BE* VERB**	A surge of power *was* responsible for the destruction of the pumps.
PASSIVE	The pumps *were destroyed* by a surge of power.
ACTIVE	A surge of power *destroyed* the pumps.

17a When to replace *be* verbs

Not every *be* verb needs replacing. The forms of *be* (*be, am, is, are, was, were, being, been*) work well when you want to link a

hackerhandbooks.com/pocket
🄴 Clarity > Exercises: 2–1 to 2–4
☑ Clarity > LearningCurve: Active and passive voice

subject to a noun that clearly renames it or to a vivid adjective that describes it: *Orchard House was the home of Louisa May Alcott. The harvest will be bountiful after the summer rains.*

If a *be* verb makes a sentence needlessly wordy, however, consider replacing it. Often a phrase following the verb will contain a word (such as *violation* or *resistant*) that suggests a more vigorous, active verb (*violate, resisted*).

▶ Burying nuclear waste in Antarctica would ~~be in~~ *violate* ^

~~violation of~~ an international treaty.

▶ When the subject ~~was resistant to~~ following the *resisted* ^

investigator's instructions, the experiment was

terminated.

NOTE: When used as helping verbs with present participles to express ongoing action, *be* verbs are fine: *She was swimming when the whistle blew.* (See 26b.)

17b When to replace passive verbs

In the active voice, the subject of the sentence performs the action; in the passive, the subject receives the action.

ACTIVE   The committee *reached* a decision.

PASSIVE   A decision *was reached* by the committee.

In passive sentences, the actor (in this case, *committee*) frequently does not appear: *A decision was reached.*

Usually, you will want to emphasize the actor, so you should use the active voice. To replace a passive verb with an active one, make the actor the subject of the sentence.

▶ The samples ~~were collected~~ daily from the *students collected the* ^

stagnant pond.

▶ ~~The land was stripped of timber before the settlers~~ *The settlers stripped the land of timber before realizing* ^

~~realized~~ the consequences of their actions.

The passive voice is appropriate when you wish to emphasize the receiver of the action or to minimize the importance of the actor. In the following sentence, for example, the writer wished to focus on the tobacco plants, not on the people spraying them: *As the time for harvest approaches, the tobacco plants are sprayed with a chemical to retard the growth of suckers.* (See also 2b.)

18   Balance parallel ideas.

If two or more ideas are parallel, they should be expressed in parallel grammatical form.

A kiss can be a comma, a question mark, or an exclamation point.   —Mistinguett

This novel is not to be tossed lightly aside, but to be hurled with great force.   —Dorothy Parker

18a   Items in a series

Balance all items in a series by presenting them in parallel grammatical form.

▶   Cross-training involves a variety of exercises,
      lifting
    such as running, swimming, and ~~weights~~.
                                      ∧

▶   Children who study music also learn confidence,
      creativity.
    discipline, and ~~they are creative.~~
                      ∧

▶   Racing to work, Sam drove down the middle of the
      ignored
    road, ran one red light, and two stop signs.
                                    ∧

18b   Paired ideas

When pairing ideas, underscore their connection by expressing them in similar grammatical form. Paired ideas are usually connected in one of three ways: (1) with a coordinating conjunction such as *and*, *but*, or *or*; (2) with

hackerhandbooks.com/pocket
e Clarity > Exercises: 3–1 to 3–4
✓ Clarity > LearningCurve: Parallelism

a pair of correlative conjunctions such as *either . . . or*, *neither . . . nor*, *not only . . . but also*, or *whether . . . or*; or (3) with a word introducing a comparison, usually *than* or *as*.

▶ Many states are reducing property taxes for home
  ~~extend~~ *extending*
  owners and extend financial aid in the form of tax
                                                    ∧
  credits to renters.

  The coordinating conjunction *and* connects two *-ing* verb forms: *reducing . . . extending.*

▶ Thomas Edison was not only a prolific inventor

  but also ~~was~~ a successful entrepreneur.

  The correlative conjunction *not only . . . but also* connects two noun phrases: *a prolific inventor* and *a successful entrepreneur.*

                                                to ground
▶ It is easier to speak in abstractions than ~~grounding~~
                                                    ∧
  one's thoughts in reality.

  The comparative term *than* links two infinitive phrases: *to speak . . . to ground.*

NOTE: Repeat function words such as prepositions (*by, to*) and subordinating conjunctions (*that, because*) to make parallel ideas easier to grasp.

▶ Our study revealed that left-handed students were

  more likely to have trouble with classroom desks
  that
  and rearranging desks for exam periods was useful.
  ∧

19 Add needed words.

Sometimes writers leave out words intentionally, without affecting meaning. But the result is often a confusing or an ungrammatical sentence. Readers need to see at a glance how the parts of a sentence are connected.

19a Words in compound structures

In compound structures, words are often omitted for economy: *Tom is a man who means what he says and [who] says what he means.* Such omissions are acceptable as long as the omitted word is common to both parts of the compound structure.

If a sentence is ungrammatical because an omitted word is not common to both parts of the compound structure, the word must be put back in.

▶ Some of the regulars are acquaintances whom we
  who
  see at work or live in our community.
  ∧

  The word *who* must be included because *whom live in our community* is not grammatically correct.

                                              accepted
▶ Mayor Davidson never has and never will accept a
                                   ∧
  bribe.

  Has . . . accept is not grammatically correct.

                                              in
▶ Many South Pacific tribes still believe and live by
                                         ∧
  ancient laws.

  Believe . . . by is not idiomatic English.

19b The word *that*

Add the word *that* if there is any danger of misreading without it.

▶ In his obedience experiments, psychologist Stanley
                          that
  Milgram discovered ordinary people were willing to
                    ∧
  inflict physical pain on strangers.

  Milgram didn't discover people; he discovered that people were willing to inflict pain on strangers.

19c Words in comparisons

Comparisons should be between items that are alike. To compare unlike items is illogical and distracting.

▶ The forests of North America are much more
                      those of
  extensive than Europe.
              ∧

Comparisons should be complete so that readers will understand what is being compared.

INCOMPLETE   The mice have less energy.

COMPLETE   The mice have less energy than the rats that were fed the same food.

Also, comparisons should leave no ambiguity about meaning. In the following sentence, two interpretations are possible.

AMBIGUOUS   Kai helped me more than my roommate.

CLEAR   Kai helped me more than *he helped* my roommate.

CLEAR   Kai helped me more than my roommate *did*.

20 Eliminate confusing shifts.

20a Shifts in point of view

The point of view of a piece of writing is the perspective from which it is written: first person (*I* or *we*), second person (*you*), or third person (*he*, *she*, *it*, *one*, or *they*). The *I* (or *we*) point of view, which emphasizes the writer, is a good choice for writing based primarily on personal experience. The *you* point of view, which emphasizes the reader, works well for giving advice or explaining how to do something. The third-person point of view, which emphasizes the subject, is appropriate in most academic and professional writing.

Writers who have difficulty settling on an appropriate point of view sometimes shift confusingly from one to another. The solution is to choose a suitable perspective and then stay with it. (See also 27a.)

▶ Our team created a new business plan. ~~You~~ *We* were graded on ~~your~~ *our* timeliness and thoroughness.

▶ ~~Travelers~~ *You* need a signed passport for trips abroad. You should also fill out the emergency information page in the passport.

20b Shifts in tense

Consistent verb tenses clearly establish the time of the actions being described. When a passage begins in one tense and then shifts without warning and for no reason to another, readers are distracted and confused.

▶ There was no way I could get the class to settle down.

Just as I was becoming frustrated, another teacher
  came   *took*
~~comes~~ in and ~~takes~~ control.
  ∧   ∧

Writers often shift verb tenses when writing about literature. The literary convention is to describe fictional events consistently in the present tense. (See p. 166.)

21   Untangle mixed constructions.

A mixed construction contains sentence parts that do not sensibly fit together. The mismatch may be a matter of grammar or of logic.

21a Mixed grammar

You should not begin a sentence with one grammatical plan and then switch without warning to another.

▶   *M*
  ~~For~~ most drivers who have a blood alcohol
      ∧

  level of .05% increase their risk of causing an

  accident.

The prepositional phrase beginning with *For* cannot serve as the subject of the verb *increase*. The revision makes *drivers* the subject.

▶ Although the United States is a wealthy nation, ~~but~~

  more than 20% of our children live in poverty.

The coordinating conjunction *but* cannot link a subordinate clause (*Although . . .*) with an independent clause (*more than 20% . . .*).

21b Illogical connections

A sentence's subject and verb should make sense together.

▶ Under the revised plan, the elderly/ ~~who now receive~~
   the double personal exemption for
   ^
   ~~a double personal exemption~~, will be abolished.

The exemption, not the elderly, will be abolished.

▶ The court decided that ~~Joe's welfare~~ would not be
   Joe
   ^
   safe living with his abusive parents.

Joe, not his welfare, would not be safe.

21c *Is when*, *is where*, and *reason . . . is because* constructions

In formal English, readers sometimes object to *is when*, *is where*, and *reason . . . is because* constructions on grammatical or logical grounds.

▶ Anorexia nervosa is ~~where people~~ think they are too
   a disorder suffered by people who
   ^
   fat and diet to the point of starvation.

Anorexia nervosa is a disorder, not a place.

▶ ~~The reason~~ /the experiment failed ~~is~~ because
   T
   ^
   conditions in the lab were not sterile.

22 Repair misplaced and dangling modifiers.

Modifiers should point clearly to the words they modify. As a rule, related words should be kept together.

22a Misplaced words

The most commonly misplaced words are limiting modifiers such as *only*, *even*, *almost*, *nearly*, and *just*. They should appear in front of a verb only if they modify the verb. If they limit the meaning of some other word in the sentence, they should be placed in front of that word.

▶ Lasers ~~only~~ destroy the target, leaving the

       only
       ∧

surrounding healthy tissue intact.

▶ I couldn't ~~even~~ save a dollar out of my paycheck.

       even
       ∧

When the limiting modifier *not* is misplaced, the sentence usually suggests a meaning that the writer did not intend.

▶ In the United States in 1860, all black southerners

       not
       ∧

were ~~not~~ slaves.

The original sentence means that no black southerners were slaves. The revision makes the writer's real meaning clear.

22b Misplaced phrases and clauses

Although phrases and clauses can appear at some distance from the words they modify, make sure your meaning is clear. When phrases or clauses are oddly placed, absurd misreadings can result.

▶ ~~There~~ are many pictures of comedians who have

       On the walls
       ∧

performed at Gavin's. ~~on the walls.~~
       ∧

The comedians weren't performing on the walls; the pictures were on the walls.

▶ The robber was described as a six-foot-tall man

       170-pound,
       ∧

with a mustache. ~~weighing 170 pounds.~~
       ∧

The robber, not the mustache, weighed 170 pounds.

22c Dangling modifiers

A dangling modifier fails to refer logically to any word in the sentence. Dangling modifiers are usually introductory word groups (such as verbal phrases) that suggest but do not name an actor. When a sentence opens with such a modifier, readers expect the subject of the next clause to name the actor. If it doesn't, the modifier dangles.

DANGLING   Upon entering the doctor's office, a skeleton caught my attention.

This sentence suggests — absurdly — that the skeleton entered the doctor's office.

To repair a dangling modifier, you can revise the sentence in one of two ways:

1. Name the actor in the subject of the sentence.
2. Name the actor in the modifier.

▶ Upon entering the doctor's office, a skeleton. *I noticed*
   ^   ^
   ~~caught my attention.~~

▶ *As I entered*
   ~~Upon entering~~ the doctor's office, a skeleton
   ^
   caught my attention.

You cannot repair a dangling modifier simply by moving it: *A skeleton caught my attention upon entering the doctor's office.* The sentence still suggests that the skeleton entered the doctor's office.

▶ Wanting to create checks and balances on power,
   the framers of
   the Constitution divided the government into three
   ^
   branches.

   The framers (not the Constitution itself) wanted to create checks and balances.

▶ After completing seminary training, *women were often denied* ~~women's~~
   ^
   access to the priesthood. ~~was often denied.~~
   ^
   The women (not their access to the priesthood) completed the training. The writer has revised the sentence by making *women* (not *women's access*) the subject.

22d Split infinitives

An infinitive consists of *to* plus a verb: *to think, to dance.* When a modifier appears between its two parts, an infinitive is said to be "split": *to slowly drive.* If a split infinitive is awkward, move the modifier to another position in the sentence.

▶   **Cardiologists encourage their patients to**
                                    more carefully.
     ~~more carefully~~ **watch their cholesterol levels.**
                                                      ^

Attempts to avoid split infinitives sometimes result in awkward sentences. When alternative phrasing sounds unnatural, most experts allow—and even encourage—splitting the infinitive. *We decided to actually enforce the law* is a natural construction in English. *We decided actually to enforce the law* is not.

23   Provide sentence variety.

When a rough draft is filled with too many same-sounding sentences, try to inject some variety—as long as you can do so without sacrificing clarity or ease of reading.

23a   Combining choppy sentences

If a series of short sentences sounds choppy, consider combining sentences. Look for opportunities to tuck some of your ideas into subordinate clauses. A subordinate clause, which contains a subject and a verb, begins with a word such as *after, although, because, before, if, since, that, unless, until, when, where, which,* or *who.* (See p. 244.)

▶   **We keep our use of insecticides to a minimum.**
                                                    because we
     ~~We~~ **are concerned about the environment.**
        ^

Also look for opportunities to tuck some of your ideas into phrases, word groups without subjects or verbs (or both). You will usually see more than one way to combine choppy sentences; the method you choose should depend on the details you want to emphasize.

▶   **The Chesapeake and Ohio Canal, ~~is~~ a 184-mile**
                                    ^
     waterway constructed in the 1800s., ~~It~~ was a major
                                        ^
     source of transportation for goods during the

     Civil War.

hackerhandbooks.com/pocket
🄴 Clarity > Exercises: 8–1 to 8–3
✅ Clarity > LearningCurve: Coordination and subordination

The revision on the bottom of page 150 emphasizes the significance of the canal during the Civil War. The first sentence, about the age of the canal, has been made into a phrase modifying *Chesapeake and Ohio Canal*.

▶ *Used as a major source of transportation for goods during the Civil War, the*
~~The~~ Chesapeake and Ohio Canal is a 184-mile
   ∧
waterway constructed in the 1800s. ~~It was a major source of transportation for goods during the Civil War.~~

This revision emphasizes the age of the canal. The second sentence, about its use for transportation of goods, has become a participial phrase modifying *Chesapeake and Ohio Canal*.

When short sentences contain ideas of equal importance, it is often effective to combine them with *and*, *but*, or *or*.

▶ Shore houses were flooded up to the first floor~~.~~/, *and*
   ∧
Brant's Lighthouse was swallowed by the sea.

23b Varying sentence openings

Most sentences in English begin with the subject, move to the verb, and continue to an object, with modifiers tucked in along the way or put at the end. For the most part, such sentences are fine. Put too many of them in a row, however, and they become monotonous.

Words, phrases, or clauses modifying the verb can often be inserted ahead of the subject.

▶ *Eventually a*
A few drops of sap ~~eventually~~ began to trickle into
   ∧
the pail.

▶ *Just as the sun was coming up, a*
A pair of black ducks flew over the pond. ~~just as the~~
   ∧   ∧
~~sun was coming up.~~

Participial phrases (beginning with verb forms such as *driving* or *exhausted*) can frequently be moved to the start of a sentence without loss of clarity.

▶ ~~The committee,~~ discouraged by the researchers'
    D
    ∧   *the committee*
apparent lack of progress, nearly withdrew funding
                                    ∧
for the prize-winning experiments.

NOTE: In a sentence that begins with a participial phrase,
the subject of the sentence must name the person or thing
being described. If it doesn't, the phrase dangles. (See 22c.)

24 Find an appropriate voice.

An appropriate voice is one that suits your subject,
engages your audience, and conforms to the conventions
of the genre in which you are writing, such as analytical
essays, lab reports, research papers, business memos, and
so on. (See also 2b and 2c.)

In writing in the social sciences and related fields,
certain language is generally considered inappropriate:
jargon, clichés, slang, and sexist language.

24a Jargon

Jargon is specialized language used among members of a
trade, profession, or group. Use jargon only when readers
will be familiar with it; even then, use it only when plain
English will not do as well.

JARGON We outsourced the work to an outfit in Ohio
because we didn't have the bandwidth to tackle it
in-house.

REVISED We hired a company in Ohio because we had too
few employees to do the work.

Broadly defined, jargon includes puffed-up language
designed more to impress readers than to inform them.
The following are common examples from business,
government, higher education, and the military, with
plain English translations in parentheses.

commence (begin)   facilitate (help)
components (parts)   finalize (finish)
endeavor (try)   impact (v.) (affect)

hackerhandbooks.com/pocket
e Clarity > Exercises: 9–1 to 9–4
☑ Clarity > LearningCurve: Word choice and appropriate language

indicator (sign)   prior to (before)
optimal (best)   utilize (use)
parameters (boundaries, limits) viable (workable)

Sentences filled with jargon are hard to read and often wordy.

▶ The CEO should ~~dialogue~~ ^{talk} with investors about
  ^{working} ∧ ~~partnering~~ with clients to buy land in ~~economically~~ ^{poor} ∧
  ^{neighborhoods.} ~~deprived zones.~~ ∧

▶ All ~~employees functioning in the capacity of~~
  ^{must prove that they are}
  work-study students ~~are required to give evidence of~~ ∧
  ^{currently enrolled.} ~~current enrollment.~~ ∧

24b Clichés

The pioneer who first announced that he had "slept like a log" no doubt amused his companions with a fresh and unlikely comparison. Today, however, that comparison is a cliché, a saying that can no longer add emphasis or surprise. To see just how predictable clichés are, put your hand over the right-hand column below and then finish the phrases given on the left.

cool as a	cucumber
beat around the	bush
busy as a	bee, beaver
crystal	clear
light as a	feather
like a bull	in a china shop
playing with	fire
nutty as a	fruitcake
selling like	hotcakes
water under the	bridge
white as a	sheet, ghost
avoid clichés like the	plague

The solution for clichés is simple: Just delete them. Sometimes you can write around a cliché by adding an element of surprise. One student who had written that she had butterflies in her stomach revised her cliché like this:

> If all of the action in my stomach is caused by butterflies, there must be a horde of them, with horseshoes on.

The image of butterflies wearing horseshoes is fresh and unlikely, not predictable like the original cliché.

24c Slang

Slang is an informal and sometimes private vocabulary that expresses the solidarity of a group such as teenagers, rap musicians, or sports fans. Although it does have a certain vitality, slang is a code that not everyone understands, and it is too informal for most written work.

▶ When the server crashed, three hours of unsaved *we lost*
 ^
 data. ~~went down the tubes.~~
 ^

24d Sexist language

Sexist language excludes, stereotypes, or demeans women or men and should be avoided.

In your writing, avoid referring to any one profession as exclusively male or exclusively female (teachers as women or engineers as men, for example). Also avoid using different conventions when identifying women and men.

▶ All executives' *spouses* ~~wives~~ are invited to the picnic.
 ^

▶ Boris Stotsky, attorney, and ~~Mrs.~~ Cynthia Jones,
 graphic designer,
 ~~mother of three,~~ are running for city council.
 ^

Traditionally, *he*, *him*, and *his* were used to refer generically to persons of either sex: *A journalist is motivated by his deadline*. You can avoid such sexist usage in one of three ways: substitute a pair of pronouns (*he or she*, *his or her*); reword in the plural; or revise the sentence to avoid the problem. Note that the terms *he or she* and *his or her* are inclusive but wordy; fine in small doses, they can become awkward when repeated throughout a paper. The other two strategies are usually more effective.

▶ A journalist is motivated by his *or her* deadline.
 ^

▶ *Journalists are* ~~A journalist is~~ motivated by ~~his deadline.~~ *their deadlines.*
 ^ ^

▶ A journalist is motivated by *a* ~~his~~ deadline.
 ^

Like *he* and *his*, the nouns *man* and *men* and related words were once used generically to refer to persons of either sex. Use gender-neutral terms instead.

INAPPROPRIATE	APPROPRIATE
chairman	chairperson, chair
congressman	representative, legislator
fireman	firefighter
mailman	mail carrier, postal worker
mankind	people, humans
to man	to operate, to staff
weatherman	meteorologist, forecaster

Grammar

25 Make subjects and verbs agree.

In the present tense, verbs agree with their subjects in number (singular or plural) and in person (first, second, or third). The present-tense ending -*s* is used on a verb if its subject is third-person singular; otherwise the verb takes no ending. Consider, for example, the present-tense forms of the verb *give*.

	SINGULAR	**PLURAL**
FIRST PERSON	I give	we give
SECOND PERSON	you give	you give
THIRD PERSON	he/she/it gives	they give
	Yolanda gives	parents give

The verb *be* varies from this pattern; it has special forms in *both* the present and the past tense.

PRESENT-TENSE FORMS OF *BE*		**PAST-TENSE FORMS OF** *BE*	
I am	we are	I was	we were
you are	you are	you were	you were
he/she/it is	they are	he/she/it was	they were

This section describes particular situations that can cause problems with subject-verb agreement.

25a Words between subject and verb

Word groups often come between the subject and the verb. Such word groups, usually modifying the subject, may contain a noun that at first appears to be the subject. By mentally stripping away such modifiers, you can isolate the noun that is in fact the subject.

The *samples* on the tray in the lab *need* testing.

▶ High levels of air pollution damages the

respiratory tract.

The subject is *levels*, not *pollution*.

▶ The slaughter of pandas for their pelts ~~have~~ caused
                                          ^ has

the panda population to decline drastically.

The subject is *slaughter*, not *pandas* or *pelts*.

hackerhandbooks.com/pocket
🄴 Grammar > Exercises: 10–1 to 10–3
☑ Grammar > LearningCurve: Subject-verb agreement

NOTE: Phrases beginning with the prepositions *as well as, in addition to, accompanied by, together with,* and *along with* do not make a singular subject plural: *The governor as well as his aide was* [not *were*] *on the plane.*

25b Subjects joined with *and*

Compound subjects joined with *and* are nearly always plural.

▶ Bleach and ammonia creates a toxic gas when mixed.

EXCEPTION: If the parts of the subject form a single unit, you may treat the subject as singular: *Bacon and eggs is always on the menu.*

25c Subjects joined with *or* or *nor*

With compound subjects joined with *or* or *nor,* make the verb agree with the part of the subject nearer to the verb.

                                              is
▶ If an infant or a child ~~are~~ having difficulty breathing,
                           ^
  seek medical attention immediately.

                                                 were
▶ Neither the lab assistant nor the students ~~was~~ able
                                              ^
  to download the program.

25d Indefinite pronouns such as *someone*

Indefinite pronouns refer to nonspecific persons or things. The following indefinite pronouns are singular: *anybody, anyone, anything, each, either, everybody, everyone, everything, neither, nobody, no one, somebody, someone, something.*

                                                    was
▶ Nobody who participated in the taste tests ~~were~~ paid.
                                              ^

            has
▶ Each of the essays ~~have~~ been graded.
                     ^

   A few indefinite pronouns (*all, any, none, some*) may be singular or plural depending on the noun or pronoun they refer to: *Some of our luggage was lost. Some of the rocks were slippery. None of his advice makes sense. None of the eggs were broken.*

25e Collective nouns such as *jury*

Collective nouns such as *jury*, *committee*, *audience*, *crowd*, *class*, *family*, and *couple* name a group. In American English, collective nouns are usually treated as singular: They emphasize the group as a unit.

meets
▶ The board of trustees ~~meet~~ in Denver twice a year.
                        ∧

Occasionally, to draw attention to the individual members of the group, a collective noun may be treated as plural: *The class are debating among themselves.* Many writers prefer to add a clearly plural noun such as *members*: *The class members are debating among themselves.*

NOTE: In general, when fractions or units of measurement are used with a singular noun, treat them as singular; when they are used with a plural noun, treat them as plural: *Three-fourths of the pie has been eaten. One-fourth of the drivers were texting.*

25f Subject after verb

Verbs ordinarily follow subjects. When this normal order is reversed, it is easy to be confused.

are
▶ Of particular concern ~~is~~ penicillin and tetracycline,
                        ∧
antibiotics used to make animals more resistant

to disease.

The subject, *penicillin and tetracycline*, is plural.

The subject always follows the verb in sentences beginning with *there is* or *there are* (or *there was* or *there were*).

were
▶ There ~~was~~ a turtle and a snake in the tank.
       ∧
The subject, *turtle and snake*, is plural, so the verb must be *were*.

25g *Who, which,* and *that*

Like most pronouns, the relative pronouns *who*, *which*, and *that* have antecedents, nouns or pronouns to which they refer. Relative pronouns used as subjects of subordinate clauses take verbs that agree with their antecedents.

ANT   PN   V

Take a *train that arrives* before 6:00 p.m.

Constructions such as *one of the students who* (or *one of the things that*) may cause problems for writers. Do not assume that the antecedent must be *one*. Instead, consider the logic of the sentence.

▶ **Our ability to use language is one of the things**

    set

  that ~~sets~~ us apart from animals.

     ∧

  The antecedent of *that* is *things*, not *one*. Several things set us apart from animals.

When the phrase *the only* comes before *one*, you are safe in assuming that *one* is the antecedent of the relative pronoun.

                                        lives

▶ **Carmen is the only one of my friends who ~~live~~**

                                         ∧

  in my building.

  The antecedent of *who* is *one*, not *friends*. Only one friend lives in the building.

25h Plural form, singular meaning

Words such as *athletics, economics, mathematics, physics, politics, statistics, measles,* and *news* are usually singular, despite their plural form.

      is

▶ **Politics ~~are~~ among my mother's favorite pastimes.**

      ∧

EXCEPTION: Occasionally some of these words, especially *economics, mathematics, politics,* and *statistics,* have plural meanings: *Office politics often affect decisions about hiring and promotion. The economics of the building plan are prohibitive.*

25i Titles, company names, and words mentioned as words

Titles, company names, and words mentioned as words are singular.

               describes

▶ *Lost Cities* ~~describe~~ the discoveries of 50 ancient

               ∧

  civilizations.

> *specializes*
> Delmonico Brothers ~~specialize~~ in organic produce
>   ^
> and additive-free meats.

> *is*
> *Controlled substances* ~~are~~ a euphemism for illegal
>   ^
> drugs.

26 Be alert to other problems with verbs.

Section 25 deals with subject-verb agreement. This section describes a few other potential problems with verbs.

26a Irregular verbs

For all regular verbs, the past-tense and past-participle forms are the same, ending in *-ed* or *-d*, so there is no danger of confusion. This is not true, however, for irregular verbs, such as the following.

BASE FORM	PAST TENSE	PAST PARTICIPLE
begin	began	begun
fly	flew	flown
ride	rode	ridden

The past-tense form, which never has a helping verb, expresses action that occurred entirely in the past. The past participle is used with a helping verb—either with *has*, *have*, or *had* to form one of the perfect tenses or with *be*, *am*, *is*, *are*, *was*, *were*, *being*, or *been* to form the passive voice.

PAST TENSE   Last July, we *began* collecting our data.

PAST PARTICIPLE   We have *begun* to collect our data.

When you aren't sure which verb form to choose (*went* or *gone*, *began* or *begun*, and so on), consult the list that begins at the bottom of page 162. Choose the past-tense form if your sentence doesn't have a helping verb; choose the past-participle form if it does.

---

hackerhandbooks.com/pocket
e Grammar > Exercises: 11–1 to 11–6
☑ Grammar > LearningCurve: Verbs

▶ Yesterday we ~~seen~~ a film about rain forests.
  saw
  ∧

Because there is no helping verb, the past-tense form *saw* is
required.

▶ By the end of the day, the stock market had ~~fell~~
  fallen
  ∧

210 points.

Because of the helping verb *had*, the past-participle form
fallen is required.

Distinguishing between *lie* and *lay*   Writers often con-
fuse the forms of *lie* (meaning "to recline or rest on a
surface") with those of *lay* (meaning "to put or place
something"). The intransitive verb *lie* does not take a
direct object: *The tax forms lie on the table*. The transitive
verb *lay* takes a direct object: *Please lay the tax forms on
the table*.

In addition to confusing the meanings of *lie* and *lay*,
writers are often unfamiliar with the standard English
forms of these verbs.

BASE FORM	PAST TENSE	PAST PARTICIPLE	PRESENT PARTICIPLE
lie	lay	lain	lying
lay	laid	laid	laying

Elizabeth was so exhausted that she *lay* down for a nap.
[Past tense of *lie*, meaning "to recline"]

The prosecutor *laid* the photograph on a table close to
the jurors. [Past tense of *lay*, meaning "to place"]

Letters dating from the Civil War were *lying* in the corner
of the chest. [Present participle of *lie*]

The patient had *lain* in an uncomfortable position all
night. [Past participle of *lie*]

Common irregular verbs

BASE FORM	PAST TENSE	PAST PARTICIPLE
arise	arose	arisen
awake	awoke, awaked	awaked, awoken
be	was, were	been
beat	beat	beaten, beat
become	became	become
begin	began	begun

BASE FORM	PAST TENSE	PAST PARTICIPLE
bend	bent	bent
bite	bit	bitten, bit
blow	blew	blown
break	broke	broken
bring	brought	brought
build	built	built
burst	burst	burst
buy	bought	bought
catch	caught	caught
choose	chose	chosen
cling	clung	clung
come	came	come
cost	cost	cost
deal	dealt	dealt
dig	dug	dug
dive	dived, dove	dived
do	did	done
draw	drew	drawn
dream	dreamed, dreamt	dreamed, dreamt
drink	drank	drunk
drive	drove	driven
eat	ate	eaten
fall	fell	fallen
fight	fought	fought
find	found	found
fly	flew	flown
forget	forgot	forgotten, forgot
freeze	froze	frozen
get	got	gotten, got
give	gave	given
go	went	gone
grow	grew	grown
hang (suspend)	hung	hung
hang (execute)	hanged	hanged
have	had	had
hear	heard	heard
hide	hid	hidden
hurt	hurt	hurt
keep	kept	kept
know	knew	known
lay (put)	laid	laid
lead	led	led
lend	lent	lent
let (allow)	let	let
lie (recline)	lay	lain
lose	lost	lost
make	made	made
prove	proved	proved, proven
read	read	read

BASE FORM	PAST TENSE	PAST PARTICIPLE
ride	rode	ridden
ring	rang	rung
rise (get up)	rose	risen
run	ran	run
say	said	said
see	saw	seen
send	sent	sent
set (place)	set	set
shake	shook	shaken
shoot	shot	shot
shrink	shrank	shrunk, shrunken
sing	sang	sung
sink	sank	sunk
sit (be seated)	sat	sat
slay	slew	slain
sleep	slept	slept
speak	spoke	spoken
spin	spun	spun
spring	sprang	sprung
stand	stood	stood
steal	stole	stolen
sting	stung	stung
strike	struck	struck, stricken
swear	swore	sworn
swim	swam	swum
swing	swung	swung
take	took	taken
teach	taught	taught
throw	threw	thrown
wake	woke, waked	waked, woken
wear	wore	worn
wring	wrung	wrung
write	wrote	written

26b Tense

Tenses indicate the time of an action in relation to the time of the speaking or writing about that action. The most common problem with tenses—shifting from one tense to another—is discussed in 20b. Other problems with tenses are detailed in this section, after the following survey of tenses.

Survey of tenses Tenses are classified as present, past, and future, with simple, perfect, and progressive forms for each.

The simple tenses indicate relatively simple time relations. The *simple present* tense is used primarily for actions occurring at the time they are being discussed or for actions occurring regularly. The *simple past* tense is used for actions completed in the past. The *simple future* tense is used for actions that will occur in the future. In the following table, the simple tenses are given for the regular verb *walk*, the irregular verb *ride*, and the highly irregular verb *be*.

SIMPLE PRESENT

SINGULAR		PLURAL	
I	walk, ride, am	we	walk, ride, are
you	walk, ride, are	you	walk, ride, are
he/she/it	walks, rides, is	they	walk, ride, are

SIMPLE PAST

SINGULAR		PLURAL	
I	walked, rode, was	we	walked, rode, were
you	walked, rode, were	you	walked, rode, were
he/she/it	walked, rode, was	they	walked, rode, were

SIMPLE FUTURE

I, you, he/she/it, we, they	will walk, ride, be

A verb in one of the perfect tenses (a form of *have* plus the past participle) expresses an action that was or will be completed at the time of another action.

PRESENT PERFECT

I, you, we, they	have walked, ridden, been
he/she/it	has walked, ridden, been

PAST PERFECT

I, you, he/she/it, we, they	had walked, ridden, been

FUTURE PERFECT

I, you, he/she/it, we, they	will have walked, ridden, been

Each of the six tenses has a progressive form used to describe actions in progress. A progressive verb consists of a form of *be* followed by the present participle.

PRESENT PROGRESSIVE

I	am walking, riding, being
he/she/it	is walking, riding, being
you, we, they	are walking, riding, being

PAST PROGRESSIVE

| I, he/she/it | was walking, riding, being |
| you, we, they | were walking, riding, being |

FUTURE PROGRESSIVE

| I, you, he/she/it, we, they | will be walking, riding, being |

PRESENT PERFECT PROGRESSIVE

| I, you, we, they | have been walking, riding, being |
| he/she/it | has been walking, riding, being |

PAST PERFECT PROGRESSIVE

| I, you, he/she/it, we, they | had been walking, riding, being |

FUTURE PERFECT PROGRESSIVE

| I, you, he/she/it, we, they | will have been walking, riding, being |

Special uses of the present tense   Use the present tense for applications or effects of your own results and for describing established knowledge.

▶ Our data indicated that concentrated poverty
   increases
   ~~increased~~ the likelihood of property crimes.
   ∧

   revolves
▶ Galileo taught that the earth ~~revolved~~ around the sun.
   ∧

See also 9b and the next section for uses of the past and present perfect tenses.

Note that in the humanities the present tense is used for writing about literary works.

   is
▶ The scarlet letter ~~was~~ a punishment placed on
   ∧
                                              is
   Hester's breast by the community, and yet it ~~was~~
   ∧

   an imaginative product of Hester's own needlework.

Special uses of the past and present perfect tenses Especially in literature reviews and primary research papers, use the past tense or present perfect tense to discuss your own findings or the work of others. (See also 9b; see the previous section for uses of the present tense.)

   explored
▶ In "On Violence," Arendt (1970) ~~explores~~ the
   ∧
   relationship between violence and power.

26c Mood

There are three moods in English: the *indicative*, used for facts, opinions, and questions; the *imperative*, used for orders or advice; and the *subjunctive*, used to express wishes, requests, or conditions contrary to fact. For many writers, the subjunctive is especially challenging.

For wishes and in *if* clauses expressing conditions contrary to fact, the subjunctive is the past-tense form of the verb; in the case of *be*, it is always *were* (not *was*), even if the subject is singular.

I wish that Jamal *drove* more slowly late at night.

If I *were* a member of Congress, I would vote for the bill.

TIP: Do not use the subjunctive mood in *if* clauses expressing conditions that exist or may exist: *If Danielle passes* [not *passed*] *the test, she will become a lifeguard.*

Use the subjunctive mood in *that* clauses following verbs such as *ask*, *insist*, *recommend*, and *request*. The subjunctive in such cases is the base form of the verb.

Dr. Chung insists that her students *be* on time.

We recommend that Dawson *file* form 1050 soon.

27 Use pronouns with care.

Pronouns are words that substitute for nouns: *he, it, them, her, me,* and so on. Pronoun errors are typically related to the four topics discussed in this section:

a. pronoun-antecedent agreement (singular vs. plural)
b. pronoun reference (clarity)
c. pronoun case (personal pronouns such as *I* vs. *me*)
d. pronoun case (*who* vs. *whom*)

27a Pronoun-antecedent agreement

The antecedent of a pronoun is the word the pronoun refers to. A pronoun and its antecedent agree when they are both singular or both plural.

hackerhandbooks.com/pocket
e Grammar > Exercises: 12–1 to 12–3
✓ Grammar > LearningCurve: Pronoun agreement and pronoun reference

SINGULAR The *doctor* finished *her* rounds.

PLURAL The *doctors* finished *their* rounds.

Indefinite pronouns Indefinite pronouns refer to nonspecific persons or things. Even though some of the following indefinite pronouns may seem to have plural meanings, treat them as singular in formal English: *anybody, anyone, anything, each, either, everybody, everyone, everything, neither, nobody, no one, nothing, somebody, someone, something.*

In this class *everyone* performs at *his or her* [not *their*] own fitness level.

When *they* or *their* refers mistakenly to a singular antecedent such as *everyone*, you will usually have three options for revision:

1. Replace *they* with *he or she* (or *their* with *his or her*).
2. Make the antecedent plural.
3. Rewrite the sentence to avoid the problem.

► If anyone wants to audition, ~~they~~ *he or she* should sign up.

► If ~~anyone wants~~ *singers want* to audition, they should sign up.

► ~~If anyone~~ *Anyone who* wants to audition / ~~they~~ should sign up.

Because the *he or she* construction is wordy, often the second or third revision strategy is more effective.

NOTE: The traditional use of *he* (or *his* or *him*) to refer to persons of either sex is now widely considered sexist. (See p. 154.)

Generic nouns A generic noun represents a typical member of a group, such as *a student*, or any member of a group, such as *any lawyer*. Although generic nouns may seem to have plural meanings, they are singular.

Every *runner* must train rigorously if *he or she wants* [not *they want*] to excel.

When a plural pronoun refers mistakenly to a generic noun, you will usually have the same revision options as for indefinite pronouns.

► A medical student must study hard if ~~they want~~ to
  he or she wants
  ^
  succeed.

► ~~A medical student~~ must study hard if they want to
  Medical students
  ^
  succeed.

► A medical student must study hard ~~if they want~~ to

  succeed.

Collective nouns   Collective nouns such as *jury, committee, audience, crowd, family,* and *team* name a group. In American English, collective nouns are usually singular because they emphasize the group functioning as a unit.

  The planning *committee* granted *its* [not *their*]
  permission to build.

If the members of the group function individually, however, you may treat the noun as plural: *The family put their signatures on the document.* Or you might add a plural antecedent such as *members* to the sentence: *The family members put their signatures on the document.*

27b Pronoun reference

In the sentence *When Andrew got home, he went straight to bed,* the noun *Andrew* is the antecedent of the pronoun *he.* A pronoun should refer clearly to its antecedent.

Ambiguous reference   Ambiguous reference occurs when the pronoun could refer to two possible antecedents.

► ~~When~~ Jo ~~put~~ the cake on the table /. ~~it collapsed.~~
  The cake collapsed when Jo put it
  ^   ^

► The manager told Arthur, ~~that he was~~ being promoted."
  "You are
                          ^   ^

What collapsed—the cake or the table? Who was being promoted—the manager or Arthur? The revisions eliminate the ambiguity.

hackerhandbooks.com/pocket
e Grammar > Exercises: 12–4 to 12–6
☑ Grammar > LearningCurve: Pronoun agreement and pronoun
         reference

Implied reference   A pronoun must refer to a specific antecedent, not to a word that is implied but not actually stated.

> After braiding Ann's hair, Sue decorated ~~them~~ with
>
> ribbons.

the braids

Vague reference of *this*, *that*, or *which*   The pronouns *this*, *that*, and *which* should ordinarily refer to specific antecedents rather than to whole ideas or sentences. When a pronoun's reference is vague, either replace the pronoun with a noun or supply an antecedent to which the pronoun clearly refers.

> Television advertising has created new demands for
>
> prescription drugs. People respond to ~~this~~ by asking
>
> for drugs they may not need.

the ads

> Romeo and Juliet were both too young to have
>
> acquired much wisdom, ~~and~~ that accounts for
>
> their rash actions.

a fact

Indefinite reference of *they*, *it*, or *you*   The pronoun *they* should refer to a specific antecedent. Do not use *they* to refer indefinitely to persons who have not been specifically mentioned.

> ~~They~~ announced an increase in sports fees for all
>
> student athletes.

The board

The word *it* should not be used indefinitely in constructions such as *In the article, it says that. . . .*

> ~~In the~~ encyclopedia ~~it~~ states that male moths can
>
> smell female moths from several miles away.

The

The pronoun *you* is appropriate only when the writer is addressing the reader directly: *Once you have kneaded the dough, let it rise in a warm place.* Except in informal contexts, however, *you* should not be used to mean "anyone in general."

> The academic handbook stipulates that
>
> ~~you~~ must complete a senior thesis to graduate.

students

27c Case of personal pronouns (*I* vs. *me* etc.)

The personal pronouns in the following list change what is known as *case form* according to their grammatical function in a sentence. Pronouns functioning as subjects or subject complements appear in the *subjective* case; those functioning as objects appear in the *objective* case; and those showing ownership appear in the *possessive* case.

SUBJECTIVE CASE	OBJECTIVE CASE	POSSESSIVE CASE
I	me	my
we	us	our
you	you	your
he/she/it	him/her/it	his/her/its
they	them	their

For the most part, you know how to use these forms correctly. The structures discussed in this section, however, may tempt you to choose the wrong pronoun.

Compound word groups You may sometimes be confused when a subject or an object appears as part of a compound structure. To test for the correct pronoun, mentally strip away all of the compound structure except the pronoun in question.

> While diving for pearls, Ikiko and ~~her~~ found a
>   _∧ *she*
> sunken boat.

> *Ikiko and she* is the subject of the verb *found*. Strip away the words *Ikiko and* to test for the correct pronoun: *she found* [not *her found*].

> The most traumatic experience for her father and
>   *me*
> ~~I~~ occurred long after her operation.
> _∧

> *Her father and me* is the object of the preposition *for*. Strip away the words *her father and* to test for the correct pronoun: *for me* [not *for I*].

When in doubt about the correct pronoun, some writers try to evade the choice by using a reflexive pronoun such as *myself*. Using a reflexive pronoun in such situations is nonstandard.

> _me_
> ▶ The cab driver gave my husband and ~~myself~~
> ∧
> some good tips on traveling in New Delhi.

My husband and me is the indirect object of the verb _gave_.

Appositives   Appositives are noun phrases that rename nouns or pronouns. A pronoun used as an appositive has the same function (usually subject or object) as the word(s) it renames.

> I,
> ▶ The chief strategists, Dr. Bell and ~~me,~~ could not
> ∧
> agree on a plan.

The appositive _Dr. Bell and I_ renames the subject, _strategists_.
Test: _I could not agree on a plan_ [not _me could not agree on a plan_].

> ▶ The reporter interviewed only two witnesses, the
> _me._
> shopkeeper and ~~I.~~
> ∧

The appositive _the shopkeeper and me_ renames the direct object, _witnesses_. Test: _interviewed me_ [not _interviewed I_].

Subject complements   Use subjective-case pronouns for subject complements, which rename or describe the subject and usually follow _be, am, is, are, was, were, being,_ or _been_.

> ▶ During the Lindberg trial, Bruno Hauptmann
> _he._
> repeatedly denied that the kidnapper was ~~him.~~
> ∧

If _kidnapper was he_ seems too stilted, rewrite the sentence: _During the Lindbergh trial, Bruno Hauptmann repeatedly denied that he was the kidnapper._

_We_ or _us_ before a noun   When deciding whether _we_ or _us_ should precede a noun, choose the pronoun that would be appropriate if the noun were omitted.

> _We_
> ▶ ~~Us~~ tenants would rather fight than move.
> ∧
> Test: _We would rather fight_ [not _Us would rather fight_].

> _us_
> ▶ Management is shortchanging ~~we~~ tenants.
> ∧
> Test: _Management is shortchanging us_ [not _Management is short-changing we_].

Pronoun after *than* or *as* When a comparison begins with *than* or *as*, your choice of pronoun will depend on your meaning. To test for the correct pronoun, mentally complete the sentence.

▶ My brother is six years older than ~~me~~. I.
^

Test: *older than I* [*am*].

▶ We respected no other candidate for city council as her.
much as ~~she~~.
^

Test: *as much as* [*we respected*] *her*.

Pronoun before or after an infinitive An infinitive is the word *to* followed by a verb. Both subjects and objects of infinitives take the objective case.

me
▶ Ms. Wilson asked John and ~~I~~ to drive the senator her
and ~~she~~ to the airport.
^

John and me is the subject and *senator and her* is the object of the infinitive *to drive*.

Pronoun or noun before a gerund If a pronoun modifies a gerund, use the possessive case: *my, our, your, his, her, its, their.* A gerund is a verb form ending in *-ing* that functions as a noun.

your
▶ The chances of ~~you~~ being hit by lightning are about
^
one in two million.

Nouns as well as pronouns may modify gerunds. To form the possessive case of a noun, use an apostrophe and *-s* (*victim's*) for a singular noun or just an apostrophe (*victims'*) for a plural noun. (See also 34a.)

▶ The old order in France paid a high price for the aristocracy's
~~aristocracy~~ exploiting the lower classes.
^

27d Who or whom

Who, a subjective-case pronoun, is used for subjects and subject complements. *Whom*, an objective-case pronoun, is used for objects. The words *who* and *whom* appear primarily in subordinate clauses or in questions.

In subordinate clauses When deciding whether to use *who* or *whom* in a subordinate clause, check for the word's function within the clause.

▶   *whoever*
He tells that story to ~~whomever~~ will listen.
                  ^

Whoever is the subject of *will listen*. The entire subordinate clause *whoever will listen* is the object of the preposition *to*.

▶   *whom*
You will work with our senior engineers, ~~who~~ you
                                            ^

will meet later.

Whom is the direct object of the verb *will meet*. This becomes clear if you restructure the clause: *you will meet whom later*.

In questions When deciding whether to use *who* or *whom* in a question, check for the word's function within the question.

▶ *Who*
~~Whom~~ was responsible for creating that computer
  ^

virus?

Who is the subject of the verb *was*.

▶ *Whom*
~~Who~~ would you nominate for council president?
  ^
Whom is the direct object of the verb *would nominate*. This becomes clear if you restructure the question: *You would nominate whom?*

28 Use adjectives and adverbs appropriately.

Adjectives modify nouns or pronouns; adverbs modify verbs, adjectives, or other adverbs.

Many adverbs are formed by adding *-ly* to adjectives (*formal, formally*). But don't assume that all words ending in *-ly* are adverbs or that all adverbs end in *-ly*. Some adjectives end in *-ly* (*lovely*, *friendly*), and some adverbs don't (*always*, *here*). When in doubt, consult a dictionary.

28a Adjectives

Adjectives ordinarily precede the nouns they modify. But they can also function as subject complements following linking verbs (usually a form of *be*: *be, am, is, are, was, were, being, been*). When an adjective functions as a subject complement, it describes the subject.

Justice is *blind.*

Verbs such as *smell, taste, look, appear, grow,* and *feel* may also be linking. If the word following one of these verbs describes the subject, use an adjective; if the word modifies the verb, use an adverb.

ADJECTIVE The detective looked *cautious.*

ADVERB The detective looked *cautiously* for the fingerprints.

Linking verbs usually suggest states of being, not actions. For example, to look *cautious* suggests the state of being cautious, whereas to look *cautiously* is to perform an action in a cautious way.

▶ Lori looked ~~well~~ *good* in her new raincoat.

▶ All of us on the debate team felt ~~badly~~ *bad* about our performance.

> The verbs *looked* and *felt* suggest states of being, not actions, so they should be followed by adjectives.

28b Adverbs

Use adverbs to modify verbs, adjectives, and other adverbs. Adverbs usually answer one of these questions: When? Where? How? Why? Under what conditions? How often? To what degree?

Adjectives are often used incorrectly in place of adverbs in casual or nonstandard speech.

▶ The manager must ensure that the office runs ~~smooth~~ *smoothly* and ~~efficient~~ *efficiently.*

▶ The chance of recovering any property lost in the

really
fire looks ~~real~~ slim.
∧

The incorrect use of the adjective *good* in place of the adverb *well* is especially common in casual or nonstandard speech.

well
▶ We were delighted that Nomo had done so ~~good~~
∧
on the exam.

28c Comparatives and superlatives

Most adjectives and adverbs have three forms: the positive, the comparative, and the superlative.

POSITIVE	COMPARATIVE	SUPERLATIVE
soft	softer	softest
fast	faster	fastest
careful	more careful	most careful
bad	worse	worst
good	better	best

Comparative vs. superlative   Use the comparative to compare two things, the superlative to compare three or more.

better?
▶ Which of these two products is ~~best?~~
∧

most
▶ Jia is the ~~more~~ qualified of the three applicants.
∧

Form of comparatives and superlatives   To form comparatives and superlatives of one-syllable adjectives, use the endings *-er* and *-est*: *smooth, smoother, smoothest*. For adjectives with three or more syllables, use *more* and *most* (or *less* and *least*): *exciting, more exciting, most exciting*. Two-syllable adjectives form comparatives and superlatives in both ways: *lovely, lovelier, loveliest; helpful, more helpful, most helpful*.

Some one-syllable adverbs take the endings *-er* and *-est*: *fast, faster, fastest*. Longer adverbs and all of those ending in *-ly* use *more* and *most* (or *less* and *least*): *quickly, more quickly, most quickly*.

Double comparatives or superlatives   When you have added *-er* or *-est* to an adjective or an adverb, do not also use *more* or *most* (or *less* or *least*).

▶ Of all her siblings, Julia is the ~~most~~ happiest about

the move.

Absolute concepts Do not use comparatives or super-latives with absolute concepts such as *unique* or *perfect*. Either something is unique or it isn't. It is illogical to suggest that absolute concepts come in degrees.

unusual
▶ That butterfly was the most ~~unique~~ specimen they
∧
had ever encountered.

29 Repair sentence fragments.

As a rule, do not treat a piece of a sentence as if it were a sentence. When you do, you create a fragment. To be a sentence, a word group must consist of at least one full independent clause. An independent clause has a subject and a verb, and it either stands alone as a sentence or could stand alone.

You can repair a fragment in one of two ways: Either pull the fragment into a nearby sentence, punctuating the new sentence correctly, or rewrite the fragment as a complete sentence.

29a Fragmented clauses

A subordinate clause is patterned like a sentence, with both a subject and a verb, but it begins with a word that tells readers it cannot stand alone—a word such as *after, although, because, before, if, so that, that, though, unless, until, when, where, who,* or *which.* (For a longer list of subordinating words, see p. 244.)

Most fragmented clauses beg to be pulled into a sentence nearby.

because
▶ We fear the West Nile virus ╱ ~~Because~~ it is transmitted
∧
by the common mosquito.

If a fragmented clause cannot be combined gracefully with a nearby sentence, try rewriting it. The simplest way to turn a fragmented clause into a sentence is to delete the opening word or words that mark it as subordinate.

▶ Uncontrolled development is taking a deadly toll on

                            In

   the environment. ~~So that in~~ many parts of the world,

               ^

   fragile ecosystems are collapsing.

29b Fragmented phrases

Like subordinate clauses, certain phrases are sometimes mistaken for sentences. They are fragments if they lack a subject, a verb, or both. Frequently a fragmented phrase may simply be pulled into a nearby sentence.

                                      examining

▶ The archaeologists worked slowly/, ~~Examining~~ and

                             ^

   labeling hundreds of pottery shards.

     The word group beginning with *Examining* is a verbal phrase, not a sentence.

                                            a

▶ Many adults suffer silently from agoraphobia/, ~~A~~

                                   ^

   fear of the outside world.

     A fear of the outside world is an appositive phrase, not a sentence.

▶ It has been said that there are only three

                                   jazz,

   indigenous American art forms/: ~~Jazz,~~ musical

                              ^

   comedy, and soap operas.

     The list is not a sentence. Notice how easily a colon corrects the problem. (See 33b.)

If the fragmented phrase cannot be attached to a nearby sentence, turn the phrase into a sentence. You may need to add a subject, a verb, or both.

▶ Researchers have discovered additional strains of the

       They also learned

   virus. ~~Also~~ how these viruses are transmitted

       ^

   and multiply.

     The revision turns the fragmented phrase into a sentence by adding a subject and a verb.

29c Acceptable fragments

Skilled writers occasionally use sentence fragments for emphasis. Although fragments are sometimes appropriate, writers and readers do not always agree on when they are appropriate. Therefore, you will find it safer to write in complete sentences.

30 Revise run-on sentences.

Run-on sentences are independent clauses that have not been joined correctly. An independent clause is a word group that stands alone or could stand alone as a sentence. When two or more independent clauses appear in one sentence, they must be joined in one of these ways:

- with a comma and a coordinating conjunction (*and, but, or, nor, for, so, yet*)
- with a semicolon (or occasionally a colon or a dash)

There are two types of run-on sentences. When a writer puts no mark of punctuation and no coordinating conjunction between independent clauses, the result is a *fused sentence*.

FUSED

Air pollution poses risks to all humans it can be deadly for people with asthma.

A far more common type of run-on sentence is the *comma splice*—two or more independent clauses joined with a comma and no coordinating conjunction. In some comma splices, the comma appears alone.

COMMA SPLICE

Air pollution poses risks to all humans, it can be deadly for people with asthma.

In other comma splices, the comma is accompanied by a joining word, such as *however*, that is *not* a coordinating conjunction. (See 30b.)

COMMA SPLICE

Air pollution poses risks to all humans, however, it can be deadly for people with asthma.

hackerhandbooks.com/pocket
e Grammar > Exercises: 15–1 to 15–4
☑ Grammar > LearningCurve: Run-on sentences

To correct a run-on sentence, you have four choices:

1. Use a comma and a coordinating conjunction.
2. Use a semicolon (or, if appropriate, a colon or a dash).
3. Make the clauses into separate sentences.
4. Restructure the sentence, perhaps by subordinating one of the clauses.

CORRECTED WITH COMMA AND COORDINATING CONJUNCTION

Air pollution poses risks to all humans, but it can be deadly for people with asthma.

CORRECTED WITH SEMICOLON

Air pollution poses risks to all humans; it can be deadly for people with asthma.

CORRECTED WITH SEPARATE SENTENCES

Air pollution poses risks to all humans. It can be deadly for people with asthma.

CORRECTED BY RESTRUCTURING

Although air pollution poses risks to all humans, it can be deadly for people with asthma.

One of these revision techniques will usually work better than the others for a particular sentence. The fourth technique, the one requiring the most extensive revision, is often the most effective.

30a Revision with a comma and a coordinating conjunction

When a coordinating conjunction (*and, but, or, nor, for, so, yet*) joins independent clauses, it is usually preceded by a comma.

▶ Most of his friends had made plans for their

   but
   retirement, Tom had not.
              ∧

30b Revision with a semicolon (or a colon or a dash)

When the independent clauses are closely related and their relation is clear without a coordinating conjunction, a semicolon is an acceptable method of revision.

▶ Tragedy depicts the individual confronted with the

   fact of death/; comedy depicts the adaptability
              ∧

   of human society.

A semicolon is required between independent clauses that have been linked with a conjunctive adverb such as *however* or *therefore* or a transitional phrase such as *in fact* or *of course*. (See 33a for longer lists.)

▶ The timber wolf looks like a large German

   shepherd/; however, the wolf has longer legs,
            ∧

   larger feet, and a wider head.

If the first independent clause introduces a quoted sentence, use a colon.

▶ Martin Luther King Jr. (1963) explained his presence

   in Birmingham this way/: "Injustice anywhere is
                       ∧

   a threat to justice everywhere."

Either a colon or a dash may be appropriate when the second clause summarizes or explains the first. (See 33b and 36d.)

30c Revision by separating sentences

If both independent clauses are long—or if one is a question and the other is not—consider making them separate sentences.

▶ Why should we spend money on space exploration/ ?
   We   ∧
   ~~we~~ have enough underfunded programs here on
   ∧
   Earth.

30d Revision by restructuring the sentence

For sentence variety, consider restructuring the run-on sentence, perhaps by turning one of the independent clauses into a subordinate clause or a phrase.

▶ One of the most famous advertising slogans is
  Wheaties cereal's "Breakfast of Champions," ~~it~~ *which*
  was penned in 1933.

▶ Mary McLeod Bethune, ~~was~~ the 17th child
  of former slaves, ~~she~~ founded the National Council
  of Negro Women in 1935.

31 Review grammar concerns for multilingual writers.

31a Verbs

This section offers a brief review of English verb forms and tenses and the passive voice.

Verb forms Every main verb in English has five forms (except *be*, which has eight). These forms are used to create all of the verb tenses in standard English. The list below shows these forms for the regular verb *help* and the irregular verbs *give* and *be*.

	REGULAR (*HELP*)	IRREGULAR (*GIVE*)	IRREGULAR (*BE*)*
BASE FORM	help	give	be
PAST TENSE	helped	gave	was, were
PAST PARTICIPLE	helped	given	been
PRESENT PARTICIPLE	helping	giving	being
-S FORM	helps	gives	is

Be also has the forms *am* and *are*, which are used in the present tense. (See also p. 165.)

Verb tense Here are descriptions of the tenses and progressive forms in standard English. See also 26b.

The simple tenses show general facts, states of being, and actions that occur regularly.

hackerhandbooks.com/pocket
ⓔ Grammar > Exercises: 16–1 to 16–3
☑ Grammar > LearningCurve: Verbs for multilingual writers

Simple present tense (base form or -s form) expresses general facts, constant states, habitual or repetitive actions, or scheduled future events: *The sun rises in the east. The plane leaves tomorrow at 6:30 a.m.*

Simple past tense (base form + -ed or -d or irregular form) is used for actions that happened at a specific time or during a specific period in the past or for repetitive actions that have ended: *She drove to Montana three years ago. When I was young, I walked to school.*

Simple future tense (will + base form) expresses actions that will occur at some time in the future and promises or predictions of future events: *I will call you next week.*

The simple progressive forms show continuing action.

Present progressive (am, is, are + present participle) shows actions in progress that are not expected to remain constant or future actions (with verbs such as *go, come, move*): *We are building our house at the shore. They are moving tomorrow.*

Past progressive (was, were + present participle) shows actions in progress at a specific past time or a continuing action that was interrupted: *Roy was driving his new car yesterday. When she walked in, we were planning her party.*

Future progressive (will + be + present participle) expresses actions that will be in progress at a certain time in the future: *Nan will be flying home tomorrow.*

TIP: Certain verbs are not normally used in the progressive: *appear, believe, belong, contain, have, hear, know, like, need, see, seem, taste, think, understand,* and *want.* There are exceptions, however, that you must notice as you encounter them: *We are thinking of buying a summer home.*

The perfect tenses show actions that happened or will happen before another time.

Present perfect tense (have, has + past participle) expresses actions that began in the past and continue to the present or actions that happened at an unspecific time in the past: *She has not spoken of her grandfather in a long time. They have traveled to Africa twice.*

Past perfect tense (*had* + past participle) expresses an action that began or occurred before another time in the past: *By the time Hakan was 15, he had learned to drive. I had just finished my walk when my brother drove up.*

Future perfect tense (*will* + *have* + past participle) expresses actions that will be completed before or at a specific future time: *By the time I graduate, I will have taken five film study classes.*

The perfect progressive forms show continuous past actions before another present or past time.

Present perfect progressive (*have, has* + *been* + present participle) expresses continuous actions that began in the past and continue to the present: *My sister has been living in Oregon since 2008.*

Past perfect progressive (*had* + *been* + present participle) conveys actions that began and continued in the past until some other past action: *By the time I moved to Georgia, I had been supporting myself for five years.*

Future perfect progressive (*will* + *have* + *been* + present participle) expresses actions that are or will be in progress before another specified time in the future: *By the time we reach the cashier, we will have been waiting in line for an hour.*

Modal verbs The nine modal verbs—*can, could, may, might, must, shall, should, will,* and *would*—are used with the base form of verbs to show certainty, necessity, or possibility. Modals do not change form to indicate tense.

▶ The art museum will ~~launches~~ its fundraising
                 launch
                           ^
   campaign next month.

▶ We could ~~spoke~~ Portuguese when we were young.
         speak
         ^

Passive voice When a sentence is written in the passive voice, the subject receives the action instead of doing it. To form the passive voice, use a form of *be*—*am, is, are, was, were, being, be,* or *been*—followed by the past participle of the main verb. (For appropriate uses of the passive voice, see 17b.)

▶ *The Protestant Ethic and the Spirit of Capitalism*

        written

  was ~~writing~~ by Max Weber.

     ^

                        be

▶ Senator Dixon will defeated.

                      ^

NOTE: Verbs that do not take direct objects—such as *occur, happen, sleep, die,* and *fall*—do not form the passive voice.

31b Articles (*a, an, the*)

Articles and other noun markers   Articles (*a, an, the*) are part of a category of words known as *noun markers* or *determiners.* Noun markers identify the nouns that follow them. Besides articles, noun markers include possessive nouns (*Elena's, child's*); possessive pronoun/adjectives (*my, your, their*); demonstrative pronoun/adjectives (*this, that*); quantifiers (*all, few, neither, some*); and numbers (*one, 26*).

          ART N

   Felix is reading a book about mythology.

        ART ADJ   N

   We took an exciting trip to Alaska last summer.

When to use *a* or *an*   Use *a* or *an* with singular count nouns that refer to one unspecific item (not a whole category). *Count nouns* refer to persons, places, things, or ideas that can be counted: *one girl, two girls; one city, three cities; one goose, four geese.*

                            a

▶ My professor asked me to bring dictionary to class.

                          ^

                 an

▶ We want to rent apartment close to the lake.

             ^

When to use *the*   Use *the* with most nouns that the reader can identify specifically. Usually the identity will be clear to the reader for one of the following reasons.

1. The noun has been previously mentioned.

                             the

▶ A truck cut in front of our van. When truck skidded

                       ^

  a few seconds later, we almost crashed into it.

hackerhandbooks.com/pocket

🅔 Grammar > Exercises: 16–4 to 16–6

☑ Grammar > LearningCurve: Articles and nouns for multilingual writers

2. A phrase or clause following the noun restricts its identity.

▶ Bryce warned me that ~~the~~ GPS in his car was not working.

3. A superlative adjective such as *best* or *most intelligent* makes the noun's identity specific. (See also 28c.)

▶ Brita had *the* best players on her team.

4. The noun describes a unique person, place, or thing.

▶ During an eclipse, viewers should not look directly at *the* sun.

5. The context or situation makes the noun's identity clear.

▶ Please don't slam *the* door when you leave.

6. The noun is singular and refers to a class or category of items (most often animals, musical instruments, and inventions).

▶ *The tin* ~~Tin~~ whistle is common in traditional Irish music.

When not to use articles Do not use *a* or *an* with non-count nouns. *Noncount nouns* refer to things or abstract ideas that cannot be counted or made plural: *salt, silver, air, furniture, patience, knowledge*. (See the chart on p. 187.)

To express an approximate amount of a noncount noun, use a quantifier such as *some* or *more*: *some water, enough coffee, less violence*.

▶ Ava gave us ~~an~~ information about the Peace Corps.

▶ Claudia said she had ~~a~~ *some* news that would surprise her parents.

Do not use articles with nouns that refer to all of something or something in general.

▶ ~~The kindness~~ *Kindness* is a virtue.

Commonly used noncount nouns

Food and drink

beef, bread, butter, candy, cereal, cheese, cream, meat, milk, pasta, rice, salt, sugar, wine

Nonfood substances

air, cement, coal, dirt, gasoline, gold, paper, petroleum, plastic, rain, silver, snow, soap, steel, wood, wool

Abstract nouns

advice, anger, beauty, confidence, courage, employment, fun, happiness, health, honesty, information, intelligence, knowledge, love, poverty, satisfaction, wealth

Other

biology (and other areas of study), clothing, equipment, furniture, homework, jewelry, luggage, machinery, mail, money, news, poetry, pollution, research, scenery, traffic, transportation, violence, weather, work

NOTE: A few noncount nouns can also be used as count nouns: *He had two loves: music and archery.*

▶ In some parts of the world, ~~the~~ rice is preferred to

all other grains.

When to use articles with proper nouns Do not use articles with most singular proper nouns: *Prime Minister Cameron, Jamaica, Lake Huron, Ivy Street, Mount Everest.* Use *the* with most plural proper nouns: *the McGregors, the Bahamas, the Finger Lakes, the United States.* Also use *the* with large regions, oceans, rivers, and mountain ranges: *the Sahara, the Indian Ocean, the Amazon River, the Rocky Mountains.*

There are, however, many exceptions, especially with geographic names. Note exceptions when you encounter them or consult a native speaker or an ESL dictionary.

31c Sentence structure

This section focuses on the major challenges that multilingual students face when writing sentences in English.

hackerhandbooks.com/pocket
e Grammar > Exercises: 16–7 and 16–8
☑ Grammar > LearningCurve: Sentence structure for multilingual
            writers

Omitted verbs Some languages do not use linking verbs (*am*, *is*, *are*, *was*, *were*) between subjects and complements (nouns or adjectives that rename or describe the subject). Every English sentence, however, must include a verb.

▶ Jim *is* intelligent.

▶ Many streets in San Francisco *are* very steep.

Omitted subjects Some languages do not require a subject in every sentence. Every English sentence, however, needs a subject.

▶ Your aunt is very energetic. *She seems* young for her age.

EXCEPTION: In commands, the subject *you* is understood but not present in the sentence: *Give me the book.*

The word *it* is used as the subject of a sentence describing the weather or temperature, stating the time, indicating distance, or suggesting an environmental fact. Do not omit *it* in such sentences.

It is raining in the valley and snowing in the mountains.

It is 9:15 a.m.

It is 340 miles to Chicago.

In July, *it* is very hot in Arizona.

In some English sentences, the subject comes after the verb, and a placeholder (called an expletive)—*there* or *it*—comes before the verb.

EXP   V ⌐— S —⌐   ⌐— S —⌐ V
There are many people here today. (Many people are

here today.)

EXP V   ⌐— S —⌐   ⌐— S —⌐   V
It is important to study daily. (To study daily is important.)

▶ As you know, *there are* many religious sects in India.

Repeated subjects, objects, and adverbs English does not allow a subject to be repeated in its own clause.

▶ The doctor ~~she~~ advised me to cut down on salt.

Do not add a pronoun even when a word group comes between the subject and the verb.

▶ The car that had been stolen ~~it~~ was found.

Do not repeat an object or an adverb in an adjective clause. Adjective clauses begin with relative pronouns (*who, whom, whose, which, that*) or relative adverbs (*when, where*). Relative pronouns usually serve as subjects or objects in the clauses they introduce; another word in the clause cannot serve the same function. Relative adverbs should not be repeated by other adverbs later in the clause.

▶ The cat ran under the car that ~~it~~ was parked on

the street.

The relative pronoun *that* is the subject of the adjective clause, so the pronoun *it* cannot be added as the subject.

If the clause begins with a relative adverb, do not use another adverb with the same meaning later in the clause.

▶ The office where I work ~~there~~ is close to home.

The adverb *there* cannot repeat the relative adverb *where*.

31d Prepositions showing time and place

The chart on page 190 is limited to three prepositions that show time and place: *at, on,* and *in*. Not every possible use is listed in the chart, so don't be surprised when you encounter exceptions and idiomatic uses that you must learn one at a time. For example, in English, we ride *in* a car but *on* a bus, plane, train, or subway.

hackerhandbooks.com/pocket
e Grammar > Exercise: 16–9
✓ Grammar > LearningCurve: Prepositions for multilingual writers

At, *on*, and *in* to show time and place

Showing time

AT   *at* a specific time: *at* 7:20, *at* dawn, *at* dinner

ON   *on* a specific day or date: *on* Tuesday, *on* June 4

IN   *in* a part of a day: *in* the afternoon, *in* the daytime [but *at* night]

    in a year or month: *in* 1999, *in* July

    in a period of time: finished *in* 13 hours

Showing place

AT   *at* a meeting place or location: *at* home, *at* the club

    at a specific address: living *at* 10 Oak Street

    at the edge of something: sitting *at* the desk

    at the corner of something: turning *at* the intersection

    at a target: throwing the snowball *at* Lucy

ON   *on* a surface: placed *on* the table, hanging *on* the wall

    on a street: the house *on* Spring Street

    on an electronic medium: *on* television, *on* the Internet

IN   *in* an enclosed space: *in* the garage, *in* an envelope

    in a geographic location: *in* San Diego, *in* Texas

    in a print medium: *in* a book, *in* a magazine

Punctuation

32   The comma

The comma was invented to help readers. Without it, sentence parts can collide into one another unexpectedly, causing misreadings.

CONFUSING   If you cook Elmer will do the dishes.

CONFUSING   While we were eating a skunk approached our campsite.

Add commas in the logical places (after *cook* and *eating*), and suddenly all is clear. No longer is Elmer being cooked, the skunk being eaten.

Various rules have evolved to prevent such misreadings and to guide readers through complex grammatical structures. According to most experts, you should use a comma in the situations described in sections 32a–32i. (Section 32j explains when not to use a comma.)

32a Before a coordinating conjunction joining independent clauses

When a coordinating conjunction connects two or more independent clauses—word groups that could stand alone as separate sentences—a comma must precede the conjunction. There are seven coordinating conjunctions in English: *and*, *but*, *or*, *nor*, *for*, *so*, and *yet*.

A comma tells readers that one independent clause has come to a close and that another is about to begin.

▶ **Respondents were given 5 minutes, but none**

   completed the survey.
   _∧

EXCEPTION: If the two independent clauses are short and there is no danger of misreading, the comma may be omitted.

   The plane took off and we were on our way.

TIP: Do *not* use a comma to separate compound elements that are not independent clauses. (See 32j. See also 32c for commas with coordinating conjunctions joining three or more elements.)

32b After an introductory word group

Use a comma after an introductory clause or phrase. A comma tells readers that the introductory word group has come to a close and that the main part of the sentence is about to begin. The most common introductory word groups are adverb clauses, prepositional phrases, and participial phrases.

▶ When Karl Marx wrote *Capital,* many societies were
   ⌃
   in the early stages of industrialization.

▶ During the past 10 years of research, scientists have
   ⌃
   made important discoveries about how humans form

   memories.

▶ Buried under layers of younger rocks, the earth's
   ⌃
   oldest rocks contain no fossils.

EXCEPTION: The comma may be omitted after a short clause or phrase if there is no danger of misreading.

In no time we were at 2,800 feet.

NOTE: Other introductory word groups include transitional expressions and absolute phrases (see 32f).

32c Between items in a series

In a series of three or more items (words, phrases, or clauses), use commas between all items, including the last two.

▶ Concentrated poverty, high rates of unemployment,

   high crime rates, and social disorder are common in
   ⌃
   urban areas.

32d Between coordinate adjectives

Use a comma between coordinate adjectives, those that each modify a noun separately.

▶ Should patients with severe, irreversible brain
   ⌃
   damage be put on life support systems?

Adjectives are coordinate if they can be connected with *and*: *severe and irreversible.*

NOTE: Do not use a comma between cumulative adjectives, those that do not each modify the noun separately.

> *Three large gray* shapes moved slowly toward us.

Cumulative adjectives cannot be joined with *and* (not *three and large and gray shapes*).

32e To set off a nonrestrictive element, but not a restrictive element

A *restrictive* element defines or limits the meaning of the word it modifies; it is therefore essential to the meaning of the sentence and is not set off with commas. A *nonrestrictive* element describes a word whose meaning is clear without it. Because it is not essential to the meaning of the sentence, it is set off with commas.

RESTRICTIVE (NO COMMAS)

Adolescents need activities *that are positive.*

NONRESTRICTIVE (WITH COMMAS)

Adolescents need positive activities, *which do not have to be expensive.*

If you remove a restrictive element from a sentence, the meaning changes significantly, becoming more general than intended. The writer of the first sample sentence does not mean that adolescents need activities in general. The meaning is more restricted: Adolescents need *positive* activities.

If you remove a nonrestrictive element from a sentence, the meaning does not change significantly. Some information may be lost, but the defining characteristics of the person or thing described remain the same: Adolescents need *positive* activities, and the activities need not be expensive.

Elements that may be restrictive or nonrestrictive include adjective clauses, adjective phrases, and appositives.

Adjective clauses   Adjective clauses, which usually follow the noun or pronoun they describe, begin with a relative pronoun (*who, whom, whose, which, that*) or a relative adverb (*when, where*). When an adjective clause is nonrestrictive, set it off with commas; when it is restrictive, omit the commas.

NONRESTRICTIVE CLAUSE (WITH COMMAS)

▶   The Kyoto Protocol, which was adopted in 1997,
              ⌃   ⌃
aims to reduce greenhouse gases.

RESTRICTIVE CLAUSE (NO COMMAS)

▶   A corporation/ that has government contracts/ must

maintain careful personnel records.

NOTE: Use *that* only with restrictive clauses and *which* only with nonrestrictive clauses.

                             that
▶   Some foods ~~which~~ are high in protein are difficult
                        ⌃
to digest.

Adjective phrases   Prepositional or verbal phrases functioning as adjectives may be restrictive or nonrestrictive. Nonrestrictive phrases are set off with commas; restrictive phrases are not.

NONRESTRICTIVE PHRASE (WITH COMMAS)

▶   The eight students, with their lab kits in hand, began
                     ⌃   ⌃
the experiment.

RESTRICTIVE PHRASE (NO COMMAS)

▶   One corner of the attic was filled with newspapers/

dating from the 1920s.

Appositives   An appositive is a noun or pronoun that renames a nearby noun. Nonrestrictive appositives are set off with commas; restrictive appositives are not.

NONRESTRICTIVE APPOSITIVE (WITH COMMAS)

▶   Darwin's most important book, *On the Origin*
                                              ⌃
of Species, was the result of many years of
         ⌃
research.

RESTRICTIVE APPOSITIVE (NO COMMAS)

▶   Selections from the book/ *Democracy and Education*/

were read aloud in class.

32f To set off transitional and parenthetical expressions, absolute phrases, and contrasted elements

Transitional expressions   Transitional expressions serve as bridges between sentences or parts of sentences. They include conjunctive adverbs such as *however, therefore,* and *moreover* and transitional phrases such as *for example* and *as a matter of fact.* For longer lists, see page 200.

When a transitional expression appears between independent clauses in a compound sentence, it is preceded by a semicolon and usually followed by a comma.

▶ **Minh did not understand our language; moreover,**
                                                    ∧
   he was unfamiliar with our customs.

When a transitional expression appears at the beginning of a sentence or in the middle of an independent clause, it is usually set off with commas.

▶ **In fact, stock values rose after the company's press**
          ∧
   release.

▶ **Natural foods are not always salt-free; celery, for**
                                                       ∧
   example, is high in sodium.
          ∧

Parenthetical expressions   Expressions that are distinctly parenthetical, interrupting the flow of a sentence, should be set off with commas.

▶ **Evolution, so far as we know, doesn't work this way.**
             ∧   ∧

Absolute phrases   An absolute phrase consists of a noun followed by a participle or participial phrase. It modifies the whole sentence and should be set off with commas.

```
┌────── ABSOLUTE PHRASE ──────┐
   N   ┌───── PARTICIPLE ─────┐
```
Our grant having been approved, we were at last

able to begin the archaeological dig.

Contrasted elements   Sharp contrasts beginning with words such as *not* and *unlike* are set off with commas.

▶ **The Epicurean philosophers sought mental, not**
                                                ∧
   bodily, pleasures.
          ∧

32g To set off nouns of direct address, the words *yes* and *no*, interrogative tags, and mild interjections

▶ Forgive me, Angela, for forgetting our meeting.
          ∧   ∧

▶ Yes, the loan will probably be approved.
     ∧

▶ The film was faithful to the book, wasn't it?
                                    ∧

▶ Well, cases like this are difficult to decide.
     ∧

32h To set off direct quotations introduced with expressions such as *he argued*

▶ Gladwell (2008) has asserted, "Those who are
                             ∧
successful . . . are most likely to be given the kinds of
special opportunities that lead to further success" (p. 30).

32i With dates, addresses, and titles

Dates   In dates, the year is set off from the rest of the sentence with commas.

▶ On December 12, 1890, orders were sent out for
                ∧   ∧
the arrest of Sitting Bull.

EXCEPTIONS: Commas are not needed if the date is inverted or if only the month and year are given: *The 15 April 2015 deadline is approaching. May 2009 was a surprisingly cold month.*

Addresses   The elements of an address or a place name are separated by commas. A zip code, however, is not preceded by a comma.

▶ The teen group met at 1113 Peoria Street, Washington,
                                           ∧   ∧
IL 61571.

Titles   If a title follows a name, set off the title with a pair of commas.

▶ Sandra Barnes, MD, was appointed to the board.
               ∧   ∧

32j Misuses of the comma

Do not use commas unless you have good reasons for using them. In particular, avoid using commas in the following situations.

WITH A COORDINATING CONJUNCTION JOINING ONLY TWO ELEMENTS

▶ Marie Curie discovered radium/ and later applied her work on radioactivity to medicine.

TO SEPARATE A VERB FROM ITS SUBJECT

▶ Zoos large enough to give the animals freedom to roam/ are becoming more popular.

BETWEEN CUMULATIVE ADJECTIVES (See p. 194.)

▶ We found an old/ maroon hatbox.

TO SET OFF RESTRICTIVE ELEMENTS (See 32e.)

▶ Drivers/ who think they own the road/ make cycling a dangerous sport.

▶ Woody Guthrie's song/ "This Land Is Your Land/ " was added to the National Recording Registry in 2002.

AFTER A COORDINATING CONJUNCTION

▶ TV talk shows are sometimes performed live, but/ more often they are taped.

AFTER *SUCH AS* OR *LIKE*

▶ Bacterial infections such as/ methicillin-resistant *Staphylococcus aureus* (MRSA) have become a serious concern in hospitals.

BEFORE *THAN*

▶ Touring Crete was more interesting/ than visiting the Greek islands frequented by the rich.

BEFORE A PARENTHESIS

▶ At InterComm, Sylvia began at the bottom/

(with only a cubicle and a swivel chair), but within

three years she had been promoted to supervisor.

TO SET OFF AN INDIRECT (REPORTED) QUOTATION

▶ Samuel Goldwyn once said/ that a verbal contract

isn't worth the paper it's written on.

WITH A QUESTION MARK OR AN EXCLAMATION POINT

▶ "Why don't you try it?/ " she coaxed.

33 The semicolon and the colon

33a The semicolon

The semicolon is used between independent clauses
not joined with a coordinating conjunction. It can also
be used between items in a series containing internal
punctuation.

The semicolon is never used between elements of
unequal grammatical rank.

Between independent clauses   When two independent
clauses appear in one sentence, they are usually linked
with a comma and a coordinating conjunction (*and*, *but*,
or, *nor*, *for*, *so*, *yet*). The coordinating conjunction signals
the relation between the clauses. If the relation is clear
without a conjunction, a writer may choose to connect
the clauses with a semicolon instead.

> In film, a low-angle shot makes the subject look power-
> ful; a high-angle shot does just the opposite.

A writer may also connect the clauses with a semicolon and a conjunctive adverb such as *however* or a transitional phrase such as *for example*.

> Many corals grow very gradually; in fact, the creation of
> a coral reef can take centuries.

hackerhandbooks.com/pocket
🄴 Punctuation > Exercises: 18–1 to 18–3
☑ Punctuation > LearningCurve: Semicolons and colons

CONJUNCTIVE ADVERBS

accordingly, also, anyway, besides, certainly, consequently, conversely, finally, furthermore, hence, however, incidentally, indeed, instead, likewise, meanwhile, moreover, nevertheless, next, nonetheless, now, otherwise, similarly, specifically, still, subsequently, then, therefore, thus

TRANSITIONAL PHRASES

after all, as a matter of fact, as a result, at any rate, at the same time, even so, for example, for instance, in addition, in conclusion, in fact, in other words, in the first place, on the contrary

NOTE: A semicolon must be used whenever a coordinating conjunction does not appear between two independent clauses. To use merely a comma — or to use a comma and a conjunctive adverb or transitional expression — creates an error known as a *comma splice*. (See section 30.)

Between items in a series containing internal punctuation Three or more items in a series are usually separated by commas. If one or more of the items contain internal punctuation, use semicolons between the items for clarity.

> Classic science fiction sagas include *Star Trek*, with Captain Kirk, Dr. McCoy, and Mr. Spock; *Battlestar Galactica*, with its Cylons; and *Star Wars*, with Han Solo, Luke Skywalker, and Darth Vader.

Misuses of the semicolon Do not use a semicolon in the following situations.

BETWEEN AN INDEPENDENT CLAUSE AND A SUBORDINATE CLAUSE

▶ The media like to portray my generation as lazy;̸, although polls show that we work as hard as the twentysomethings before us.

BETWEEN AN APPOSITIVE AND THE WORD IT REFERS TO

▶ We were fascinated by the species *Argyroneta aquatica*;̸, a spider that lives underwater.

TO INTRODUCE A LIST

▶ Some public-sector professions require specialized training;̸: teaching, law enforcement, and firefighting.

BETWEEN INDEPENDENT CLAUSES JOINED BY *AND*, *BUT*, *OR*, *NOR*, *FOR*, *SO*, OR *YET*

▶ Five of the applicants had used spreadsheets/,
  ∧

but only one was familiar with databases.

33b The colon

Main uses of the colon A colon can be used after an independent clause to direct readers' attention to a list, an appositive, or a quotation.

A LIST

The routine includes the following: 20 knee bends, 50 leg lifts, and 5 minutes of running in place.

AN APPOSITIVE

My roommate is guilty of two of the seven deadly sins: gluttony and sloth.

A QUOTATION

Consider the words of Benjamin Franklin: "There never was a good war or a bad peace."

For other ways of introducing quotations, see pages 207–08.

A colon may also be used between independent clauses if the second clause summarizes or explains the first clause.

Faith is like love: It cannot be forced.

When an independent clause follows a colon, begin the independent clause with a capital letter. (See 37f.)

Conventional uses Use a colon after the salutation in a formal letter, to indicate hours and minutes, to show proportions, between a title and a subtitle, to separate location and publisher in reference list entries, and between chapter and verse in citations of sacred texts.

Dear Sir or Madam:

5:30 p.m.

The ratio of women to men was 2:1.

Alvin Ailey: A Life in Dance

Boston, MA: Bedford/St. Martin's

Luke 2:14, Qur'an 67:3

Misuses of the colon   A colon must be preceded by an independent clause. Therefore, avoid using it in the following situations.

BETWEEN A VERB AND ITS OBJECT OR COMPLEMENT

▶   Some important vitamins found in vegetables are⫶

vitamin A, thiamine, niacin, and vitamin C.

BETWEEN A PREPOSITION AND ITS OBJECT

▶   The two sides of the heart each consist of⫶ an

upper chamber, or atrium, and a lower chamber,

or ventricle.

AFTER *SUCH AS, INCLUDING,* **OR** *FOR EXAMPLE*

▶   The NCAA regulates college athletic sports,

including⫶ basketball, baseball, softball, and football.

34   The apostrophe

The apostrophe indicates possession and marks contractions. In addition, it has a few conventional uses.

34a   To indicate possession

The apostrophe is used to indicate that a noun or an indefinite pronoun is possessive. Possessives usually indicate ownership, as in *Tim's hat, the writer's desk,* or *someone's gloves.* Frequently, however, ownership is only loosely implied: *the tree's roots, a day's work.* If you are not sure whether a word is possessive, try turning it into an *of* phrase: *the roots of the tree, the work of a day.*

When to add -'s   Add -'s if the noun does not end in -s or if the noun is singular and ends in -s or an s sound.

Luck often propels a rock musician's career.

Thank you for refunding the children's money.

Lois's sister spent last year in India.

Her article presents an overview of Marx's teachings.

EXCEPTION: If pronunciation would be awkward with an apostrophe and an -*s*, some writers use only the apostrophe: *Sophocles'*.

When to add only an apostrophe   If the noun is plural and ends in -*s*, add only an apostrophe.

Both diplomats' briefcases were searched by guards.

Joint possession   To show joint possession, use -'*s* (or -*s'*) with the last noun only; to show individual possession, make all nouns possessive.

Have you seen Joyce and Greg's new camper?

Hernando's and Maria's expectations were quite different.

Compound nouns   If a noun is compound, use -'*s* (or -*s'*) with the last element.

Her father-in-law's sculpture won first place.

Indefinite pronouns such as *someone*   Use -'*s* to indicate that an indefinite pronoun is possessive. Indefinite pronouns refer to no specific person or thing: *anyone, everyone, someone, no one,* and so on.

This diet will improve almost anyone's health.

NOTE: Possessive pronouns (*its, his,* and so on) do not use an apostrophe. (See 34d.)

34b To mark contractions

In a contraction, an apostrophe takes the place of missing letters.

It's unfortunate that many children can't get the services they need.

It's stands for *it is, can't* for *cannot.*

The apostrophe is also used to mark the omission of the first two digits of a year (*the class of '13*) or years (*the '60s generation*).

34c Conventional uses

An apostrophe typically is not used to make plural numbers, abbreviations, letters, or words mentioned as words. Note the few exceptions and be consistent in your writing.

Plural numbers and abbreviations   Do not use an apostrophe in the plural of any numbers (including decades) or of any abbreviations.

> Peggy skated nearly perfect figure 8s.

> We've paid only four IOUs out of six.

Plural letters   Italicize the letter and use roman (regular) font style for the *-s* ending.

> Two large *J*s were painted on the door.

You may use an apostrophe to avoid misreading: *A*'s.

Plural of words mentioned as words   Italicize the word and use roman (regular) font style for the *-s* ending.

> We've heard enough *maybe*s.

34d Misuses of the apostrophe

Do not use an apostrophe in the following situations.

WITH NOUNS THAT ARE PLURAL BUT NOT POSSESSIVE

> ▶ Some ~~outpatient's~~ *outpatients* have special parking permits.
> ^

IN THE POSSESSIVE PRONOUNS *ITS*, *WHOSE*, *HIS*, *HERS*, *OURS*, *YOURS*, AND *THEIRS*

> ▶ Each area has ~~it's~~ *its* own conference room.
> ^

> ▶ We attended a reading by Junot Díaz, ~~who's~~ *whose*
> ^
> work focuses on the Dominican immigration
> experience.

> *It's* means "it is"; *who's* means "who is" (see 34b). Possessive pronouns such as *its* and *whose* contain no apostrophes.

35   Quotation marks

Quotation marks are used to enclose direct quotations. They are also used around some titles.

35a   To enclose direct quotations

Direct quotations of a person's words, whether spoken or written, must be enclosed in quotation marks.

> "The contract talks are stalled," the mediator told reporters, "but I'll work hard to bring both sides together."

NOTE: Do not use quotation marks around indirect quotations, which report what a person said without using the person's exact words.

> The mediator pledged to find a compromise even though negotiations had broken down.

Quotation within quotation   Use single quotation marks to enclose a quotation within a quotation.

> Marshall (2006) noted that Elizabeth Peabody wanted her school to focus on "not merely 'teaching' but 'educating children morally and spiritually as well as intellectually from the first'" (p. 107).

Indented (block) quotations   In an APA-style paper, when a long quotation (40 or more words) has been set off from the text by indenting, do not use quotation marks around the quotation. (See p. 36.) However, use double quotation marks around quoted words that appear within a block quotation.

A report by the Henry J. Kaiser Family Foundation (2004) outlined trends that may have contributed to the childhood obesity crisis:

> a reduction in physical education classes and after-school athletic programs, an increase in the availability of sodas and snacks in public schools, the growth in the number of fast-food outlets . . . , the trend toward "super-sizing" food portions in restaurants, and the increasing number of highly processed high-calorie and high-fat grocery products. (p. 1)

35b Around titles of short works

In the text of a paper, use quotation marks around titles of short works such as journal and newspaper articles, poems, short stories, songs, episodes of television and radio programs, and chapters or subdivisions of books. (For titles of short works in the reference list, see 11b.)

> The story "Pushcart Man" is by Langston Hughes.

NOTE: Titles of books, plays, Web sites, television and radio programs, films, journals, magazines, and newspapers are put in italics. (See 40a.)

35c Other punctuation with quotation marks

This section describes the conventions to observe in placing various marks of punctuation inside or outside quotation marks. It also explains how to punctuate when introducing quoted material.

Periods and commas   Place periods and commas inside quotation marks.

> "I'm here for my service-learning project," I told the teacher. "I'd like to become a reading specialist."

This rule applies to single and double quotation marks, and it applies to quotation marks around words, phrases, and clauses.

EXCEPTION: In parenthetical in-text citations, the period follows the citation in parentheses.

> According to Cole (1999), "The instruments of science have vastly extended our senses" (p. 53).

Colons and semicolons   Put colons and semicolons outside quotation marks.

> Harold wrote, "I regret that I cannot attend the fundraiser for AIDS research"; his letter, however, contained a contribution.

Question marks and exclamation points   Put question marks and exclamation points inside quotation marks unless they apply to the whole sentence.

> On the first day of class, the psychology professor always posed the question "What three goals do you have for the course this term?"

Have you heard the old proverb "Do not climb the hill until you reach it"?

In the first sentence, the question mark applies only to the quoted question. In the second sentence, the question mark applies to the whole sentence.

Introducing quoted material After a word group introducing a quotation, use a colon, a comma, or no punctuation at all, whichever is appropriate in context.

If a quotation is formally introduced, a colon is appropriate. A formal introduction is a full independent clause, not just an expression such as *he wrote* or *she argued*.

> Thomas Friedman (2006) provided a challenging yet optimistic view of the future: "We need to get back to work on our country and on our planet. The hour is late, the stakes couldn't be higher, the project couldn't be harder, the payoff couldn't be greater" (p. 25).

If a quotation is preceded or followed by an expression such as *he wrote* or *she argued*, use a comma.

> Phillips (1993) claimed, "The idea of the unconscious is, among other things, a way of describing the fact that there are things we didn't know we could say" (p. 25).

> "Unless another war is prevented it is likely to bring destruction on a scale never before held possible," Einstein predicted (1947, p. 29).

When you blend a quotation into your own sentence, use either a comma or no punctuation, depending on the way the quotation fits into your sentence structure.

> The champion could, as he put it, "float like a butterfly and sting like a bee."

> Virginia Woolf wrote in 1928 that "a woman must have money and a room of her own if she is to write fiction" (p. 4).

If a quotation appears at the beginning of a sentence, use a comma after it unless the quotation ends with a question mark or an exclamation point.

> "I've always thought of myself as a reporter," claimed American poet Gwendolyn Brooks (1987, p. 162).

> "What is it?" I asked, bracing myself.

If a quoted sentence is interrupted by explanatory words, use commas to set off the explanatory words.

> "With regard to air travel," Stephen Ambrose (1997) noted, "Jefferson was a full century ahead of the curve" (p. 53).

If two successive quoted sentences from the same source are interrupted by explanatory words, use a comma before the explanatory words and a period after them.

> "Everyone agrees journalists must tell the truth," Kovach and Rosenstiel (2001) wrote. "Yet people are befuddled about what 'the truth' means" (p. 37).

NOTE: Quotations of 40 or more words are set off from the text by indenting. See "Setting off long quotations" in 9a.

35d Misuses of quotation marks

Avoid using quotation marks in the following situations.

FAMILIAR SLANG, TRITE EXPRESSIONS, OR HUMOR

▶ The economist emphasized that 5% was a

/"ballpark figure./"

INDIRECT QUOTATIONS

▶ After finishing the exam, Chuck said that/"he was

due for a coffee break./"

36 Other marks

36a The period

Use a period to end all sentences except direct questions or genuine exclamations.

> Celia asked whether class would be canceled.

> A period is conventionally used with personal titles, Latin abbreviations, and designations for time.

Mr.	i.e.	a.m.
Ms.	e.g.	p.m.
Dr.	etc.	

NOTE: If a sentence ends with a period marking an abbreviation, do not add a second period.

A period is not used for most other abbreviations (see also section 38).

CA	UNESCO	FCC	NATO	PhD	cm
NY	AFL-CIO	IRS	USA	BCE	min

36b The question mark

Use a question mark after a direct question.

Which economists have argued for free markets?

NOTE: Use a period, not a question mark, after an indirect question, one that is reported rather than asked directly.

He asked me who taught the engineering course.

36c The exclamation point

Use an exclamation point after a sentence that expresses exceptional feeling or deserves special emphasis.

We yelled to the attending physician, "He's not drunk! He's in diabetic shock!"

Do not overuse the exclamation point.

▶ **In the fisherman's memory, the fish lives on,**

increasing in length and weight each year, until it is

big enough to shade a fishing boat!.
                                       ∧

This sentence doesn't need to be pumped up with an exclamation point. It is emphatic enough without it.

36d The dash

The dash may be used to set off parenthetical material that deserves special emphasis. When typing, use two hyphens to form a dash (--), with no space before or after them. If your word processing program has what is known as an "em-dash" (—), you may use it instead, with no space before or after it.

Use a dash to introduce a list, to signal a restatement or an amplification, or to indicate a striking shift in tone or thought.

> Along the wall are the bulk liquids—sesame seed oil, honey, safflower oil, and half-liquid peanut butter.

> Peter decided to focus on his priorities—applying to graduate school, getting financial aid, and finding a roommate.

> Kiere took a few steps back, came running full speed, kicked a mighty kick—and missed the ball.

In the first two examples, the writer could also use a colon. (See 33b.) The colon is more formal than the dash and not quite as dramatic.

Use a pair of dashes to set off parenthetical material that deserves special emphasis or to set off an appositive that contains commas.

> Everything in the classroom—from the pencils on the desks to the books on the shelves—was in perfect order.

> In my hometown, people's basic needs—food, clothing, and shelter—are less costly than in Denver.

TIP: Unless you have a specific reason for using the dash, avoid it. Unnecessary dashes create a choppy effect.

36e Parentheses

Parentheses have several conventional uses.

Supplemental information   Use parentheses to enclose supplemental material, minor digressions, and afterthoughts.

> Nurses record patients' vital signs (temperature, pulse, and blood pressure) several times a day.

Abbreviations   Use parentheses around an abbreviation following the spelled-out form the first time you mention the term. Use the abbreviation alone in subsequent references.

> Data from the Uniform Crime Reports (UCR) indicate that homicide rates have been declining. Because most murders are reported to the police, the data from the UCR are widely viewed as a valid indicator of homicide rates.

Technical notation   Statistical values, degrees of freedom, and other technical expressions are often enclosed in parentheses.

The relationship between these variables was statistically significant ($p = .021$).

$t(80) = 2.22$

$F(2, 118) = 4.55$

Series   Use parentheses to enclose letters or numbers labeling items in a series.

Freudians recognize three parts to a person's psyche: (a) the unconscious id, where basic drives such as hunger reside; (b) the ego, which controls many of our conscious decisions; and (c) the superego, which regulates behavior according to internalized societal expectations.

Documentation   Parentheses are used around dates and page numbers in in-text citations and around dates in reference list entries. (See sections 13 and 14.)

Inappropriate use   Do not overuse parentheses. Often a sentence reads more gracefully without them.

> *from*
> ► **Research shows that 17 million ~~(estimates run as~~**
>   *to*   ∧
> **~~high as 23 million~~) Americans have diabetes.**
>   ∧

36f Brackets

Use brackets to enclose any words or phrases you have inserted into an otherwise word-for-word quotation.

As Simon (2007) has argued, "Perhaps the most important feature of this change has been an enormous expansion of power [for prosecutors] at the expense of judges, paroling authorities, and defense lawyers" (p. 35).

Simon's book did not contain the words *for prosecutors* in the sentence quoted.

The Latin word *sic* in brackets indicates that an error in a quoted sentence appears in the original source.

According to the review, the book was "an important contribution to gender studies, suceeding [*sic*] where others have fallen short."

36g The ellipsis mark

Use an ellipsis mark, three spaced periods, to indicate that you have deleted material from an otherwise word-for-word quotation.

> Harmon (2011) noted, "During hibernation, heart rate would drop to nine beats per minute between breaths . . . and then speed up with each inhale."

If you delete a full sentence or more in the middle of a quoted passage, use a period before the three ellipsis dots.

NOTE: Do not use the ellipsis mark at the beginning or end of a quotation unless it is important, for clarity, to indicate that the passage quoted is from the middle of a sentence.

36h The slash

Use the slash to separate two or three lines of poetry that have been run into your text. Add a space both before and after the slash.

> In the opening lines of "Jordan," George Herbert pokes fun at popular poems of his time: "Who says that fictions only and false hair / Become a verse? Is there in truth no beauty?"

A slash is used in an in-text citation for the dates of a republished work: (1867/2011).

Use the slash sparingly, if at all, to separate options: *pass/fail, producer/director*. Put no space around the slash. Avoid using expressions such as *he/she* and *his/her* and the awkward construction *and/or*.

Mechanics

37 Capitalization

In addition to reading the following guidelines, consult a good dictionary for help in determining when to use capital letters.

37a Proper vs. common nouns

Proper nouns and words derived from them are capitalized; common nouns are not. Proper nouns name specific persons, places, and things. All other nouns are common nouns.

The following types of words are usually capitalized: names of deities, religions, religious followers, and sacred books; words of family relationships used as names; particular places; nationalities and their languages, races, and tribes; educational institutions, departments, and particular courses; government departments, organizations, and political parties; historical movements, periods, events, and documents; the Web and specific electronic sources; and trade names.

PROPER NOUNS	COMMON NOUNS
God (used as a name)	a god
Book of Common Prayer	a sacred book
Uncle Pedro	my uncle
Father (used as a name)	my father
Lake Superior	a picturesque lake
the Capital Center	a center for the arts
the South	a southern state
Wrigley Field	a baseball stadium
Swedish	a nationality
Pinghua	a dialect
University of Wisconsin	a good university
Geology 101	a geology course
Veterans Administration	a federal agency
Phi Kappa Psi	a fraternity
the Democratic Party	a political party
the Enlightenment	the eighteenth century
the Great Depression	a recession
the Treaty of Versailles	a treaty
Xerox	a photocopy

Months, holidays, and days of the week are capitalized: *May, Labor Day, Monday.* The seasons and numbers of the days of the month are not: *summer, the fifth of June.*

Names of school subjects are capitalized only if they are names of languages: *English, French, geology, history.*

NOTE: Do not capitalize common nouns to make them seem important: *Our company is currently hiring technical support staff* [not *Company, Technical Support Staff*].

37b Titles with proper names

Capitalize a title when used as part of a proper name but usually not when used alone.

Prof. Margaret Burnes; Dr. Sinyee Sein; John Scott Williams Jr.; Anne Tilton, LLD

District Attorney Mill was ruled out of order.

The district attorney was elected for a two-year term.

Usage varies when the title of a public figure is used alone: *The president* [or *President*] *vetoed the bill.*

37c Titles of works

In titles and subtitles of works mentioned in the text of a paper, capitalize all major words (nouns, pronouns, verbs, adjectives, and adverbs) as well as all words of four letters or more. Minor words of fewer than four characters (articles, prepositions, and coordinating conjunctions) are not capitalized unless they are the first or last word of a title or subtitle.

The Impossible Theater: A Manifesto

"The Truth About the National Debt"

A Guide to Working With Adolescents

Titles of works are handled differently in the APA reference list. See section 14.

37d Special terms

In the social sciences, the following terms are typically capitalized.

SPECIFIC TITLES OF TESTS   Myers-Briggs Type Indicator

NOUNS FOLLOWED BY LETTERS OR NUMBERS   Type 2 diabetes, Trial 5

TRADE NAMES OF DRUGS   Advil, Benadryl

The following are typically lowercase.

GENERIC TITLES OF TESTS   career preference test

NOUNS FOLLOWED BY VARIABLES   type x, trial y

GENERIC NAMES OF DRUGS   ibuprofen, diphenhydramine

NAMES OF THEORIES   social disorganization theory, Marxian economics

NOTE: Terms (such as *Marxian*) derived from proper nouns are capitalized.

37e First word of a sentence or quoted sentence

The first word of a sentence should be capitalized. Capitalize the first word of a quoted sentence but not a quoted phrase.

> Loveless (2011) wrote, "If failing schools are ever to be turned around, much more must be learned about how schools age as institutions" (p. 25).

> Russell Baker (1967) has written that sports are "the opiate of the masses" (p. 46).

If a quoted sentence is interrupted by explanatory words, do not capitalize the first word after the interruption.

> "When we all think alike," he said, "no one is thinking."

When a sentence appears within parentheses, capitalize the first word unless the parentheses appear within another sentence.

> Early detection of breast cancer increases survival rates. (See Table 2.)

> Early detection of breast cancer increases survival rates (see Table 2).

37f First word following a colon

Capitalize the first word after a colon if it begins an independent clause.

> Suddenly the political climate changed: The voters rejected the previously popular governor.

37g Abbreviations

Capitalize abbreviations for departments and agencies of government, organizations, and corporations, as well as the call letters of radio and television stations.

EPA, FBI, DKNY, IBM, WERS, KNBC-TV

38 Abbreviations

In the text of a paper, use abbreviations only when they are clearly appropriate and universally understood (such as *Dr.*, *mm*, *IQ*).

38a Before and after a name

Use standard abbreviations for titles immediately before and after proper names.

TITLES BEFORE PROPER NAMES	TITLES AFTER PROPER NAMES
Ms. Nancy Linehan	Thomas Hines Jr.
Dr. Margaret Simmons	Anita Lor, PhD
Rev. John Stone	Robert Simkowski, MD
St. Joan of Arc	William Lyons, MA
Prof. James Russo	Polly Stern, LPN

Do not abbreviate a title if it is not used with a proper name: *My criminology professor* [not *prof.*] *was an expert in constitutional law.*

38b Organizations, companies, countries

Familiar abbreviations for names of organizations, companies, and countries are generally acceptable: *CIA, FBI, NAACP, EPA, YMCA, NBC, USA.*

If you have any doubt about whether your readers will understand an abbreviation or whether the abbreviation is potentially unfamiliar or ambiguous, write the full name followed immediately by the abbreviation in parentheses the first time you mention it. Then just use the abbreviation in the rest of the paper. *AMA*, for instance, could refer to the American Medical Association or the American Management Association.

hackerhandbooks.com/pocket
e Mechanics > Exercise: 23–1

38c Units of measurement and time

Use abbreviations for units of measurement and of time that are preceded by a number. Spell out units if they are used alone.

> 5 cm
>
> 20 μA
>
> 10-km race
>
> 10:00 p.m.
>
> Doses were specified in milliliters.
>
> Results were measured in seconds.

The following are typical abbreviations for units of measurement. While most social science and related fields use metric measures, you may have occasion to use U.S. standard units in some of your work.

m, cm, mm	km, kph	g, kg, mg, μg	L, mL, dL
dB	ppm	Hz, kHz	W, kW
°C, °F	A, μA	hr, min	s, ms, ns
lb	yd, ft, in.	mi, mph	

Do not use periods after abbreviations for units of measurement or time (except the abbreviations *in.* for inch and *a.m.* and *p.m.*).

Do not abbreviate *day*, *week*, *month*, or *year*, even when preceded by a number.

38d Latin abbreviations

Although Latin abbreviations are appropriate in footnotes and reference lists, use the appropriate English phrases in the text of a paper.

> cf. (*confer*, "compare")
>
> e.g. (*exempli gratia*, "for example")
>
> et al. (*et alii*, "and others")
>
> etc. (*et cetera*, "and so forth")
>
> i.e. (*id est*, "that is")
>
> N.B. (*nota bene*, "note well")

38e Plural of abbreviations

For the plural of most abbreviations, add -*s* (do not use an apostrophe): *PhDs, RTs, EMTs.*

Do not add -*s* to indicate the plural of units of measurement.

mm (*not* mms)

L (*not* Ls)

in. (*not* ins.)

38f Other uses of abbreviations

Other commonly accepted abbreviations and symbols include *BC, AD, No.,* and *$*. The abbreviation *BC* ("before Christ") follows a date, and *AD* ("*anno Domini*") precedes a date. Acceptable alternatives are *BCE* ("before the common era") and *CE* ("common era"). Both follow a date.

40 BC (or 40 BCE)   No. 12 (or no. 12)
AD 44 (or 44 CE) $150

Avoid using *No.* or *$* when not accompanied by a specific figure.

38g Inappropriate abbreviations

In the text of a paper, abbreviations for the following are not commonly accepted.

PERSONAL NAME   Charles (*not* Chas.)

DAYS OF THE WEEK   Monday (*not* Mon.)

HOLIDAYS   Christmas (*not* Xmas)

MONTHS   January, February (*not* Jan., Feb.)

COURSES OF STUDY   political science (*not* poli. sci.)

DIVISIONS OF WRITTEN WORKS   chapter, page (*not* ch., p.)

STATES AND COUNTRIES   Florida (*not* FL or Fla.)

PARTS OF A BUSINESS NAME   Adams Lighting Company (*not* Adams Lighting Co.)

NOTE: For use of abbreviations in documenting sources, see sections 13 and 14.

39 Numbers

In a paper, you may need to communicate statistics, survey results, or other data. In some cases, you will use numerals (*15*, for instance); in others, you will spell out the numbers (*eight*).

39a Using numerals

Use numerals to represent all numbers 10 and above and for all numbers that precede a unit of measurement. (See 39b for exceptions.)

> 12 mm, 4 cm
>
> 5-ft gap

Use numerals for all numbers in the abstract of a paper. The following are other acceptable uses of numerals.

DATES July 4, 1776; 56 BC; AD 30

ADDRESSES 77 Latches Lane, 519 West 42nd Street

PERCENTAGES 5%

FRACTIONS, DECIMALS ¹/₂, 0.047

SCORES 7 to 3, 21–18

AGES 5-year-old, average age 37

SURVEYS 4 out of 5

EXACT AMOUNTS OF MONEY $105.37, $0.05

DIVISIONS OF BOOKS volume 3, chapter 4, page 189

DIVISIONS OF PLAYS act 3, scene 3

TIME OF DAY 4:00 p.m., 1:30 a.m.

ORDINALS ABOVE 10 12th

39b Using words for numbers

Spell out the numbers one through nine (unless they are used in the ways noted in 39a).

Spell out numbers for approximate quantities: *about twelve weeks, almost thirty minutes*.

A number at the beginning of a sentence should be spelled out, but it is preferable to reword the sentence to avoid the number at the beginning.

NOTE: Numerals and spelled-out numbers may appear together in the same sentence or paragraph. Use the rules in 39a and 39b to determine whether each number should be spelled out or expressed as a numeral.

> Of 35 students taking the test, only three finished in the allotted time.

40   Italics

This section describes conventional uses for italics.

40a   Titles of works

Titles of the following types of works are italicized.

TITLES OF BOOKS   *The Invisible Line, Governing Through Crime, Freakonomics*

JOURNALS AND MAGAZINES   *Psychological Review, Journal of Social Work, American Journal of Political Science*

NEWSPAPERS   the *Baltimore Sun,* the *Wall Street Journal*

PAMPHLETS   *Common Sense, Facts About Marijuana*

PLAYS   *King Lear, Wicked*

FILMS   *A Beautiful Life, An Inconvenient Truth*

TELEVISION PROGRAMS   *American Idol, Frontline*

RADIO PROGRAMS   *All Things Considered*

MUSICAL COMPOSITIONS   *Porgy and Bess*

WORKS OF VISUAL ART   *American Gothic*

COMIC STRIPS   *Dilbert*

WEB SITES   *ZDNet, Google*

VIDEO GAMES   *Dragon Age, Call of Duty*

Titles of other works, such as journal or newspaper articles, short stories, essays, and songs, are enclosed in quotation marks in the text of a paper. (See also 35b.)

For guidelines on formatting titles in the reference list, see 11b.

NOTE: Do not use italics when referring to the Bible; titles of books in the Bible (Genesis, not *Genesis*); the titles of legal documents (the Constitution, not the *Constitution*); or the titles of your own papers.

40b Words as words and other uses

Italicize words and letters used in the following ways.

WORDS AS WORDS   The 3-year-old could pronounce *know* but not *snow*.

LETTERS AS LETTERS   Many children with dyslexia cannot distinguish *b* from *d*.

VARIABLES AND STATISTICAL NOTATION $F(1, 14)$, $p = .04$

GENERA, SPECIES, VARIETIES   *Alligator sinensis*

FIRST USE OF KEY TERM   The process is called *photosynthesis*.

40c Ships, aircraft, spacecraft

Italicize names of specific ships, aircraft, and spacecraft.

> *Arbella, Spirit of St. Louis, Challenger*

40d Foreign words

Italicize foreign words used in an English sentence.

> *Gemeinschaften* are communities in which members are strongly attached to the values and beliefs of the group.

EXCEPTION: Do not italicize foreign words that have become part of the English language.

laissez-faire	per diem
fait accompli	modus operandi
et al.	per se

41 Spelling

A spell checker is a useful tool when you are working on a computer, but be aware of its limitations. A spell checker will not tell you how to spell words not listed in its dictionary; nor will it help you catch words commonly confused, such as *accept* and *except*, or common typographical errors, such as *own* for *won*. You will still need to proofread, and for some words you may need to turn to the dictionary.

NOTE: To check for correct use of commonly confused words (*accept* and *except*, *its* and *it's*, and so on), consult the glossary of usage in the appendices at the back of the book.

41a Major spelling rules

If you need to improve your spelling, review the following rules and exceptions.

i before e In general, use *i* before *e* except after *c* and except when sounded like "ay," as in *neighbor* and *weigh*.

I BEFORE *E*	relieve, believe, sieve, niece, fierce, frieze
E* BEFORE *I	receive, deceive, sleigh, freight, eight
EXCEPTIONS	seize, either, weird, height, foreign, leisure

Adding suffixes Generally, drop a final silent *-e* when adding a suffix that begins with a vowel. Keep the final *-e* if the suffix begins with a consonant.

desire, desiring   achieve, achievement
remove, removable   care, careful

Words such as *changeable, judgment, argument,* and *truly* are exceptions.

If a final consonant is preceded by a single vowel *and* the consonant ends a one-syllable word or a stressed syllable, double the consonant when adding a suffix beginning with a vowel.

bet, betting   occur, occurrence
commit, committed

Adding *-s* and *-ed* When adding *-s* or *-ed* to words ending in *-y*, ordinarily change *-y* to *-ie* when the *-y* is preceded by a consonant. Add just an *-s* or add *-ed* when *-y* is preceded by a vowel.

comedy, comedies   monkey, monkeys
dry, dried   play, played

With proper names ending in *-y,* however, do not change the *-y* to *-i* even if it is preceded by a consonant: *the Dougherty family, the Doughertys*.

Plurals   Add -s to form the plural of most nouns; add -es to singular nouns ending in -s, -sh, -ch, and -x.

table, tables	church, churches
paper, papers	dish, dishes
agenda, agendas	fox, foxes

Ordinarily add -s to nouns ending in -o when the -o is preceded by a vowel. Add -es when the -o is preceded by a consonant.

radio, radios	hero, heroes
video, videos	tomato, tomatoes

To form the plural of a hyphenated compound word, add the -s to the chief word even if it does not appear at the end.

mother-in-law, mothers-in-law

NOTE: English words derived from other languages such as Latin, Greek, or French sometimes form the plural as they would in their original language.

medium, media	chateau, chateaux
criterion, criteria	

41b Spelling variations

Following is a list of some common words spelled differently in American and British English. Consult a dictionary for others.

AMERICAN	BRITISH
canceled, traveled	cancelled, travelled
color, humor	colour, humour
judgment	judgement
check	cheque
realize, apologize	realise, apologise
defense	defence
anemia, anesthetic	anaemia, anaesthetic
theater, center	theatre, centre
fetus	foetus
mold, smolder	mould, smoulder
civilization	civilisation
connection, inflection	connexion, inflexion

42 Hyphenation

In addition to the following guidelines, a dictionary can provide help with hyphenation.

42a Compound words

The dictionary will tell you whether to treat a compound word as a hyphenated compound (*water-repellent*), as one word (*waterproof*), or as two words (*water table*). If the compound word is not in the dictionary, treat it as two words.

> The prosecutor did not cross-examine any witnesses.

> The research committee considered the pros and cons of a crossover trial.

> The sample represented a cross section of voters in the third district.

42b Words functioning together as an adjective

When two or more words function together as an adjective before a noun, connect them with a hyphen. Generally, do not use a hyphen when such compounds follow the noun.

> well-known candidate, candidate who is well known

> stress-inducing activity

> middle-school students

> low-impact agriculture

> 10th-grade assignments, sixth-grade teacher

> 1-mm tolerance

> three-fifths representation

Do not use a hyphen after an adverb ending in *-ly*, in a compound that includes a comparative or superlative, with chemical compounds, with foreign phrases, and with a compound ending in a number.

> rapidly growing bacteria

> longest running experiment

> sodium hydroxide production

> a priori condition

> Type 2 diabetes

NOTE: In a series of hyphenated adjectives modifying the same noun, hyphens are suspended: *The test was administered to all second-, third-, and fourth-year students.*

42c Suffixes and prefixes

Most suffixes and prefixes do not require a hyphen.

PREFIXES	SUFFIXES
*anti*war	human*like*
*inter*scholastic	search*able*
*non*consenting	
*semi*circle	
*un*sustainable	

There are some exceptions. Hyphens are used with the prefixes *all-*, *ex-*, and *self-* and the suffix *-elect*; with prefixes before capitalized words or numbers; with prefixes of more than two words; and with terms that would otherwise be confusing.

all-encompassing	un-American
ex-president	non-stress-inducing
self-effacing	re-create (create again)
senator-elect	re-sent (sent again)

A hyphen is usually used to avoid a double vowel, but most *pre-* and *re-* words and some other words that are well established do not use the hyphen in such a case.

anti-inflammatory	reenter
anti-intellectual	reemerge
co-opt	preexisting
co-owner	cooperate
intra-arterial	microorganism

42d Hyphenation at ends of lines

Set your word processing program to not hyphenate words at the end of a line of text. This setting ensures that only words that already contain a hyphen may be broken at the end of a line.

E-mail addresses, URLs, and other electronic addresses need special attention when they occur at the end of a line of text. Do not insert a hyphen to divide electronic addresses. Instead, break an e-mail address after the @ symbol or before a period. Break a URL after a double slash or before any other mark of punctuation.

Appendices

Glossary of usage

This glossary includes words commonly confused, words commonly misused, and words that are nonstandard. It also lists colloquialisms that may be appropriate in informal speech but are inappropriate in formal writing.

a, an   Use *an* before a vowel sound, *a* before a consonant sound: *an apple, a peach.* Problems sometimes arise with words beginning with *h* or *u*. If the *h* is silent, the word begins with a vowel sound, so use *an*: *an hour, an heir, an honest senator.* If the *h* is pronounced, the word begins with a consonant sound, so use *a*: *a hospital, a historian, a hotel.* Words such as *university* and *union* begin with a consonant sound, so use *a*: *a union.* Words such as *uncle* and *umbrella* begin with a vowel sound, so use *an*: *an underground well.* When an abbreviation or acronym begins with a vowel sound, use *an*: *an EKG, an MRI.*

accept, except   *Accept* is a verb meaning "to receive." *Except* is usually a preposition meaning "excluding." *I will accept all the packages except that one. Except* is also a verb meaning "to exclude." *Please except that item from the list.*

adapt, adopt   *Adapt* means "to adjust or become accustomed"; it is usually followed by *to. Adopt* means "to take as one's own." *Our family adopted a Vietnamese child, who quickly adapted to his new life.*

adverse, averse   *Adverse* means "unfavorable." *Averse* means "opposed" or "reluctant"; it is usually followed by *to. I am averse to your proposal because it could have an adverse impact on the economy.*

advice, advise   *Advice* is a noun, *advise* a verb. *We advise you to follow John's advice.*

affect, effect   *Affect* is usually a verb meaning "to influence." *Effect* is usually a noun meaning "result." *The drug did not affect the disease, and it had adverse side effects. Effect* can also be a verb meaning "to bring about." *Only the president can effect such a change.*

all ready, already   *All ready* means "completely prepared." *Already* means "previously." *Susan was all ready for the concert, but her friends had already left.*

all right   *All right,* written as two words, is correct. *Alright* is nonstandard.

all together, altogether   *All together* means "everyone gathered." *Altogether* means "entirely." *We were not altogether sure that we could bring the family all together for the reunion.*

allusion, illusion   An *allusion* is an indirect reference; an *illusion* is a misconception or false impression. *Did you catch my allusion to Shakespeare? Mirrors give the room an illusion of depth.*

a lot   *A lot* is two words. Do not write *alot.*

among, between   Ordinarily, use *among* with three or more entities, *between* with two. *The prize was divided among several contestants. You have a choice between carrots and beans.*

amoral, immoral   *Amoral* means "neither moral nor immoral"; it also means "not caring about moral judgments." *Immoral* means "morally wrong." *Many business courses are taught from an amoral perspective. Murder is immoral.*

amount, number   Use *amount* with quantities that cannot be counted; use *number* with those that can. *This recipe calls for a large amount of sugar. We have a large number of toads in our garden.*

an   See *a, an.*

and/or   Avoid *and/or* except in technical or legal documents.

anxious   *Anxious* means "worried" or "apprehensive." In formal writing, avoid using *anxious* to mean "eager." *We are eager* (not *anxious*) *to see your new house.*

anybody, anyone   See sections 25d and 27a.

anyone, any one   *Anyone*, an indefinite pronoun, means "any person at all." *Any one* refers to a particular person or thing in a group. *Anyone in the class may choose any one of the books to read.*

anyways, anywheres   *Anyways* and *anywheres* are nonstandard for *anyway* and *anywhere.*

as   *As* is sometimes used to mean "because." But do not use it if there is any chance of ambiguity. *We canceled the picnic because* (not *as*) *it began raining. As* here could mean "because" or "when."

as, like   See *like, as.*

averse   See *adverse, averse.*

awful   The adjective *awful* and the adverb *awfully* are too colloquial for formal writing.

awhile, a while   *Awhile* is an adverb; it can modify a verb, but it cannot be the object of a preposition such as *for.* The two-word form *a while* is a noun preceded by an article and therefore can be the object of a preposition. *Stay awhile. Stay for a while.*

back up, backup   *Back up* is a verb phrase. *Back up the car carefully. Be sure to back up your hard drive. Backup* is a noun often meaning "duplicate of electronically stored data." *Keep your backup in a safe place. Backup* can also be used as an adjective. *I regularly create backup disks.*

bad, badly *Bad* is an adjective, *badly* an adverb. *They felt bad about being early and ruining the surprise. Her arm hurt badly after she slid into second.* See section 28.

being as, being that *Being as* and *being that* are non-standard expressions. Write *because* instead.

beside, besides *Beside* is a preposition meaning "at the side of" or "next to." *Annie sleeps with a flashlight beside her bed. Besides* is a preposition meaning "except" or "in addition to." *No one besides Terrie can have that ice cream. Besides* is also an adverb meaning "in addition." *I'm not hungry; besides, I don't like ice cream.*

between See *among, between.*

bring, take Use *bring* when an object is being transported toward you, *take* when it is being moved away. *Please bring me a glass of water. Please take these magazines to Mr. Scott.*

can, may *Can* is traditionally reserved for ability, *may* for permission. *Can you speak French? May I help you?*

capital, capitol *Capital* refers to a city, *capitol* to a building where lawmakers meet. *The residents of the state capital protested the development plans. The capitol has undergone extensive renovations. Capital* also refers to wealth or resources.

censor, censure *Censor* means "to remove or suppress material considered objectionable." *Censure* means "to criticize severely." *The school's policy of censoring books has been censured by the media.*

cite, site *Cite* means "to quote as an authority or example." *Site* is usually a noun meaning "a particular place." *He cited the zoning law in his argument against the proposed site of the gas station.* Locations on the Internet are usually referred to as *sites.*

coarse, course *Coarse* means "crude" or "rough in texture." *The hand-knit sweater had a coarse weave. Course* usually refers to a path, a playing field, or a unit of study. *I plan to take a course in car repair this summer.* The expression *of course* means "certainly."

complement, compliment *Complement* is a verb meaning "to go with or complete" or a noun meaning "something that completes." As a verb, *compliment* means "to flatter"; as a noun, it means "flattering remark." *Her skill at rushing the net complements his skill at volleying. Sheiying's music arrangements receive many compliments.*

conscience, conscious *Conscience* is a noun meaning "moral principles"; *conscious* is an adjective meaning "aware or alert." *Let your conscience be your guide. Were you conscious of his love for you?*

continual, continuous   *Continual* means "repeated regularly and frequently." *She grew weary of the continual telephone calls. Continuous* means "extended or prolonged without interruption." *The broken siren made a continuous wail.*

could care less   *Could care less* is a nonstandard expression. Write *couldn't care less* instead.

could of   *Could of* is nonstandard for *could have.*

council, counsel   A *council* is a deliberative body, and a *councilor* is a member of such a body. *Counsel* usually means "advice" and can also mean "lawyer"; a *counselor* is one who gives advice or guidance. *The councilors met to draft the council's position paper. The pastor offered wise counsel to the troubled teenager.*

criteria   *Criteria* is the plural of *criterion*, which means "a standard, rule, or test on which a judgment or decision can be based." *The only criterion for the scholarship is ability.*

data   *Data* is a plural noun meaning "facts or results." But *data* is increasingly being accepted as a singular noun. *The new data suggest* (or *suggests*) *that our theory is correct.* (The singular *datum* is rarely used.)

different from, different than   Ordinarily, write *different from. Your sense of style is different from Jim's.* However, *different than* is acceptable to avoid an awkward construction. *Please let me know if your plans are different than* (to avoid *from what*) *they were six weeks ago.*

don't   *Don't* is the contraction for *do not. I don't want milk. Don't* should not be used as the contraction for *does not,* which is *doesn't. He doesn't* (not *don't*) *want milk.*

due to   *Due to* is an adjective phrase and should not be used as a preposition meaning "because of." *The trip was canceled because of* (not *due to*) *lack of interest. Due to* is acceptable as a subject complement and usually follows a form of the verb *be. His success was due to hard work.*

each   See sections 25d and 27a.

effect   See *affect, effect.*

either   See sections 25d and 27a.

elicit, illicit   *Elicit* is a verb meaning "to bring out" or "to evoke." *Illicit* is an adjective meaning "unlawful." *The reporter was unable to elicit any information from the police about illicit drug traffic.*

emigrate from, immigrate to   *Emigrate* means "to leave one place to settle in another." *My great-grandfather emigrated from Russia to escape the religious pogroms. Immigrate* means "to enter another place and reside there." *Thousands of Bosnians immigrated to the United States in the 1990s.*

enthused   As an adjective, *enthusiastic* is preferred. *The children were enthusiastic* (not *enthused*) *about going to the circus.*

etc.   Avoid ending a list with *etc.* It is more emphatic to end with an example, and usually readers will understand that the list is not exhaustive. When you don't wish to end with an example, *and so on* is more graceful than *etc.*

everybody, everyone   See sections 25d and 27a.

everyone, every one   *Everyone* is an indefinite pronoun. *Everyone wanted to go. Every one*, the pronoun *one* preceded by the adjective *every*, means "each individual or thing in a particular group." *Every one* is usually followed by *of. Every one of the missing books was found.*

except   See *accept, except.*

farther, further   *Farther* describes distances. *Further* suggests quantity or degree. *Detroit is farther from Miami than I thought. You extended the curfew further than necessary.*

fewer, less   *Fewer* refers to items that can be counted; *less* refers to items that cannot be counted. *Fewer people are living in the city. Please put less sugar in my tea.*

firstly   *Firstly* sounds pretentious, and it leads to the ungainly series *firstly, secondly, thirdly, fourthly*, and so on. Write *first, second, third* instead.

further   See *farther, further.*

good, well   See section 28b.

graduate   Both of the following uses of *graduate* are standard: *My sister was graduated from UCLA last year. My sister graduated from UCLA last year.* It is nonstandard to drop the word *from: My sister graduated UCLA last year.*

grow   Phrases such as *to grow a business* are jargon. Usually the verb *grow* is intransitive (it does not take a direct object). *Our business has grown very quickly.* When *grow* is used in a transitive sense, with a direct object, it means "to cultivate" or "to allow to grow." *We plan to grow tomatoes. John is growing a beard.* (See also "direct object" on p. 240 and "transitive and intransitive verbs" on p. 244.)

hanged, hung   *Hanged* is the past-tense and past-participle form of the verb *hang*, meaning "to execute." *The prisoner was hanged at dawn. Hung* is the past-tense and past-participle form of the verb *hang*, meaning "to fasten or suspend." *The stockings were hung by the chimney with care.*

hardly   Avoid expressions such as *can't hardly* and *not hardly*, which are considered double negatives. *I can* (not *can't*) *hardly describe my elation at getting the job.*

he   At one time *he* was used to mean "he or she." Today such usage is inappropriate. See sections 24d and 27a for alternative constructions.

hisself   *Hisself* is nonstandard. Use *himself.*

hopefully   *Hopefully* means "in a hopeful manner." *We looked hopefully to the future.* Some usage experts object to the use of *hopefully* as a sentence adverb, apparently on grounds of clarity. To be safe, avoid using *hopefully* in sentences such as the following: *Hopefully, your son will recover soon.* Instead, indicate who is doing the hoping: *I hope that your son will recover soon.*

however   Some writers object to *however* at the beginning of a sentence, but experts advise placing the word according to the meaning and emphasis intended. Any of the following sentences is correct, depending on the intended contrast. *Pam decided, however, to attend the lecture. However, Pam decided to attend the lecture.* (She had been considering other activities.) *Pam, however, decided to attend the lecture.* (Unlike someone else, Pam opted for the lecture.)

hung   See *hanged, hung.*

illusion   See *allusion, illusion.*

immigrate   See *emigrate from, immigrate to.*

immoral   See *amoral, immoral.*

imply, infer   *Imply* means "to suggest or state indirectly"; *infer* means "to draw a conclusion." *John implied that he knew all about computers, but the interviewer inferred that John was inexperienced.*

in, into   *In* indicates location or condition; *into* indicates movement or a change in condition. *They found the lost letters in a box after moving into the house.*

in regards to   Use either *in regard to* or *as regards*. *In regard to* (or *As regards*) *the contract, ignore the first clause.*

irregardless   *Irregardless* is nonstandard. Use *regardless.*

is when, is where   See section 21c.

its, it's   *Its* is a possessive pronoun; *it's* is a contraction for *it is. It's always fun to watch a dog chase its tail.*

kind of, sort of   Avoid using *kind of* or *sort of* to mean "somewhat." *The movie was a little* (not *kind of*) *boring.* Do not put *a* after either phrase. *That kind of* (not *kind of a*) *salesclerk annoys me.*

lay, lie   See page 162.

lead, led   *Lead* is a metallic element; it is a noun. *Led* is the past tense of the verb *lead. He led me to the treasure.*

learn, teach   *Learn* means "to gain knowledge"; *teach* means "to impart knowledge." *I must teach* (not *learn*) *my sister to read.*

leave, let   *Leave* means "to exit." Avoid using it with the nonstandard meaning "to permit." *Let* (not *Leave*) *me help you with the dishes.*

less   See *fewer, less.*

let, leave   See *leave, let.*

liable   *Liable* means "obligated" or "responsible." Do not use it to mean "likely." *You're likely* (not *liable*) *to trip if you don't tie your shoelaces.*

lie, lay   See page 162.

like, as   *Like* is a preposition, not a subordinating conjunction. It should be followed only by a noun or a noun phrase. *As* is a subordinating conjunction that introduces a subordinate clause. In casual speech, you may say *She looks like she has not slept.* But in formal writing, use *as. She looks as if she has not slept.*

loose, lose   *Loose* is an adjective meaning "not securely fastened." *Lose* is a verb meaning "to misplace" or "to not win." *Did you lose your only loose pair of work pants?*

may   See *can, may.*

maybe, may be   *Maybe* is an adverb meaning "possibly"; *may be* is a verb phrase. *Maybe the sun will shine tomorrow. Tomorrow may be a brighter day.*

may of, might of   *May of* and *might of* are nonstandard for *may have* and *might have.*

media, medium   *Media* is the plural of *medium. Of all the media that cover the Olympics, television is the medium that best captures the spectacle of the events.*

must of   *Must of* is nonstandard for *must have.*

myself   *Myself* is a reflexive or intensive pronoun. Reflexive: *I cut myself.* Intensive: *I will drive you myself.* Do not use *myself* in place of *I* or *me: He gave the plants to Melinda and me* (not *myself*).

neither   See sections 25d and 27a.

none   See section 25d.

nowheres   *Nowheres* is nonstandard for *nowhere.*

number   See *amount, number.*

off of   *Off* is sufficient. Omit *of.*

passed, past   *Passed* is the past tense of the verb *pass. Emily passed me a slice of cake. Past* usually means "belonging to a former time" or "beyond a time or place." *Our past president spoke until past 10:00 p.m. The hotel is just past the station.*

plus   *Plus* should not be used to join independent clauses. *This raincoat is dirty; moreover* (not *plus*), *it has a hole in it.*

precede, proceed   *Precede* means "to come before." *Proceed* means "to go forward." *As we proceeded up the mountain, we saw evidence that some hikers had preceded us.*

principal, principle   *Principal* is a noun meaning "the head of a school or an organization" or "a sum of money." It is also an adjective meaning "most important." *Principle* is a noun meaning "a basic truth or law." *The principal expelled her for three principal reasons. We believe in the principle of equal justice for all.*

proceed, precede   See *precede, proceed*.

quote, quotation   *Quote* is a verb; *quotation* is a noun. Avoid using *quote* as a shortened form of quotation. *Her quotations* (not *quotes*) *from Shakespeare intrigued us.*

real, really   *Real* is an adjective; *really* is an adverb. *Real* is sometimes used informally as an adverb, but avoid this use in formal writing. *She was really* (not *real*) *angry.* See also section 28.

reason . . . is because   See section 21c.

reason why   The expression *reason why* is redundant. *The reason* (not *The reason why*) *Jones lost the election is clear.*

respectfully, respectively   *Respectfully* means "showing or marked by respect." *He respectfully submitted his opinion. Respectively* means "each in the order given." *John, Tom, and Larry were a butcher, a baker, and a lawyer, respectively.*

sensual, sensuous   *Sensual* means "gratifying the physical senses," especially those associated with sexual pleasure. *Sensuous* means "pleasing to the senses," especially involving art, music, and nature. *The sensuous music and balmy air led the dancers to more sensual movements.*

set, sit   *Set* means "to put" or "to place"; *sit* means "to be seated." *She set the dough in a warm corner of the kitchen. The cat sits in the warmest part of the room.*

should of   *Should of* is nonstandard for *should have*.

since   Do not use *since* to mean "because" if there is any chance of ambiguity. *Because* (not *Since*) *we won the game, we have been celebrating. Since* here could mean "because" or "from the time that."

sit   See *set, sit*.

site, cite   See *cite, site*.

somebody, someone, something   See sections 25d and 27a.

suppose to   Write *supposed to*.

sure and   *Sure and* is nonstandard for *sure to.* Be sure to (not *sure and*) *bring a gift for the host.*

take   See *bring, take.*

than, then   *Than* is a conjunction used in comparisons; *then* is an adverb denoting time. *That pizza is more than I can eat. Tom laughed, and then we recognized him.*

that   See *who, which, that.*

that, which   Many writers reserve *that* for restrictive clauses, *which* for nonrestrictive clauses. (See p. 195.)

theirselves   *Theirselves* is nonstandard for *themselves.*

them   The use of *them* in place of *those* is nonstandard. *Please send those* (not *them*) *letters to the sponsors.*

then   See *than, then.*

there, their, they're   *There* is an adverb specifying place; it is also an expletive (placeholder). Adverb: *Sylvia is sitting there patiently.* Expletive: *There are two plums left.* (See also "expletive" on p. 240.) *Their* is a possessive pronoun. *Fred and Jane finally washed their car. They're* is a contraction of *they are. They're late today.*

to, too, two   *To* is a preposition; *too* is an adverb; *two* is a number. *Too many of your shots slice to the left, but the last two were right on the mark.*

toward, towards   *Toward* and *towards* are generally interchangeable, although *toward* is preferred in American English.

try and   *Try and* is nonstandard for *try to. I will try to* (not *try and*) *be better about writing to you.*

unique   See page 177.

use to   Write *used to. We used to live in an apartment.*

utilize   *Utilize* is often a pretentious substitute for *use;* in most cases, *use* is sufficient. *I used* (not *utilized*) *the best workers to get the job done fast.*

wait for, wait on   *Wait for* means "to be in readiness for" or "await." *Wait on* means "to serve." *We're waiting for* (not *waiting on*) *Ruth before we can leave.*

ways   *Ways* is colloquial when used in place of *way* to mean "distance." *The city is a long way* (not *ways*) *from here.*

weather, whether   The noun *weather* refers to the state of the atmosphere. *Whether* is a conjunction indicating a choice between alternatives. *We wondered whether the weather would clear up in time for our picnic.*

well, good   See section 28b.

where   Do not use *where* in place of *that*. *I heard that* (not *where*) *the crime rate is increasing.*

which   See *that, which* and *who, which, that.*

while   Avoid using *while* to mean "although" or "whereas" if there is any chance of ambiguity. *Although* (not *While*) *Gloria lost money in the slot machine, Tom won it at roulette.* Here *While* could mean either "although" or "at the same time that."

who, which, that   Use *who*, not *which*, to refer to persons. Generally, use *that* to refer to things or, occasionally, to a group or class of people. *The player who* (not *that* or *which*) *made the basket at the buzzer was named MVP. The team that scores the most points in this game will win the tournament.*

who, whom   See section 27d.

who's, whose   *Who's* is a contraction of *who is; whose* is a possessive pronoun. *Who's ready for more popcorn? Whose coat is this?*

would of   *Would of* is nonstandard for *would have.*

you   See page 170.

your, you're   *Your* is a possessive pronoun; *you're* is a contraction of *you are. Is that your bike? You're in the finals.*

Glossary of grammatical terms

This glossary gives definitions for parts of speech, such as nouns; parts of sentences, such as subjects; and types of sentences, clauses, and phrases.

If you are looking up the name of an error (sentence fragment, for example), consult the index or the table of contents instead.

absolute phrase   A word group that modifies a whole clause or sentence, usually consisting of a noun followed by a participle or participial phrase: *Her words echoing in the large arena,* the senator mesmerized the crowd.

active vs. passive voice   When a verb is in the active voice, the subject of the sentence does the action: *Hernando caught* the ball. In the passive voice, the subject receives the action: The *ball was caught* by Hernando. Often the actor does not appear in a passive-voice sentence: The *ball was caught.* See also section 17.

adjective   A word used to modify (describe) a noun or pronoun: the *frisky* horse, *rare old* stamps, *sixteen* candles. Adjectives usually answer one of these questions: Which one? What kind of? How many or how much? See also section 28.

adjective clause   A subordinate clause that modifies a noun or pronoun. An adjective clause begins with a relative pronoun (*who, whom, whose, which, that*) or a relative adverb (*when, where*) and usually appears right after the word it modifies: The book *that goes unread* is a writer's worst nightmare.

adverb   A word used to modify a verb, an adjective, or another adverb: rides *smoothly, unusually* attractive, *very* slowly. An adverb usually answers one of these questions: When? Where? How? Why? Under what conditions? To what degree? See also section 28.

adverb clause   A subordinate clause that modifies a verb (or occasionally an adjective or adverb). An adverb clause begins with a subordinating conjunction such as *although, because, if, unless,* or *when* and usually appears at the beginning or the end of a sentence: *When the sun went down,* the hikers prepared their camp. See also *subordinate clause; subordinating conjunction.*

agreement   See sections 25 and 27.

antecedent   A noun or pronoun to which a pronoun refers: When the *battery* wears down, we recharge *it.* The noun *battery* is the antecedent of the pronoun *it.*

appositive   A noun or noun phrase that renames a nearby noun or pronoun: Bloggers, *conversationalists at heart*, are the online equivalent of talk show hosts.

article   The word *a*, *an*, or *the*, used to mark a noun. Also see section 31b.

case   See sections 27c and 27d.

clause   A word group containing a subject, a verb, and any objects, complements, or modifiers. See *independent clause*; *subordinate clause*.

collective noun   See sections 25e and 27a.

common noun   See section 37a.

complement   See *object complement*; *subject complement*.

complex sentence   A sentence consisting of one independent clause and one or more subordinate clauses. In the following example, the subordinate clause is italicized: We walked along the river *until we came to the bridge*.

compound-complex sentence   A sentence consisting of at least two independent clauses and at least one subordinate clause: Jan dictated a story, and the children wrote whatever he said. In the preceding sentence, the subordinate clause is *whatever he said*. The two independent clauses are *Jan dictated a story* and *the children wrote whatever he said*.

compound sentence   A sentence consisting of two independent clauses. The clauses are usually joined with a comma and a coordinating conjunction (*and, but, or, nor, for, so, yet*) or with a semicolon: The car broke down, *but* a rescue van arrived within minutes. A shark was spotted near shore; people left the water immediately.

conjunction   A joining word. See *conjunctive adverb*; *coordinating conjunction*; *correlative conjunction*; *subordinating conjunction*.

conjunctive adverb   An adverb used with a semicolon to connect independent clauses: The bus was stuck in traffic; *therefore*, the team was late for the game. The most commonly used conjunctive adverbs are *consequently, furthermore, however, moreover, nevertheless, then, therefore*, and *thus*. See page 200 for a longer list.

coordinating conjunction   One of the following words, used to join elements of equal grammatical rank: *and, but, or, nor, for, so, yet*.

correlative conjunction   A pair of conjunctions connecting grammatically equal elements: *either . . . or, neither . . . nor, whether . . . or, not only . . . but also*, and *both . . . and*. See also section 18b.

count noun   A noun that refers to persons, places, things, or ideas that can be counted. See also section 31b.

demonstrative pronoun   A pronoun used to identify or point to a noun: *this, that, these, those. This* is my favorite chair.

direct object   A word or word group that receives the action of the verb: The hungry cat clawed *the bag of dry food*. The complete direct object is *the bag of dry food*. The simple direct object is always a noun or a pronoun, in this case *bag*.

expletive   The word *there* or *it* when used at the beginning of a sentence to delay the subject: *There* are eight planes waiting to take off. *It* is healthy to eat breakfast every day. The delayed subjects are the noun *planes* and the infinitive phrase *to eat breakfast every day*.

gerund   A verb form ending in *-ing* used as a noun: *Reading* aloud helps children appreciate language. The gerund *reading* is used as the subject of the verb *helps*.

gerund phrase   A gerund and its objects, complements, or modifiers. A gerund phrase always functions as a noun, usually as a subject, a subject complement, or a direct object. In the following example, the phrase functions as a direct object: We tried *planting tulips*.

helping verb   One of the following words, when used with a main verb: *be, am, is, are, was, were, being, been; has, have, had; do, does, did; can, will, shall, should, could, would, may, might, must*. Helping verbs always precede main verbs: *will work, is working, had worked*. See also *modal verb*.

indefinite pronoun   A pronoun that refers to a nonspecific person or thing: *Something* is burning. The most common indefinite pronouns are *all, another, any, anybody, anyone, anything, both, each, either, everybody, everyone, everything, few, many, neither, nobody, none, no one, nothing, one, some, somebody, someone, something*. See also sections 25d and 27a.

independent clause   A word group containing a subject and a verb that can or does stand alone as a sentence. In addition to at least one independent clause, many sentences contain subordinate clauses that function as adjectives, adverbs, or nouns. See also *clause; subordinate clause*.

indirect object   A noun or pronoun that names to whom or for whom the action of a sentence is done: We gave *her* some leftover yarn. An indirect object always precedes a direct object, in this case *some leftover yarn*.

infinitive   The word *to* followed by the base form of a verb: *to think, to dream*.

infinitive phrase   An infinitive and its objects, complements, or modifiers. An infinitive phrase can function as a
noun, an adjective, or an adverb. Noun: *To live without health
insurance* is risky. Adjective: The Nineteenth Amendment
gave women the right *to vote*. Adverb: Volunteers knocked
on doors *to rescue people from the flood*.

intensive or reflexive pronoun   A pronoun ending in *-self*
(or *-selves*): *myself, yourself, himself, herself, itself, ourselves,
yourselves, themselves.* An intensive pronoun emphasizes a
noun or another pronoun: I *myself* don't have a job. A reflexive pronoun names a receiver of an action identical with the
doer of the action: Did Paula cut *herself*?

interjection   A word expressing surprise or emotion: *Oh!
Wow! Hey! Hooray!*

interrogative pronoun   A pronoun used to introduce a
question: *who, whom, whose, which, what. What* does history
teach us?

intransitive verb   See *transitive and intransitive verbs*.

irregular verb   See *regular and irregular verbs*. See also
section 26a.

linking verb   A verb that links a subject to a subject complement, a word or word group that renames or describes the
subject: The winner *was* a teacher. The cherries *taste* sour.
The most common linking verbs are forms of *be*: *be, am, is,
are, was, were, being, been.* The following sometimes function
as linking verbs: *appear, become, feel, grow, look, make, seem,
smell, sound, taste.* See also *subject complement*.

modal verb   A helping verb that cannot be used as a main
verb. There are nine modals: *can, could, may, might, must,
shall, should, will,* and *would.* We *must* shut the windows
before the storm. The verb phrase *ought to* is often classified
as a modal as well. See also *helping verb*.

modifier   A word, phrase, or clause that describes or quali-
fies the meaning of a word. Modifiers include adjectives,
adverbs, prepositional phrases, participial phrases, some
infinitive phrases, and adjective and adverb clauses.

mood   See section 26c.

noncount noun   A noun that refers to things or abstract ideas
that cannot be counted or made plural. See also section 31b.

noun   The name of a person, place, thing, or concept (*freedom*): The *lion* in the *cage* growled at the *zookeeper*.

noun clause   A subordinate clause that functions as a
noun, usually as a subject, a subject complement, or a direct
object. In the following sentence, the italicized noun clause

functions as the subject: *Whoever leaves the house last* must lock the door. Noun clauses usually begin with *how, who, whom, whoever, that, what, whatever, whether,* or *why.*

noun equivalent   A word or word group that functions like a noun: a pronoun, a noun and its modifiers, a gerund phrase, some infinitive phrases, or a noun clause.

object   See *direct object; indirect object.*

object complement   A word or word group that renames or describes a direct object. It always appears after the direct object: The kiln makes clay *firm and strong.*

object of a preposition   See *prepositional phrase.*

participial phrase   A present or past participle and its objects, complements, or modifiers. A participial phrase always functions as an adjective describing a noun or pronoun. Usually it appears before or after the word it modifies: *Being a weight-bearing joint,* the knee is often injured. Plants *kept in moist soil* will thrive.

participle, past   A verb form usually ending in *-d, -ed, -n, -en,* or *-t: asked, stolen, fought.* Past participles are used with helping verbs to form perfect tenses (had *spoken*) and the passive voice (were *required*). They are also used as adjectives (the *stolen* car).

participle, present   A verb form ending in *-ing.* Present participles are used with helping verbs in progressive forms (is *rising,* has been *walking*). They are also used as adjectives (the *rising* tide).

parts of speech   A system for classifying words. Many words can function as more than one part of speech. See *adjective, adverb, conjunction, interjection, noun, preposition, pronoun, verb.*

passive voice   See *active vs. passive voice.*

personal pronoun   One of the following pronouns, used to refer to a specific person or thing: *I, me, you, she, her, he, him, it, we, us, they, them.* After Julia won the award, *she* gave half of the prize money to a literacy program. See also *antecedent.*

phrase   A word group that lacks a subject, a verb, or both. Most phrases function within sentences as adjectives, as adverbs, or as nouns. See *absolute phrase; appositive; gerund phrase; infinitive phrase; participial phrase; prepositional phrase.*

possessive case   See section 34a.

possessive pronoun   A pronoun used to indicate ownership: *my, mine, your, yours, her, hers, his, its, our, ours, your, yours, their, theirs.* The guest made *his* own breakfast.

predicate A verb and any objects, complements, and modifiers that go with it: The horses *exercise in the corral every day*.

preposition A word placed before a noun or noun equivalent to form a phrase modifying another word in the sentence. The preposition indicates the relation between the noun (or noun equivalent) and the word the phrase modifies. The most common prepositions are *about, above, across, after, against, along, among, around, at, before, behind, below, beside, besides, between, beyond, by, down, during, except, for, from, in, inside, into, like, near, of, off, on, onto, out, outside, over, past, since, than, through, to, toward, under, unlike, until, up, with, within,* and *without*.

prepositional phrase A phrase beginning with a preposition and ending with a noun or noun equivalent (called the *object of the preposition*). Most prepositional phrases function as adjectives or adverbs. Adjective phrases usually come right after the noun or pronoun they modify: The road *to the summit* was treacherous. Adverb phrases usually appear at the beginning or the end of the sentence: *To the hikers*, the brief shower was a welcome relief. The brief shower was a welcome relief *to the hikers*.

progressive verb forms See pages 165–66 and 183–84.

pronoun A word used in place of a noun. Usually the pronoun substitutes for a specific noun, known as the pronoun's *antecedent*. In the following example, *alarm* is the antecedent of the pronoun *it*: When the *alarm* rang, I reached over and turned *it* off. See also *demonstrative pronoun; indefinite pronoun; intensive or reflexive pronoun; interrogative pronoun; personal pronoun; possessive pronoun; relative pronoun*.

proper noun See section 37a.

regular and irregular verbs When a verb is regular, both the past tense and the past participle are formed by adding *-ed* or *-d* to the base form of the verb: *walk, walked, walked*. The past tense and past participle of irregular verbs are formed in a variety of other ways: *ride, rode, ridden; begin, began, begun; go, went, gone;* and so on. Also see section 26a.

relative adverb The word *when* or *where*, when used to introduce an adjective clause. The park *where* we had our picnic closes on October 1. See also *adjective clause*.

relative pronoun One of the following words, when used to introduce an adjective clause: *who, whom, whose, which, that*. The writer *who* won the award refused to accept it.

sentence A word group consisting of at least one independent clause. See also *complex sentence; compound sentence; compound-complex sentence; simple sentence*.

simple sentence   A sentence consisting of one independent clause and no subordinate clauses: Without a passport, Eva could not visit her parents in Poland.

subject   A word or word group that names who or what the sentence is about. In the following example, the complete subject (the simple subject and all of its modifiers) is italicized: *The devastating effects of famine* can last for many years. The simple subject is *effects*. See also *subject after verb; understood subject.*

subject after verb   Although the subject normally precedes the verb, sentences are sometimes inverted. In the following example, the subject *the sleepy child* comes after the verb *sat*: Under the table *sat the sleepy child*. When a sentence begins with the expletive *there* or *it*, the subject always follows the verb. See also *expletive.*

subject complement   A word or word group that follows a linking verb and either renames or describes the subject of the sentence. If the subject complement renames the subject, it is a noun or a noun equivalent: That signature may be *a forgery*. If it describes the subject, it is an adjective: Love is *blind*.

subjunctive mood   See section 26c.

subordinate clause   A word group containing a subject and a verb that cannot stand alone as a sentence. Subordinate clauses function within sentences as adjectives, adverbs, or nouns. They begin with subordinating conjunctions such as *although, because, if,* and *until* or with relative pronouns such as *who, which,* and *that*. See *adjective clause; adverb clause; independent clause; noun clause.*

subordinating conjunction   A word that introduces a subordinate clause and indicates the relation of the clause to the rest of the sentence. The most common subordinating conjunctions are *after, although, as, as if, because, before, even though, if, since, so that, than, that, though, unless, until, when, where, whether,* and *while*. Note: The relative pronouns *who, whom, whose, which,* and *that* also introduce subordinate clauses.

tenses   See section 26b.

transitive and intransitive verbs   Transitive verbs take direct objects, nouns or noun equivalents that receive the action. In the following example, the transitive verb *wrote* takes the direct object *a story*: Each student *wrote* a story. Intransitive verbs do not take direct objects: The audience *laughed*. If any words follow an intransitive verb, they are adverbs or word groups functioning as adverbs: The audience *laughed* at the talking parrot.

understood subject   The subject *you* when it is understood but not actually present in the sentence. Understood subjects occur in sentences that issue commands or advice: [*You*] Put your clothes in the hamper.

verb   A word that expresses action (*jump, think*) or being (*is, was*). A sentence's verb is composed of a main verb possibly preceded by one or more helping verbs: The band *practiced* every day. The report *was* not *completed* on schedule. Verbs have five forms: the base form, or dictionary form (*walk, ride*); the past-tense form (*walked, rode*); the past participle (*walked, ridden*); the present participle (*walking, riding*); and the -*s* form (*walks, rides*).

verbal phrase   See *gerund phrase; infinitive phrase; participial phrase.*

Checklist for global revision

Focus

▶ Are the main point or points of your paper — the thesis or the hypothesis and results — clearly stated in the abstract or in the opening paragraph (if the paper does not have an abstract)?

▶ Does each part of the paper support and expand on the main points without adding unnecessary detail?

Organization

▶ Can readers easily follow the structure?

▶ Do you use headings appropriately for the genre in which you are writing, to help readers follow the flow of your ideas?

▶ Does each paragraph contain a new idea that clearly connects to ideas in surrounding paragraphs?

▶ Do you present ideas in a logical order?

Content

▶ Are your methods, data, results, and supporting ideas logical and persuasive?

▶ Do you acknowledge ideas contrary to your thesis or hypothesis? Do you suggest limitations of your own work and suggest directions for further research?

▶ Do you fully develop important ideas?

▶ Is the draft free of irrelevant or repetitious material?

Style

▶ Are your sentences clear, direct, objective, and formal?

▶ Do you avoid stereotypical, biased, or sexist language?

Use of sources

▶ Do you use sources to inform, support, or extend your points?

▶ Have you varied the function of sources — to provide background, explain concepts, lend authority, and counter objections? Do you introduce sources with signal phrases that indicate these functions?

▶ Is it clear how your sources relate to your main points?

▶ Is the draft free of plagiarism? Are summaries and paraphrases in your own words? Is quoted material enclosed in quotation marks or set off from the text?

▶ Have you documented source material that is not common knowledge?

Checklist for visiting the writing center

Step 1: Gather your materials.

► Gather materials your instructor has provided: the assignment, sample papers, your syllabus.

► Gather your own materials: a copy of your draft, copies of sources you have cited in your paper, previous papers with instructor comments.

Step 2: Organize your materials and prepare questions.

► Reread the assignment. If you are confused, ask your instructor to clarify the assignment before you visit the writing center.

► Look at previous papers with instructor comments. Can those comments help you think about your current paper?

► Create a list of specific questions to focus your writing center conversation.

Step 3: Visit the writing center.

► Be on time and treat your tutor or consultant with courtesy and respect.

► Participate actively by asking questions and taking notes.

► Understand the limitations of your visit. Be prepared to cover one or two major issues.

► Understand the purpose of your visit. Most writing center staff are trained to give you suggestions and feedback, but they will not write or edit your paper for you.

Step 4: Reflect on your visit.

► As soon as possible after your visit, make sure you understand your notes from the session and add anything you didn't have time to write during your visit.

► As you revise, apply your notes to your entire paper. Don't focus only on the parts of your paper you looked at in the session.

► Do not feel obligated to follow advice that you disagree with. Writing center staff are trained to provide helpful feedback, but you are the author; you decide which changes will help you best express your meaning.

► As you revise, keep track of questions or goals for your next writing center visit.

Index

Documentation Directories

Continued >

Charts and Lists for Quick Reference

List of Sample Pages from Student Papers

hackerhandbooks.com/pocket
e APA papers > Sample student writing
e APA papers > Sample student writing (APA version)

Revision Symbols

Detailed Menu